ABOUT THE AUTHOR

P.G. Maxwell-Stuart is Senior Lecturer in History at the University of St Andrews. He lives in St Andrews.

PRAISE FOR P.G. MAXWELL-STUART

Ghosts: A History of Phantoms, Ghouls, & Other Spirits of the Dead
'Scholarly and well-written ... a wide ranging account' *THES*

Witch Hunters
'The lurid tales of orgies and other debauchery told by these individuals still make for shocking reading today' *THE DAILY MAIL*
'Based on massive erudition ... a learned, informative, at times very subtle book'
JAMES SHARPE, author of *Dick Turpin*

Wizards: A History
'An excellent pioneering work ... fascinating and entertaining'
RONALD HUTTON
'A fascinating, well-researched and lucid book'
THE ENGLISH HISTORICAL REVIEW

Witchcraft: A History
'Combines scholarly rigour with literary flair'
THE INDEPENDENT ON SUNDAY

Satan

A Biography

P.G. MAXWELL-STUART

AMBERLEY PUBLISHING

First published 2008

Amberley Publishing Plc
Cirencester Road, Chalford,
Stroud, Gloucestershire, GL6 8PE

www.amberley-books.com

British Library Cataloguing in Publication Data.
A catalogue record for this book is available from the British Library.

ISBN 978 1 84868 082 1

Typesetting and Origination by diagrafmedia
Printed in Great Britain

Contents

Author's Note

The history of the Devil – and in what follows I have elided 'the Devil' and 'Satan', since this has been a common merger for most of the Christian period – is long, complex, and in some respects controversial, and as he has been the object of discussion from the earliest Christian years; the relevant bibliography is vast. For both these reasons, the narrative presented here does not claim to be comprehensive or definitive. It is, rather, a series of snapshots, each intended to give some idea of how people in succeeding Christian centuries tried to grapple with the idea of personified evil, to explain his workings and motives, and to express their notions of him through visual images. Such a personification is not peculiar to Christianity, of course, but 'the Devil' to all intents and purposes is, and I have therefore seen fit to present his history through Christian eyes while, at the same time, including those personifications of other faiths in as far as Christians have come across them or had experience of them. There may be those who have reservations about these choices, but here perhaps the old saying holds good: *de gustibus non est disputandum*.

Translations: I have used existing translations duly acknowledged in the Notes or Bibliography, but in many instances, after consulting the original text, I have felt at liberty to alter them in the interests of greater clarity or accuracy. Otherwise, all translations are my own.

CHAPTER 1

The Devil's Ancient Origins

On Thursday 19 June 1664, Cecilia Ferrazzi, a woman about fifty years old, appeared before members of the Venetian Inquisition and answered questions about her life. Unable to become a nun as she had wanted, Cecilia remained unmarried and opened houses of refuge in the city for young women who were in danger of drifting into prostitution. Her health had been bad, her spiritual life dramatic, filled on the one hand with visits from demons in the form of dreadful animals and on the other with visions of the Blessed Virgin and other saints. So it was not really surprising that she had eventually been brought to the notice of the Inquisition. One incident in particular demands our attention. It happened during the mid 1630s. Cecilia was under close confinement in a private house, put there because she was physically ill with bladder stones and because her spiritual condition was giving cause for alarm. One day, she told the inquisitors, she saw twenty or thirty people enter her room at about midday. They were not dream-figures or visions, she said, but as real as the interrogators she was addressing, and were dressed in black, like the members of a local religious confraternity whose role was to accompany condemned prisoners to execution. She heard them singing, and watched as they laid a life-size crucifix on the ground; but when Cecilia begged the figure on the cross forgiveness for her sins, it bowed its head and rebuffed her more than once with one of its arms.

This whole experience lasted for about six hours, after which the crucifix and company left her, (the English translation says 'disappeared' which may or may not be ambiguous), and were succeeded by a hermit dressed in grey. The hood of his garment was pulled low over his forehead, but Cecilia could see that he had a big beard and that his hands were hairy - a sign which should perhaps have warned her that appearances could be deceptive. The hermit told Cecilia he had come from God, (perhaps a necessary pacification of initial alarm), and, after failing to persuade her to come away with him, in order to perform penance, stayed with her for eight days, talking, talking, talking, all the while kneeling upon a prie-dieu and turning the pages of a breviary. He did not look at her throughout this time – indeed, he turned his back on her – and as he talked, Cecilia scourged herself, (a regular mode of performing penance), never hearing a word he said. At the end of the eight days, however, the hermit revealed his true nature. For at midnight, he insisted Cecilia leave with him after renouncing the Virgin Mary and openly cursing the obedience she had sworn to her confessor. Realising at last that this was the Devil, not someone sent by God, Cecilia called on Jesus and the Virgin and was immediately subjected to extreme violence as the hermit beat her, seized her by the hair, and dashed her head violently against the walls of her room, spattering them with blood.[1]

The type of reality being described here is of no consequence to us. What matters is the reality Cecilia felt and believed herself to be experiencing, and as far as that reality is concerned, she was for a prolonged period of time the focus of a non-human entity's attention. This entity was able to take on the outward characteristics of a recognisable human person, (albeit with a tell-tale trait of excessive hairiness which, had Cecilia been alert, might have provided a warning-sign of his true nature), handle physical objects – first the breviary, then Cecilia herself – and utter comprehensible speech at the beginning and end of his lengthy visitation, if not during the intervening days. That Cecilia was not alert can be ascribed partly to her physical exhaustion, but perhaps mainly to her emotional, mental, and spiritual state at the time of the visitation. She had just witnessed, over a period of several hours, a multiplicity of signs, which persuaded her she was seeing members of a religious confraternity, a life-size crucifix, and above all the figure of Jesus who moved, and in such a way as to reject her pleas for remission of sins. At just such a point, one could suggest, she would be open to deception and spiritual assault by an entity ill-disposed towards her. Hence his adoption of a religious guise and religious accoutrements, and his apparent imitation of Christ's rejection of her until he judged her to be in a condition of physical and emotional weakness sufficiently profound to let him reveal himself and begin an attack upon her spirit and body.

Satan is conventionally portrayed as a feral or semi-bestial figure, clearly not of this world, self-evidently fearsome and immediately repellent. Art, however, has its own perfectly good reasons for picturing him thus, as we shall discuss later. Most people's experience of meeting or being accosted by Satan, as they themselves describe it, is, on the other hand, completely different. To them he tends to appear in human guise, as he did to Cecilia, and in such a non-threatening, matter-of-fact, even winsome fashion, that the object of his attentions either does not realise anything is amiss, or is willing, for whatever reason, to suspend alarm and be wooed into calm and compliance. One is reminded of the myth of Semele and Zeus. The father of the gods initiated a love affair with her by appearing to her in the form of a mortal man. But after a while, Semele conceived the idea of seeing Zeus as he actually was, in full divine splendour, and when he showed himself to her thus, her humanity was unable to sustain the shock and so she died. Satan's aping the appearance of humanity can be said to aim at avoiding a similar catastrophe, at least while the person undergoing temptation is still alive and open to seduction. Post-mortem will be the time for reality. Hence, even when Satan turns violent and hales Cecilia about the room, he maintains his human shape, even though it is dawning on her that she is being attacked by the Devil and if not by the Devil himself, at least by some dreadful spirit.

One of the great problems faced by those who admit the existence of forms of being other than the purely material is to know when (and indeed if) a given experience represents a genuine interpenetration of a non-material reality into one that is material and, if the happening is real, how to gauge the nature of that occurrence – amicable, hostile, dangerous, monitory, accidental? So there develops a science devoted to collecting, understanding, and interpreting materials derived from or based upon such experiences, so that decisions anent the nature of both those and of subsequent experiences can be made, and strategies formulated to guide the human objects of these experiences in dealing with them, whether to avoid their attendant harm or benefit from any good they may bring or represent. This science of demonology – an unfortunate term, since it ought to include visions of or visitations from God, the saints, and the dead, as well as spirits with evil intent, and entities of unknown nature and provenance – is one which may seem abstruse and perhaps somewhat fanciful to the modern 'rationalist' mind, but for the majority of humankind both now and in the past it represents a serious repository of knowledge upon which, under the guidance of experts, (just as though it were medicine or surgery), the individual can draw for rational explanations of phenomena beyond his or her normal ken, and for practical solutions to any problems those phenomena might be causing. In Cecilia's case, as in the cases of so many before and after her, then, it was demonology which could help provide an answer to the question which rose and troubled both her and those around her as a result of her experiences: did those experiences come from God or from the Devil?

Cecilia was, of course, a Christian and therefore her question has to be expressed in Christian terms. These are clear enough, the result of long centuries of both accumulated experiences and theological deductions and speculation: the Devil is Satan, the greatest and most dangerous embodiment of evil, commander of a host of other entities like him in nature and intention, but less powerful, through whom, when he does not act himself, he may choose to operate against human beings, seeking their ultimate downfall and thus their companionship in perpetual exclusion from God's presence. Satan is thus, as his name suggests, the antagonist, engaged in unceasing combat against God who created him in the first place, and in whose heavenly Court he once occupied a particular place and fulfilled a specific role. For Cecilia, as for her mentors and her inquisitors, Satan was no stranger. He could be seen, encountered, heard, spoken to, and felt in a multitude of guises, not all of them immediately frightening, and these visions and meetings might happen at any time without warning, either when their object was off guard and preoccupied with other thoughts or business, or when circumstances conjoined to make him or her peculiarly susceptible to a demonic experience. So in the mid seventeenth century in Christian Europe, manifestations of personified evil were not unusual, and strategies for recognising and dealing with them had long been developed.

But how had the theories underlying those strategies emerged in the first place, and why had personification of evil taken the form it had in Christian thought? Ancient religions of the Middle East tended to picture their divinities as members of an immense supernatural Court ruled over by a supreme deity and his wife or female counterpart, and expressed as a hierarchy stretching from a pinnacle of theocratic power to a 'servants' hall' of spirits, (either non-human beings or dead humans who had transmogrified into a greater-than-human form once they had passed over the threshold of death), and even hybrid entities born of congress between a human and some kind of spirit. Divinities also ebbed and flowed as civilisations rose and fell, one becoming identified as another or being made to absorb the qualities of a different deity. Thus, Nanna, the Sumerian Moon God, and Utu, the Sun God, surrendered to their Akkadian equivalents, and Sumerian Inanna turned into Akkadian Ishtar who then, like some monstrous fish, swallowed the supernatural roles of countless other female deities and grew so immense that at last her very name turned into the word for 'goddess'.

So too Akkadian Marduk displaced Sumerian Enlil as the supreme divinity and quickly added to the range of his potency the attributes of other deities:

Marduk is Ninurta, the god of agriculture;
He is Nergal, the god of battles;
Zababa, the god of war;
Nabu, the god of accountants;
Enlil, the god of governing;
Sin, the god who lights the night;
Samas, the god of justice;
And Adad, the god of rain.[2]

Now, this diverse multiplicity of supernatural beings does not appear to have begun with any notable structure. The change from inchoate crowd to ordered hierarchy was gradually imposed on it – or, perhaps more accurately, realised – partly by generations of priests and religious thinkers who made a deliberate effort to tease out sense from apparent disorder and then codify their conclusions, such as is done in the opening section of the Sumerian *Epic of Creation*, which describes the lineage of the gods and the emergence of Marduk, the last of them to be born, who, it says, was many times worthier than the others to preside over them: and partly by the long passage of legend-telling and the magnification of detail in protective or curative rituals which listed and codified the spirits thought to be hostile or responsible for an illness:

I drive away Ishire, I drive away Aghuire, I drive away Aghra, I drive away Ughra; I drive away sickness, I drive away death, I drive away pain and fever; I drive away Sarana, I drive away Sarasti, I drive away Azana, I drive away Azahva, I drive away Kurugha, I drive away Azivaka, I drive away Duruka, I drive away Astairya; I drive away the disease, rottenness, and infection which Anghra Mainyu has created by his witchcraft against the bodies of mortals. I drive away all manner of diseases and deaths, all the Yatus and Pairikas, and all the wicked Gainis.

The deities met in assembly or council, presided over by its most powerful member, a divinity who in later mythologies tended to become lodged uncomfortably between being an absolute monarch and *primus inter pares*. The meeting-place is described frequently as a mountain-top, although Ugaritic literature suggests it could also have been at or near the source of rivers leading to the Underworld; and there 'they opened the domed tent of 'El and entered the tent-shrine of the King, the Father of Years'. Among their other activities, members of this particular council drew up plans for the creation of heaven and earth, and both human and animal life. But in their plans these gods forgot to limit human life, and so humanity multiplied to such an extent that its constant noise and laughter prevented the King of the gods from sleeping; so he sent illness and drought and famine and flood to control their numbers, an exercise of absolute power coloured by the god's apparent indifference to the harshness of his punishment when compared with the relatively slight nature of humanity's offence. (One is reminded of the extraordinary imbalance between cause and effect in many early modern witchcraft cases, when a dismissive word or look, or the refusal of alms, might result in the breaking of limbs or the destruction of crops or the death of a child. Anger, it seems, had scarcely any gradations. However small the affront, the offence to the witch's personal dignity or 'face' was likely to evoke a rage unbridled by patience or Christian forbearance, and call for immediate and crushing retribution).[3]

But was the constant noise of humans a 'sin', and did the entry of illness and sudden death into their lives constitute punishment for sin? What, too, was the relationship between these controlling disasters and the humans themselves? Here we must prepare ourselves for the notion of divinity as the source of everything, whether good or bad. Thus, when Tiamat, goddess of the primeval waters, was angered by the noise and laughter of her own children, she produced an immense number of demons with the aim of destroying them, and was prevented from doing so only because she herself was killed by Marduk, the younger son of the god who killed and supplanted her own husband. The Hittite religion too, contains a narrative of rage, in which the storm god vents himself upon humankind, destroying crops so that people and animals will die. This he does, as the myth makes clear, not because humanity has done anything wrong, but simply because the god is feeling angry and chooses to express his anger in this way. So although there may be demons in these mythologies, the principal cause of misfortune and death among humans and the gods themselves are the principal deities of the heavenly Court, who lash out because they can and show no remorse for or compunction about exercising their limitless power in pursuit of revenge or assuagement of damaged honour. No wonder, then, that the Middle East saw what Thorkild Jacobsen has called 'a barbarization of the idea of divinity', and that people grew increasingly fearful of everyday existence. 'Witchcraft and sorcery were suspected everywhere, demons and evil spirits threatened life unceasingly'. 'Evil' as a set of actions separate from divinity and thus not originating with it does not as yet seem to have been conceived, and so these early manifestations of the Divine – Sumerian, Babylonian, Hittite – cannot really be said to have contributed directly to the concept and figure of Satan.

Nevertheless, contained in these early Middle Eastern religions there were indeed notions, which would later flow into Judaism and thence into Christianity, thereby providing an ambience for the rise of Satan, and indirectly sow seeds from which his character could grow. One such stems from the belief that divinity, rather than containing within itself equal capacities for 'good' and 'bad', can alter its basic character and turn from expressing itself benevolently to behaving in ways which are more or less maleficent. In Babylonian myth, for example, the ruler of the underworld and his consort or female counterpart were both originally deities of the sky. Enthroned as subchthonic deities, however, even though the male was sometimes portrayed as willing to heal as well as to kill, they turned to inflicting destruction, disease, war, and death upon the world above; and so we find the emergence of gods and goddesses who are conceived in terms of habitual hostility to everyone, supernatural or human.

One of the most obvious examples of this type is Lilith, a female demon who preys upon men and children. Originally a Mesopotamian spirit of winds, who existed in a multiplicity of forms both male and female, Lilith developed into a single monstrous creature with a complex history of her own. She appears once in the Bible (*Isaiah* 34.14), although the Authorised Version's translation does not make this clear. 'The wild beasts of the desert shall also meet with the wild beasts of the island, and the satyr shall cry to his fellow; and the screech owl also shall rest there, and find for herself a place of rest'. More recognisable is the Latin Vulgate which says, 'Demons will meet ass-centaurs and one hairy creature will cry out to a second. There *Lamia* [Lilith] will lie down and find her rest'. 'Lamia' is one of the Latin words, which would later be used for 'witch', and is a carefully calculated version of the Hebrew, which carries a somewhat similar burden of significance. The principal source for her legend, however, is an anonymous text of the ninth or tenth century AD, attributed to Ben Sira, *Alphabeticum Siracidis*, which lists twenty-two proverbs in Aramaic and twenty-two in Hebrew, and offers commentaries upon them and stories about Ben Sira himself. Lilith occurs in the fifth of the Hebrew set. Ben Sira has been summoned to the Court of King Nebudchadnezzar:

> Soon afterwards the young son of the king took ill. Nebudchadnezzar said, "Heal my son. If you don't, I will kill you". Ben Sira immediately sat down and wrote an amulet with the Holy Name, and he inscribed on it the angels in charge of medicine by their names, forms, and images, and by their wings, hands, and feet. Nebudchadnezzar looked at the amulet. "Who are these?" "The angels who are in charge of medicine ... After God created Adam, who was alone, He said, 'It is not good for man to be alone'. He then created a woman for Adam, from the earth, as He had created Adam himself, and called her Lilith. Adam and Lilith immediately began to fight. She said, 'I will not lie below', and he said, 'I will not lie beneath you, but only on top. Or you are fit only to be in the bottom position, while I am to be the superior one'. Lilith replied, 'We are equal to each other, in as much as we were both created from the earth'. But they would not listen to one another. When Lilith saw this, she pronounced the Ineffable Name and flew away into the air. Adam stood in prayer before his Creator. 'Sovereign of the universe', he said, 'the woman you gave me has run away'. At once the Holy One, (blessed be He), sent these three angels to bring her back.
> The Holy One said to Adam, 'If she agrees to come back, what is made is good. If not, she must permit one hundred of her children to die every day'. The angels left God and pursued Lilith, whom they overtook in the midst of

the sea, in the mighty waters wherein the Egyptians were destined to drown. They told her God's word, but she did not wish to return. The angels said, 'We shall drown you in the sea'. 'Leave me', she said. 'I was created only to cause sickness to infants. If the infant is male, I shall have dominion over him for eight days after his birth; and if female, for twenty days'.

When the angels heard Lilith's words, they insisted she go back. But she swore to them by the name of the eternal and living God. 'Whenever I see you or your forms in an amulet, I shall have no power over that infant'. She also agreed to have one hundred of her children die every day. Accordingly, every day one hundred demons perish, and for the same reason we write the angels' names on the amulets of young children. When Lilith sees their names, she remembers her oath and the child recovers".

We can see from this at once whence the connection with child killing was derived, and it reminds us of the killing of children by witches at a Sabbat. (The terminology 'Sabbat' and 'synagogue' applied to these mass meetings of witches, while not actually originating in the Lilith story, does make an overt connection with Jews and Jewish mythology, real or imagined, which the use of the Latin *lamia* = 'Lilith/witch' would echo and encourage.) But the story also makes two other important points: (i) that certain created individuals rebel against the natural order of things ordained by God – for this is how Lilith's refusal to be subject to Adam is meant to be understood, albeit her tale occurs in a set of irreverent, sometimes vulgar burlesques of traditional rabbinic scholarship; and (ii) that the disobedient rebel can be controlled by magic.[4]

It is now a cliché of Biblical commentaries that Satan developed into the great rebel against God. The ancient notion of divinity as many powerful, non-human forces constituting a heavenly Court presided over by a divine monarch invited comparison with human behaviour under parallel conditions. Thus, family struggles between siblings, or attempts to overthrow and supplant the Father, or conspiracies against the divine overlord by younger ambitious deities, are all to be met with in the mythologies. In Egypt, Seth manages to kill his brother Osiris who is then resurrected by Isis, their sister, whereupon Horus, Seth's nephew, conceived magically while Osiris was dead, becomes Seth's adversary and there follows a long period of vicious, destructive battles between the two. In Babylonia, Anzu is sent to the palace of Enlil, the father god, and sees with increasing jealousy 'the crown of his sovereignty, the robe of his godhead, his divine tablet of destinies'. Constant sight of this kingship makes him determined to remove Enlil and usurp his place, an ambition in which he succeeds, although the rest of the gods soon rally from their shock and debate the best way to kill, (and therefore supplant in turn), the rebellious Anzu. As for younger gods supplanting older, we have seen this already in the relationship between Babylonian Apsu and Tiamat who are slain by Ea and Marduk.

Struggles and rebellions within the divine 'family' or at least the heavenly Court, then, open the way to elide concepts of deities who are capable of performing some actions which may be viewed as benevolent and others as malevolent, with different concepts which turn benevolence into 'good' and malevolence into 'bad', and then in turn transfer the goodness or the badness of the deeds to the divinity him or herself, so that the deity becomes associated with goodness or badness as his or her predominant characteristic. This we can see happening in the case of Marduk who elevated himself to divine supremacy by rebellion and assassination, and thereafter created Earth and was worshipped as supreme lord of creation. Horus and Seth in Egypt went even more clearly in separate directions, with Horus, the falcon-headed child of Isis, avenging his father Osiris's death and engaging in combat against his wicked uncle Seth who, having once been regarded as a beneficent god, turned into the divine ruler of everything the Egyptians feared, especially the desert – that place of sterility and death, which constantly threatened to encroach upon and overwhelm the black land of fertility and life.[5]

Divine, semi-divine, heroic, and angelic figures are all thus capable of change of status and often subsequent change of character, and since Satan sprang out of this religious mind-set common to the theologies and mythopoesis of the Middle East, it will not be surprising if we find some of these themes developing in his emergent personality. One particular influence which has been claimed for a dualistic view of good and evil – God and Satan, even though Satan should not be elevated beyond his status as a created, not a divine being – lies in the Zoroastrianism of ancient Persia. The prophet and leader of this religion, Zarathushtra, (or 'Zoroaster' in his Greek form), made it clear that God is good and does not produce evil. Evil stems from a separate entity altogether, Angra Mainyu or, in Middle Iranian, Ahriman, who is entirely malignant and exists of himself, not as an entity created by the good god, Ahura Mazdā:

> Now, these are the two original Spirits who, as twins, have been perceived through a vision. In both thought and speech [and] in deed, these two are what is good and evil. Between these two, the wise, not the foolish, will choose rightly.
>
> Furthermore, the two Spirits confronted each other. In the beginning [each] created for himself life and non-life, so that in the end there will be the worst existence for those who cling to delusion, but the best purpose for those who cling to the truth.

Of these two Spirits, he-who-is-wicked chose the worst course of action, [while] the most beneficent Spirit who is clothed in the hardest stones [chose] truth, and [so do they] who would satisfy Ahura Mazdā by honest deeds (*Yasna* 30.3-5)

Angra Mainyu is 'the spirit who causes someone to suffer (*angra*, from *anj/ang* = 'to torment', and *mainyu* = 'spirit'). He has no physical body, is actively malignant, and presides over a dark, subterranean region where sinners go for punishment. During the deadly struggle he constantly pursues with Ahura Mazdā, he once did his best to destroy the good god's seven creations by turning the waters filthy and the lands into a desert, thereby bringing death to any life which existed there; and although the creations rallied and launched a counter attack, Angra Mainyu continues to do his best to blight all life, aided by evil spirits he himself has begotten, who first seduce and then enter those beings created by Ahura Mazdā and thus aggressively pursue the evil ends of their father. Here at least, if not in the origin and status of Angra Mainyu, we can see parallels with the later development of Satan as a figure implacably hostile to humanity, willing and eager to make use of the demonic spirits subordinate to him as instruments whereby he may, quite literally, take possession of humans and animals, and thus cause them to participate in their own destruction.[6]

Certain themes, then, emerge from this very brief review of some of the religions local to ancient Israel, and thus liable to have influenced the development of her religious concepts. Gods and goddesses formed part of a royal Court which was presided over by a powerful deity acting both as an absolute monarch and as a father to the rest of his fellow divinities, and his Court was composed, not of equals but of male and female deities arranged in hierarchic order, with varying responsibilities. The divine hierarchy was not stable, and many of its members could be replaced as human empires fell and rose; but the greatest change might happen as the result of internal struggle or rebellion among the deities themselves, with the father-monarch frequently the target for usurpation. Initially, the deities were not thought of as good or evil in themselves, but as beings capable of doing good or wreaking harm in accordance with their own will and desire, either as simple exercises of power or in response to prayers, offerings, sacrifices, magical compulsion, slights, insults, or omissions. Some divinities, however, were seen as either good or evil from the start, or took on characteristics which settled the view of their characters as either predominantly 'good' or predominantly 'bad', and so evil – largely conceived as consisting of deeds hostile to humankind, and deliberately and aggressively malevolent, or as the expression of characteristics in supernatural or natural entities, tending to the same tormenting or destructive ends – became associated with one divinity or more in particular, thus releasing that 'good' divinity or those 'good' divine beings from responsibility for the production and performance of evil.

So let us now turn to the Old Testament to see how, if at all, these trends and concepts are reflected in its developing perception and narrative of God. The first parallel is obvious. God is an absolute monarch and presides over a heavenly Court. 'I saw the Lord sitting on His throne', says Micaiah, 'and all the host of Heaven standing by Him on His right hand and on His left', and when God wants something done, His courtiers discuss it. 'And one said, "This is how it should be done", and another said, "No, this is how it should be done"'. Among these courtiers are those willing to do wrong if that will see God's wishes carried out. 'There came forth a spirit and stood before the Lord and said, "I will entice Ahab to fight and die at Ramoth-gilead". And the Lord said unto him, "How will you do that?" And he said, "I shall go forth, and I shall be a lying spirit in the mouth of all his prophets". And [God] said, "You will entice him and prevail also. Go forth and do so"', (3 *Kings* 22.19-22). This reference to a spirit of false prophecy reminds us of the later concept of Satan as 'the father of lies', with the scene as a whole indicating that murky stage of theological understanding where it is implied that God is capable of doing bad actions as well as good; and yet He is separated from the actual performance of the bad action by having a subordinate carry it out on His behalf, albeit with His consent.

'Enticing' is an interesting verb to describe this *satan's* actions. He is to be seen doing it again in the Babylonian Talmud when, we are told, David 'ventured forth to Sekhor Bizzae [and] Satan appeared before him in the guise of a deer. [David] shot arrows at him, but did not reach him, and was thus led on until inveigled into the land of the Philistines'; or again, 'Bath Sheba was cleansing her hair behind a screen, when Satan came to [David], appearing in the shape of a bird. [David] shot an arrow at him, which broke the screen, and she stood revealed, and he saw her', (*Sanhedrin* 95a, 107a). Enticement and deception with a view to causing unhappiness, mayhem, and death – these are becoming characteristics particularly associated with the *satan*, whichever *satan* he might be. But the root of the Hebrew name or word 'satan' takes us in a slightly different direction. *Śtn* means 'someone who obstructs or objects or acts as an adversary', and whenever *satan* appears in the Old Testament texts, we may have to decide whether the *satan* in question is non-human or human, and note the identity of the person or persons he is opposing, and his motives for doing so. For example, 1 *Kings* 29.4 says that the Philistines were afraid that David, who was fighting for them, would return to the Israelites and so become a *satan*, an adversary; in 2 *Kings* 19.22, King David complains that in opposing his will, some of his subjects are behaving as *satans* against him; in 3 *Kings* 5.4, by contrast, King Solomon says he is glad he has no *satan*, no adversary, a happy situation which does not last, because later Hadad the Edomite and Rezon, son of Eliada, both turn *satan* and oppose him, (3 *Kings*

11.14, 25). All these 'satans' are clearly human and operate in the material world. In *Numbers* 22.20-35, however, we find a different example. There God tells Balaam not to go to Moab and curse some Egyptian interlopers, but then changes His mind and tells him to go, as long as he obeys His instructions. Balaam accordingly saddles his ass and departs, only to incur God's sudden anger by doing so – here perhaps we have an echo of the notion that Divinity may be capricious, and that a deity may change his mind and become angry without warning or immediately apprehensible reason – 'and the angel of the Lord took his stand in the road as his [Balaam's] *satan*'. In other words, the angel blocks Balaam's path and prevents him from going further. The ass sees this divine messenger, but Balaam does not until he has beaten his ass three times for apparent disobedience. But then the Lord opens the eyes of Balaam who prostrates himself at the sight of God's messenger. So the *satan* here is one of God's non-human servants, and is opposing a human at God's express wish and command.

Satan acts as an angel, (literally 'messenger'), because he is a member of the heavenly Court and has his allotted place within the hierarchy of spirits. 'There was a day', says *Job* 1.6 (repeated 2.1), 'when the sons of God [*Bene ha-Elohîm*] came to present themselves before the Lord, and *ha-satan* came also among them': *ha-satan*, that is to say, 'the angel or spirit whose task it is to offer opposition or be a stumbling-block in someone's way'. What follows – a short conversation between God and *ha-satan* – has been interpreted as a report offered to God-as-monarch by a spirit whose particular task resembles that of a spy or secret policeman such as was an integral part of the Persian King's system of gathering intelligence. Here the writer (or one of the writers) of *Job* has a play upon words. *Ha-satan* tells God he has just come back from roaming the earth and strolling about on it, (*Job* 1.7). 'Roaming' is the verb *sût*, a clear pun on *śtn* ('satan'), used again in *Zacharias* 4.10 where seven lamps are described as 'the eyes of the Lord which roam through the whole earth'. This roving commission, then, precipitates a view of the Devil, which, in combination with 1 *Peter* 5.8 – 'Be sober, be vigilant, because your adversary the Devil, as a roaring lion, walketh about, seeking whom he may devour' – informs the later Mediaeval and Early Modern perception of Satan as a dangerous figure on the loose whom one may meet round any corner. After *ha-satan* has explained what he has just been doing, God praises Job to him, commending in the highest terms Job's moral integrity and steadfast faith, a speech of confidence which causes *ha-satan* to issue an immediate challenge: test Job as hard as you can, and you will find he will fail and curse you to your face. It is a challenge God allows to proceed, with what results are well known: 'the Lord gave Job twice as much as he had before ... [and] the Lord blessed the latter end of Job more than his beginning', (*Job* 42.10, 11).

It is remarkable to see how far God allows *ha-satan* to go in crippling Job financially, emotionally, physically, before calling an end to his torments. How much personal malice is there in the Satan's challenge? Is he inherently malevolent, is he jealous of God's praising of Job, or is he indifferent, as an automaton is indifferent? We can dismiss this last, for *ha-satan's* reply to God's encomium begins with what sounds like a piece of sarcasm. 'Does Job venerate the Lord for no good reason?' [*Septuagint*], or 'Can it be said that Job is needlessly afraid of the Lord?' [*Vulgate*]. After all, says *ha-satan*, God is protecting Job all the time. Take that protection away and his reverence will soon disappear. There is a touch of arrogance in this assumption that Job will fail the test, so we are beginning to see a possible change of character, (assuming this particular *satan* was not wholly given to maleficence from the start), such as we have noted in certain Middle Eastern deities during their period of transition.

Other examples of 'Satan' as a spirit-member of the heavenly Court are not hard to find. In *Zacharias* 3.1, for example, the prophet sees a vision of Joshua, the High Priest, 'standing before the angel of the Lord, and *ha-satan* standing at his right hand to accuse him', the accusation being one of failing in the duties proper to his office. Elaine Pagels sees this *satan* as a somewhat sinister figure. 'His role begins to change from God's agent to that of His opponent', as he takes sides in a conflict internal to the Israelites at a crucial juncture in their history, or, as Neil Forsyth puts it, 'a cosmic projection of the groups hostile to the Temple hierocracy'. Whatever the specific interpretation of his role in this visionary episode, however, the import of the passage is clear. *Ha-satan* and the angel of the Lord are both servants of God and are operating in judicial capacities, thereby constituting a court of law. But, if Elaine Pagels is right in seeing this *satan* as a spirit in process of change, the *satan* of 1 *Chronicles* 21.1 looks as though he has accomplished that change altogether. The episode in question deals with David's offence of taking a census of the Israelites whereby he incurs severe punishment from God, having the people of Israel counted being a divine prerogative, as is made clear in *Numbers* 1.2, 3.15, 26.2. But David did not commit this sin entirely of his own volition. He was provoked into it. 'And Satan stood up against Israel and moved David to number Israel'. The word *satan* here has no accompanying definite article, which means it may be understood either as a common or as a proper noun. So 'satan' in this verse could mean 'an adversary' or 'Satan'. Either way, he is behaving as an agent provocateur and is acting independently of God's wish or command. So we can see in this figure not only a distinct entity moved to act by some malice inherent in him, but also a spirit whose principal attribute ('opposition') has become his defining name.[7]

Here, then, we discern the outline of Satan as he was perceived by later generations. It will be noted that no mention has been made of the serpent of

Genesis, who tempted Eve and, through her, Adam into disobeying God's strict injunctions. This is because identification of the serpent with Satan is a much later gloss on the original text, and is therefore not relevant to these early stages of Satan's emergence. It is the same with other spirits whose characteristics were later absorbed into those of the predominant figure of evil who was termed 'Satan' or 'the Devil'. Hence Belial ('wickedness'), identified with death by drowning and with crimes and committers of crimes against God, crimes such as apostasy, perjury, and usurpation, gradually turned into another name for the Devil; while Mastemah ('hostility') has etymological connections with 'Satan', and represents not only the hostile acts of Belial against the children of light as described by the Dead Sea Scrolls, but in the apocryphal Book of Jubilees, composed in the second century BC, turns into the prince of those evil spirits who are a danger to humankind, and is thus identified with Satan.[8]

So by the time they reached the first century AD, the Jews had accumulated a grand sweep of apocalyptic literature which provided ample opportunity to work out what 'evil' meant and how it might be portrayed, and to produce a range of figures who personified either evil in itself or aspects of evil intent and behaviour. A hierarchy of wicked spirits begins to emerge, and since a hierarchy has a leader or monarch, so the entity who was going to be called 'Satan' as though the attribute were his proper name, gradually took shape. One fact remained constant throughout, however. Unlike Zoroastrianism with its two self-created spirits of good and evil, Judaism never intruded upon the singleness of God. Satan was a created being from the start and therefore always a subordinate, no matter how powerful he was envisaged as being, and no matter how large he loomed in human consciousness. So when it came to Christianity, whatever the tempter, the enticer, the opponent, the adversary, the enemy, might do or say, he could never prevail in his perpetual struggle with God because however dualistic the appearance of Christian theology, in reality the conflict between good and evil is the conflict between the Creator and one of His creatures. The New Testament, however, certainly makes good use of the adversarial nature of creation's chief demon. He appears 568 times, challenging Jesus' authority, endeavouring to entice those around Him into betrayal or dereliction of trust and belief, and dominant in the vision of the Last Days; and since the New Testament was written in Greek, the *lingua franca* of the region during the Hellenistic and early Roman period, terms equivalent to *ha-satan* were employed to designate him. *Diabolē* in Greek means 'a false accusation, a slander, a quarrel, a fraud', and *diabolos* (which has passed into various European languages – diavolo, diablo, diable, duivel, Teufel, diabhal, devil – is a person who does such things. But while the Old Testament tends to distinguish between its names for perpetration of evil intention, the tendency to elision which is evident in Jewish apocalyptic literature and the Dead Sea Scrolls becomes much more evident in the New Testament, where Satan, the Devil, the Enemy, Beelzebub, Belial, the Prince of this World, the Tempter, the Accuser, the Evil One, the Prince of Demons, and the Prince of the Air, all clearly refer to the same entity.

This composite Satan is the one who tempts Jesus in the desert. Mark (1.12-13) does not go into details, but Matthew (4.1-9) expands Jesus' test into three distinct episodes during which Satan suggests He satisfy His hunger by turning stones into bread, work an essentially pointless miracle by throwing Himself off the roof of the Temple in Jerusalem – presumably in full sight of the crowds who would be thronging the area – so that angels would be obliged to come to His rescue, and bow down in homage to Satan in return for earthly command of a temporal empire. Luke (4.1-7) repeats the account in a different order. The portrait of Satan here is familiar: he entices, he seeks to corrupt, and his motives are entirely malevolent. But is he, as he seems to suggest during his offer of temporal kingship, the ruler of the world? 'I shall give to you all this power and all the glory of these kingdoms, because it has been handed over to me, and I give it to anyone I please', (*Luke* 4.6). (It is at this point, incidentally, that Jesus addresses the tempting spirit by name in both Matthew's account and Luke's: 'Get thee hence, Satan', 'Get thee behind me, Satan'.) According to the first episode of *John* 5.19, 'the whole world lies in the Evil One'. The word here translated as 'lies' has a variety of possible meanings in Greek: lies still, lies sick or wounded, lies dead, lies neglected, lies at the mercy of. But 'lies in' suggests another – 'is dependent on', and this strongly implies a connection between what Luke and John are saying at this point, and John's further 'Now shall the ruler of this scheme of things [*kosmos*] be driven out', (12.31). Henry Kelly suggests that this notion of Satan as ruler of the earth may have more than one source in earlier Jewish religious literature, particularly a passage in *Jeremiah* (27.5-8) where God, by way of punishment for rebelliousness, delivers both Jews and non-Jews into the hands of Nebuchadnezzar, King of Babylon, a ruler who is scarcely the pattern of an ideal monarch but whose rule is destined to come to an end once the allotted term of punishment is fulfilled.

Satan, then, feels secure enough in what he sees as his dominant worldly position to tempt Jesus with the prospect of earthly rule, and is sufficiently unabashed by his failure on this occasion to be prepared to try again – in the words of St Luke, 'When the Devil had finished every test, he departed from Him *until an opportune time*', (4.13, my italics). Apart from this role of apparently self-confident aristocrat, however, Satan's activities in relation to Jesus, as depicted in the Gospels, are those we have come to expect, including his possession of people in order to continue his dire work through a human agent, as he does, for example, through Judas, ('and Satan entered into him', *John* 13.27); and even when Jesus calls St Peter a 'satan' for protesting against His destiny of arrest, trial, and crucifixion, (*Matthew* 16.21-3), He is repeating the common Hebrew usage whereby *satan* is a common noun meaning 'obstacle' rather than a proper name, as Matthew's immediate translation of *satana* by *skandalon* ('stumbling-block') makes clear. This sense of 'obstruction' or 'obstructer' continues in the letters of St Paul who constantly sees the Devil as a force working through human agents to throw up obstacles to the preaching and spreading of the Gospel. 'I appeal to you, brethren, to keep an eye on those who create dissensions and stumbling-blocks contrary to the teaching you have learned, and avoid them. People such as these serve as slaves not of our Lord, Christ, but of their own stomach, and through fair words and fine phrases they deceive the hearts of the innocent ... The God of peace will grind Satan to pieces under your feet', (*Romans* 16.18, 20).

But it is the *Apocalypse* of St John, which provides us with further insights into the character of Satan, along with a context which underlines his dominance as *the* spiritual embodiment and exorciser of evil in this world, and a narrative which tells us of his attempted coup against God and his subsequent punishment:

And there was war in heaven: Michael and his angels fought against the serpent, and the serpent fought, and his angels, and prevailed not; neither was their place found in any more in heaven. And the great serpent was cast out, and that old serpent called "the Devil" and "Satan" which deceiveth the whole world, he was cast out into the earth and his angels were cast out with him ... And I saw an angel come down from heaven, having the key of the bottomless pit, and a great chain in his hand. And he laid hold on the serpent, that old serpent which is "the Devil" and "Satan", and bound him 1000 years, and cast him into the bottomless pit, and shut him up, and set a seal upon him, that he should deceive the nations no more, till the thousand years should be fulfilled ... And fire came down from God out of heaven and devoured them. And the Devil that deceived them was cast into the lake of fire and brimstone, there the beast and the false prophet are, and shall be tormented day and night for ever and ever, (*Apocalypse* 12.7-9; 20.1-3, 9-10).

Here St John gives us the material not only for a narrative of Satan's fall from Heaven, but also for the composite image of him as angel-and-beast. He takes his cue, as Elaine Pagels points out, from *Isaiah* 26.17 - 27.1 wherein the prophet tells us of the day when God will come to punish the inhabitants of the earth for their iniquity, and will also punish Leviathan, 'the piercing serpent, even Leviathan that crooked serpent: and He shall slay the serpent that is in the sea'. This cosmic war is therefore the ultimate rebellion, waged by someone or something who can be envisaged only in terms of bestial imagery, and who is now perceived as that most shudderingly dreadful of creatures, one which can kill by crushing to death or injecting a fatal poison. Such a figure is much more than a subordinate in the Court of Heaven, a servant who can be sent to test someone's faith, or an advocate in a law-court however exalted. He is also no longer in a group of people who oppose the Temple hierarchy in Jerusalem or the missionary efforts of an Apostle such as St Paul. He is now truly a prince in his own right, commander of armies consisting of evil spirits and terrifying monsters, engaged in a battle with God which ranges far beyond this world into other created realms where he and his legions are met by the hierarchy of Heaven, and a demonic overlord with his own kingdom, the earth, and his own dwelling-place, Hell. No wonder, therefore, if St Paul warned the Ephesians that 'our contest is not against flesh and blood, but against the authorities, against the powers, against the world-rulers of this darkness, against the spiritual forces of evil in heavenly places', (6.12). For by this time, Satan had emerged from his origins, more or less fully fledged as the Fiend of later commentary and interpretation.[9]

CHAPTER 2

Demons in the Desert:
The Early Christian Centuries

Between c.AD 271 and 285, St Antony of Egypt was subject to several attacks by the Devil. He had left home after the death of his parents, entrusted his sister to the care of local virgins, sold all he had, and was now living the life of an ascetic in the desert not far from his native village. 'The Devil', says the *Life of St Antony* by St Athanasius, 'who hates and envies what is good, could not bear to see such purpose in the young man, so he now initiated his usual practices against [him]'. They started with memories of possessions and family and friends, and when these had no effect were followed by sexual temptations which began with Satan's whispering foul thoughts in St Antony's ear and then appearing to him in the form of a woman who 'imitated all a woman's ways, solely for the purpose of deceiving Antony'. Once again, however, St Antony resisted and the Devil, now referred to as 'the serpent' (*drakōn*), changed his shape to that of a black child and spoke directly to the saint in tones at once pitiful and whining (*oiktras phōnas*) as he complained that his usual tricks had not worked. But St Antony, not devoid of courage, however disconcerted, answered, 'You are completely despicable because you are black in mind and like a feeble child'; at which that black individual (*ho melas ekeinos*) immediately fled this frightening tone of voice and was thereafter afraid of coming near St Antony again.

Not that the fear put him off permanently. The saint had decided to go and live among tombs at some distance from his village, and shut himself up in one of them in order to be alone. But 'the Enemy' was unable to endure the thought that St Antony might turn the desert into a city of ascetics, and so one night he came out with a numerous mob of demons and rained down so many blows on the saint that Antony was left lying on the ground, speechless with pain. The verb St Athanasius uses here for 'strike' also means 'cut', and so we may be meant to see St Antony not only bruised but bleeding from a large number of weals. He recovered from this attack, however, only to be subjected to another. 'The Enemy' was amazed at his courage and 'summoned his dogs', that is, his faithful demons, who thereupon swarmed round the saint in various shapes – lions, bears, leopards, bulls, and poisonous snakes – and made such a din that the tomb seemed to be disintegrating around them. Once again they appeared to have inflicted physical damage on St Antony for the *Life* says he was 'flogged' and 'stabbed as though by goads', expressions which seem to reflect the slashing of big cats' teeth and the biting of snakes, until his courage and prayers saved him. The roof seemed to open, a beam of light shone down on him, and suddenly the demons vanished, and with them the pain they had caused.

Now came a further trial. St Antony decided to retreat still further into the desert and set off for Mount Pispir. The Devil tried tempting him with gold and silver – an illusory silver dish and a pile of gold lying upon the road – but St Antony ignored both of them. He arrived at a deserted military outpost, (presumably a stockade with a small building in which the soldiers, off guard, could rest or shelter), laid in sufficient bread and water for six months, and then blocked up the entrance. He stayed there for a year and at some point – apparently more than one – the Devil attacked him again, sending wave upon wave of demons to interrupt the saint's prayers and meditations. Friends who came to visit St Antony in his retreat heard voices and crashing inside, as though a mob had invaded and was fighting him; but when they looked through a hole in the wall, they saw nothing and realised the noise came from demons. By now St Antony was so used to these phenomena that he ignored them. He came to the door of his refuge and told his friends to go away and not be afraid. 'Demons make phantasms in this fashion [as an act of hostility] against those who are afraid', he said. 'So cross yourselves, go away with fresh courage, and leave these entities to play games for their own amusement'.[10]

There are various points worth noting here. The first is that St Antony chooses to go and live in the desert where he will be surrounded by snakes and wild animals, which present potential physical danger. This is territory, which in the old religion used to belong to Seth, the evil god who presided over death and sterility, and is therefore terrain in which appearances of Satan and demonic activity are entirely to be expected. Secondly, St Athanasius calls Satan 'the serpent' in what is surely meant to be a reference to *Genesis* 3.1-5 and 14-15. Actually there is no overt link in the Hebrew text identifying the serpent of Eden with the Devil, but the *Apocalypse* certainly does so: 'that ancient snake who is called the Devil and Satan', (12.9), 'the serpent, that ancient snake who is called the Devil and Satan', (20.2). St Justin Martyr (died 165 AD) seems to have been the first to make the connection, and yet he does so in an offhand way which suggests that the notion was not his, but had been current for a while; for in his *Dialogue with Trypho the Jew*, he mentions that Christ had existed from before the creation of the world and submitted to becoming incarnate, 'so that by this dispensation of God the serpent (*ophis*) who did evil in the beginning, and the angels who became like him, might be destroyed and death be brought into contempt', (chapter 45).

A snake, however, is only one of the forms taken by the Devil in St Antony's *Life*. He also appears as a woman and as a black child, and this shape-changing raises interesting questions not so much about why the Devil behaves thus as how. One of the constant preoccupations of later centuries, the sixteenth and early seventeenth in particular, was the problem of how spirits who, by definition, had no physical body were able to manifest themselves in the world of matter and to perform functions apparently possible only by an individual in possession of a physical body – speaking in such a way as to be heard and understood, touching and being touched, having sexual intercourse with a human, such intercourse often being corporeal enough to result in pregnancy and birth. This last, of course, refers to incubi and succubi, those spirits who take the forms of men or women in order to seduce human beings into committing sins of a particular kind – adultery or fornication. 'I am a friend of fornication', the Devil says to St Antony, using a word that means 'prostitution'. 'I have taken it upon myself to trap youngsters into fornication and titillate them with it'. (One should perhaps remember that St Antony himself was no more than twenty at this time). Since spirits have no corporeal bodies, they cannot of themselves be locatable in the world of matter, and therefore they become locatable only by what they do; and in order to do anything on the physical plane, they must either manufacture for themselves a body from the dense air which exists between the moon and the earth, or borrow a human body either alive or dead, or create an illusion capable of being transmitted via the image-making capability of the human mind to a point in space in which the illusion will seem to be real.

We shall come back to these questions later, but it should be noted here that dismissing St Antony's diabolic and demonic experiences as hallucinations brought on by a combination of ascetic practices and psychological strain will miss the point. Importing nineteenth- or twentieth-century jargon into the third and fourth centuries explains nothing, and certainly does not allow us to understand why St Antony himself interpreted his experiences the way he did, and how they prompted him to offer the kind of advice he gave to other people. As far as he was concerned, the shape-changing Devil and demons were as real as the desert around him. He could hear their voices, smell them, see the various forms in which they appeared – hyena, hybrid, a tall human being, or even another monk – and so the principal question for him to ask himself was whether these were real, (in the sense of their having a separate objectivity outwith himself), or illusory. In both those parts of the *Life* which are narrative by St Athanasius, and in those which purport to reproduce the words of St Antony, there are many instances wherein the Devil or his demons are described as manufacturing illusions or apparitions, and many in which the phenomena are presented as real. Thus, the appearance of the Devil as a black child is an illusion (*phantasia*), and so is the large silver dish St Antony sees in the road on his way to Mount Pisper. But the gold he sees there a little while later is specifically said to be real, ('genuine' or 'true'), and the pains he suffers from the demons' assaults on his person are by no means fantasy. *Phantasia*, however, the word which frequently appears in the *Life* in connection with these phenomena, is not an easy term to grasp. The verb from which it is derived, *phantazō*, means both 'I make something visible to the eye' and 'I imagine', and it therefore straddles the border between the world of physical objects and the world of images. Similarly, *phantasia* refers to the outward appearance of someone or something, or to a movement of the mind generated by sensation – '*phantasia* seems to be a movement of some kind and does not appear to happen without sensation', said Aristotle while at the same time repeating that *phantasia* may turn out to be false, and therefore the opposite of sensation, sensation being always 'genuine' or 'true'. The appearance, then, may be real in itself or generated from elsewhere, and so be real only to sight but not in actuality.

This can best be understood by reference to one of St Antony's similes in which he presents the demons' actions in terms of theatre. If demons were genuinely powerful, he says, they would not conjure up apparitions or change their shapes, because they would not need to resort to such subterfuges. 'Unable to do anything [of their own power and authority], demons play about as though they were on a stage, changing their shapes and frightening children by [creating] the illusion of undisciplined mobs, and by taking on different appearances', (28). Now, an actor is a real person but, having entered upon a stage, assumes different roles and different appearances, and is likely to perform all kinds of actions he or she might be unlikely to do in real life. The actor therefore leads a double life and, *mutatis mutandis*, so does the demon; for he exists really enough in his own plane of spirit, but is prepared to take on a variety of different roles on the plane of matter, as though the corporeal world were a stage and its inhabitants the demon's audience. As far as that audience is concerned, the demon is a reality, while the illusions he creates are both real and unreal, just as an actor's performance is both real and unreal at the same time. Hence the apparent paradox of one demonic attack on St Antony. While he was in his tomb-cell, demons made a dreadful racket and entered the cell in the forms of various wild animals and reptiles, described by St Athanasius as 'illusory' (*phantasia*). Each animal made as though to attack St Antony, but stopped short before making physical contact. This is to be expected. These shapes were unreal, in as much as they were parts played by the demons. But the cacophony, which accompanied their appearance, was no illusion, and neither was the pain St Antony was suffering – 'lacerated and stabbed by them ... He groaned because of the pain in his body', (9). But who are 'them'? At first it seems as though 'they' should be the animals and reptiles, but we have just been told they failed to touch the saint. 'They' must therefore be the demons, capable, as we have been informed before, of inflicting physical damage without necessarily taking on different forms. In other words, these actors do not need to assume other roles in order to achieve their purpose, but do so for their own amusement or diversion; and while the parts they play may be 'illusory', the actor-demons themselves are undeniably real."

One of these theatrical parts, as we have seen, was that of a black child, a role assumed by the Devil himself during his first assault on St Antony. The child in this instance is actually a boy, and it is in this guise that the Devil makes his speech about being 'the friend of fornication'; but before we make the mistake of thinking there is a paederastic connection between these two facts, we must bear in mind Dom Nugent's observation that 'the demon of fornication is depicted as a boy ... simply because he is, as St Antony remarks, "powerless and a child"'. Nugent sees the depiction of demons as boys in early Christian literature as little more than an indication that they are simply pests trying to distract monks and other devout people from their devotions by a string of naughtinesses – pulling the hem of their garment, creating a diversion by running about in church, sticking their fingers into monks' mouths to make them yawn. All this is pertinent, of course, but the Greek text tells us something important: 'the way he existed in [St Antony's] mind was the way he appeared to him next'.

So the Devil read the saint's mind, so to speak, taking his cue from that, and reaching into St Antony's memory where images of children he had seen were stored, abstracting one of these, and presenting it to the common sense, (that is, a kind of centralised place in the brain where the sensations are organised for immediate use or reservation), and the faculty of imagination, (that is, the ability to create mental pictures), in so violent a fashion that the exterior sense of sight was jolted or forced into accepting this image of a child as real. Such, at any rate, is the process as envisaged later by Heinrich Institoris. Why was St Antony thinking of a child at this juncture? Children are smaller and weaker than adults, and biddable. Essentially, they are not to be feared. As St Antony explained to his monks, 'We need have no fear at all of [demons'] illusions, for they are nothing and they disappear quickly, especially if each person creates a protective barrier round him or herself with faith and the sign of the cross'; and he dismisses the Devil's attempts to deceive the faithful in language redolent with contempt, likening him to a tethered farmyard animal or 'a little sparrow to be mocked by us'. As for the child's being black, we have to bear in mind the geography of Egypt and its relationship with Biblical texts. On the one hand, 'Ethiopians' – a catch-all word referring to black people living in desert areas remote from the centres of Egyptian civilisation – were described by St Augustine as 'the most remote and most offensive of human beings': while on the other, 'Ethiopians' were considered to be descendants of Noah's cursed son Ham and thus to have inherited, in the words of the fifth-century monk and theologian, John Cassian, 'profanity and perpetual sin'. Indeed, more than once Cassian refers to a demon as an 'Ethiopian' or a loathsome Ethiopian', and his near contemporary, St Augustine of Hippo, noted an incident in Carthage when a doctor suffering from gout, who was about to be baptised, saw black, curly-haired boys in his sleep. He realised they were demons and, although they forbade him to receive baptism, ignored them and proceeded with the sacrament in spite of the pain they caused him by stamping on his feet. Many of the slaves in Egypt at this time will have come from sub-Saharan Africa, and we are told that St Antony's family was wellborn and quite well off. So one of his childhood memories may have been of small black slaves in and around the house. Possible links between these various strands are not peculiar to St Antony, of course, but envisaging demons as black and small does seem to be a common thread in the accounts of Egyptian and other north African desert Fathers and theologians, so perhaps we may regard this particular aspect of St Antony's experience as one rooted both in his personal and his cultural history.[12]

The complex mixture of real and 'imagined' in St Antony's experiences with the Devil, then, gives us some indication of how he himself perceived them, and indeed provides a guide to understanding what Cecilia Ferrazzi and her contemporaries so many centuries later thought such experiences were making them undergo. Cecilia said that the twenty or thirty people who entered her room and sang while they laid a life-size crucifix on the floor were neither dream-figures nor visions, and until the 'hermit' vanished she took him to be real as well. Indeed, why should she not, since she heard him address her and talk constantly as though in prayer, and then felt his violence as he laid hands on her and dashed her head against the walls of her room? Once again, a 'rationalist' explanation will fail to let us appreciate the experience from Cecilia's point of view, the really important one for an historian; and perhaps the most notable feature that unites St Antony's experience and Cecilia's, is the intense physicality attendant upon intercourse with the Devil. St Antony, (as well as St Athanasius, his biographer), recognises the dual nature of these encounters which, spiritual in origin, are physical in effect, and thus give rise to the ambiguous duality wherein lies the most alarming aspect of the experience for the humans involved.

Satan, however, did not always appear in an immediately frightening shape, as Cecilia found out, and this brings us to one of his names – *Lucifer*, 'bringer of light'. The prophet Isaiah recounts that the Israelites are to end their exile in Babylon and return to Jerusalem, and then puts a long cry of triumph into their mouths, urging them to exult over their late master, the King of Babylon. This cry contains a key verse: 'How art thou fallen from Heaven, o Lucifer, son of the morning! How art thou cut down to the ground, which didst weaken the nations!' Why did this Lucifer fall? From overweening pride. 'Thou hast said in thy heart, I will ascend unto Heaven, I will exalt my throne above the stars of God ... I will be like the Most High'. But the result of this arrogance will be deadly. 'Thou shalt be brought down to Hell, to the sides of the pit', (14.12-15). Certain of the Church Fathers, St Justin Martyr, Tertullian, and Origen in particular, seized upon this passage and its quotation in *Luke* 10.15, and applied it to Satan, and once this interpretation had been made, it quickly established itself as the standard account. Here, of course, we have the rebel against the divine monarch, the dissident in the heavenly Court, and the perception that if Satan and his fellow-conspirators could no longer inhabit the spirit-realm of Heaven, they must inhabit somewhere else – Hades, Hell, She'ol, the Pit – a state of existence referred to by *Mark* (9.43-8), *Luke* (16.19-26), *Matthew* (13.40-3, 49-50), and *Apocalypse* (20.10), who together reveal it as a state of post-mortem misery, wailing, and 'the eternal fire prepared for the Devil and his angels'.

But where was this Hell, and did Satan and his demons exist there all the time, or were they able, as daily Christian experience suggested, to manifest themselves in some way in the world of matter? These were questions of great importance and significance, and yet they do not seem to have been addressed with any degree of urgency. The reason is not that people at the time were not interested, but that they had what they regarded as somewhat more pressing questions to consider and resolve. The early Christian centuries were plagued by a large number of heresies, which speculated on almost every aspect of the Godhead and the nature of Jesus. Who, or perhaps what exactly was Jesus: God or man, or some combination of the two? How could spirit and matter co-exist in the same individual? Did it, in fact, do so? Debates expanded and were conducted in the manner of wars between those of orthodox and unorthodox persuasion. In the second century, for example, the Marcionites repudiated the Old Testament and the God described therein whom they viewed as a demiurge, a creator, not wicked in himself, yet nevertheless the cause of the world and its evil. In the third century, adherents of Manichaeism had a dualistic conception of the structure of the world – one is reminded of Zoroastrianism, perhaps not surprisingly since Mani, the heresy's originator, came from Media – and envisaged three stages for creation: (i) the beginning, when the two kingdoms of light and darkness existed separately; (ii) the middle (i.e. the present), when light and darkness have commingled; and (iii) the end, when the original separation will be restored. There are two equally balanced and opposite powers – Good and Evil – in constant struggle with one another, said the Manichaeans, with the human individual as their main battleground, while Satan, (although he is not so called), becomes a creature born from the sperm of the spirit-son of primeval darkness. In this narrative, Jesus is simply one among several prophets, the others being Seth, Enoch, Noah, the Buddha, Zoroaster, and Mani himself. The Manichaean Jesus, (at least in the West), did not really die on the cross, but merely feigned death, suffering only in appearance, while the real Son of God stood by at a distance, 'laughing because someone else was suffering in His place'. Likewise in the third century, Arians denied the divinity of Jesus altogether, maintaining that God the Father alone is true God, a theory pursued in the fourth century by Eutyches, a monk, who said that Christ had one nature only, and in the fifth by Nestorius who sought to be yet more subtle and made a distinction between the 'nature' and the 'person' of Christ.

With every aspect of Christian belief under constant debate, therefore, it is scarcely surprising to find the nature of evil and Satan's ultimate fate are also subject to discussion. Indeed, the fifth- or sixth-century pseudo-Dionysios went as far as to suggest that demons are not evil by nature. 'Devils cannot be evil since they owe their origin to God. The Good is the creator and preserver of good things. If they are called evil, it is not in respect of their being, since they owe their origin to the Good and were the recipients of a good being, but rather because being is lacking to them by virtue of their inability, as Scripture puts it, "to hold on to their original source"'. Hence the notion of universal redemption floated by Valentinus (second century) and tentatively pursued by Origen, which included the idea that in the end everyone, even Satan, would be redeemed and return to the essential purity of the beginning. For the most part, however, any attempt to take the Zoroastrian position of having a personified evil independent of and equal to the divine monarch was condemned by the Church, as happened at the Council of Braga in 563: 'Whoever denies that the Devil was originally a good angel created by God, contending instead that he arose from the chaos and the darkness and has no creator, but is himself the principle and the substance of evil ... Let him be anathema'. Similarly, the prediction of Satan's ultimate fate, contained in *Apocalypse* 20.1-10, which envisages his being bound and confined in a pit for a thousand years, then released to cause havoc upon earth before being defeated in battle and imprisoned in a place of perpetual punishment, became orthodox doctrine, facing down a variety of contrary suppositions and interpretations.[13]

But where was this pit, this fiery place of eternal punishment? The Bible uses various words for it – She'ol, Gehinnom, *shahat, tehom*, Hades – and between them they give a somewhat conflicting picture of what was being envisaged. She'ol is a word of uncertain etymology, but clearly refers to the region of the dead. It is located very deep under the earth – hence its identification with *shahat*, 'pit', and *tehom*, 'abyss' – is guarded by gates, and is a place of silence and darkness where the dead are restrained, like animals caught in a snare. Gehinnom, (Latin Gehenna), was originally a valley to the south of Jerusalem, where children were sacrificed to Moloch, an Ammonite deity, whose worship rendered the spot thereafter defiled. The children were burned on altars, and thus Gehenna became associated with fire. In later times, the place was used for the burning of all kinds of rubbish and detritus. Hence Jesus' observation that 'if thy hand offend thee, cut it off: it is better for thee to enter into life maimed than, having two hands, to go to Hell [Geënnan], into the fire that never shall be quenched', (*Mark* 9,43). Hades, in Greek the house of a person, the brother of Zeus, and ruler of the underworld, was also the region of the dead, and in this sense it is close to She'ol, as in *Matthew* 16.18, 'the gates of Hell shall not prevail against [the Church]', and *Apocalypse* 20.13, 'and death and Hell delivered up the dead which were in them'.

Darkness, misery, and silence characterised She'ol and to some extent these features can still be detected in Gehenna with its seven names – She'ol, Destruction, Pit, Tumultuous Pit, Miry Clay, Shadow of Death, and Underworld – and the darkness, fire, snow, and ice described by the patriarch Levi in his *Testament*. But it was the fires of Gehenna, which informed later developed ideas of what Hell was like. The Jewish tradition of the Babylonian Talmud, for example, emphasised this. The fire of Gehenna was created by God on the second day and will never be extinguished. There are two palm trees in the Ravine of Ben Himmon and smoke rises between them, indicating the presence of one of the gates of Gehenna. The *Testament of Isaac* goes further. '[The angel] brought me to a river of fire. I saw it throbbing, with its waves rising to about thirty cubits: and its sound was like rolling thunder. I looked upon many souls being immersed in it to a depth of about nine cubits. They were weeping and crying out with a loud voice and great groaning, those who were in the river. And that river had wisdom in its fire. It would not harm the righteous, but only the sinners by burning them. It would burn every one of them because of the stench and repugnance of the odour surrounding the sinners'. Ezra, too, had similar visions of Gehenna. 'I saw boiling fires there, and a multitude of sinners in them', he recorded in his *Apocalypse*, although more detailed and more extraordinary is his *Vision* which is devoted almost entirely to this revelation:

He saw fiery gates and at these gates he saw two lions lying there, from whose mouth and nostrils proceeded the most powerful flames ... He saw in that place people standing in torments. Some [of the angels] were throwing fire in their faces; others, however, were whipping them with fiery scourges ... He saw a cauldron in which were sulphur and bitumen, and it was boiling just like the waves of the sea ... And the sinners came, wishing to pass over, and the angels of Hell came and submerged them in the fiery stream ... He saw visions of a furnace, against the setting sun, burning with great fire, into which were sent many kings and princes of this world.

This is basically Jewish tradition with Christian additions and interpolations. But purely Christian tradition repeated these themes, virtually without embellishment. 'I saw there a river of fire burning with heat', says the *Apocalypse of Paul*, 'and in it was a multitude of men and women sunk up to their knees, and other men up to the navel ... I saw on the north side a place of sundry and diverse torments, full of men and women, and a river of fire flowed down upon them ... I saw not far off another old man whom four evil angels brought, running quickly, and they sunk him up to his knees in the river of fire, and smote him with stones, and wounded his face like a tempest'. The *Apocalypse of Peter* presents the same picture: sinners of various kinds subjected to a variety of tortures, but over and over again to the accompaniment of fire a searing heat – even miscarried bastards are steeped in a lake of faeces and shoot rays of fire into the eyes of their guilty mothers – while the *Acts of Thomas* presents us with the eye-witness testimony of a woman raised from the dead:

And the Apostle said to her: Tell us where you have been. And she answered: Do you want to hear who was with me and to whom I was delivered? And she began to say: A man who was hateful to look at took me. [He was] altogether black, and his raiment exceedingly foul. He took me away to a place wherein were many pits, and a great stench and hateful odour issued thence. And he made me look into every pit, and I saw in the [first] pit flaming fire, and wheels of fire ran round there, and souls were hanged upon those wheels, and were dashed against each other.

Coptic *Apophthegmata*, too, followed the same pattern of fire and punishment. According to one of them, an old woman relates a turning-point in her life when she was visited in sleep by someone 'great in his body, frightful in his appearance ... [and] furious in his aspect', who took her into Hell to see the sufferings of her dead mother:

The one who had brought me there took me in his grasp, saying, "Come and see your mother also, being burned with fire, so that you shall perceive what is the good and profitable life so that you may choose it for yourself". He set me over a house of gloom and all darkness, filled with the chattering of teeth and distress. He showed me a fiery cauldron which was giving forth flame and bubbling over. Certain ones were standing over it, they being very afraid. I looked down. I saw my mother in the cauldron up to her shoulders, her teeth chattering and striking against each other, and the fire was burning her up and many worms were eating her.[14]

Clearly, then, Hell, like the Devil, was conceived in remarkably physical terms and the question must arise whether these were taken literally or metaphorically. In as much as Hell is a spirit-state, and the Devil, his demons, and indeed the human souls who occupy that state are also spirits, it can be said that the language of physical matter in which they are described must be a figurative attempt to convey to corporeal sensibilities and comprehension experiences which are incorporeal. But, as we shall see, the borderline between metaphorical and literal was easily blurred, and the appearance of spirit-forms in the world of matter meant that the barriers between the worlds of matter and of spirit must be considered porous, or that these incompatible states of being were constantly drifting in and out of each other's ambience, thereby enabling elements from one to occupy space in the other. Such drift or interpenetration could not but affect the way experiences of the spirit-worlds were felt and then described, and a kind of unease permeates this type of literature as the reader becomes increasingly aware, if only at a subliminal level, that neither a literal nor a metaphorical reading of the text is satisfactory, and that the words on the page are like fingers grasping for sunlight.

So if Hell was 'real' in more senses than one, and so were those who inhabited it, how were they able to leave and where else could they be found? Let us leave on one side the question of human souls consigned to Hell, since they do not concern us here. The 'where else' is clear. St Antony's experiences alone tell us that demons could enter and leave the desert, so that we know they were capable of appearing on earth, whether visibly or invisibly. But there was also a long-standing learned debate on their occupation of the sky or air. It stems from St Paul's letter to the Ephesians, which says, 'We wrestle not against flesh and blood, but against principalities, against powers, against the rulers of the darkness of this world, against the spirits of wickedness in the places of the heavens/the sky/the air', (6.12). It is the precise meaning of that last phrase, *en tois epouraniois*, which produces the need for alternatives, and since spirits of wickedness could scarcely be envisaged as inhabiting Heaven, Church Fathers and several modern commentators have been drawn to choosing between 'sky' and 'air', with St Basil and St Jerome favouring the former and St John Chrysostom and Theodore of Mopsuestia the latter. Proliferation of heresies during the early centuries meant there were further complications to consider. The Marcionites, for example, proposed the existence of two heavens, and the Manichaeans ten, while a Christian addition to the *Martyrdom of Isaiah*, (the *Ascension*), composed some time during the first three centuries, describes a vision in which the author sees Christ descending through seven heavens on His way to be born a human, and then entering the region (called 'the firmament') where the Prince of this world lives:

> He gave the password to those who were on the left and His form [was] like theirs, and they did not praise Him there; but in envy they were fighting one another, for there is there a power of evil and envying about trifles. And I saw when He descended and made Himself like the angels of the air, that He was like one of them.

This is reminiscent of *Ephesians* 2.2, 'In time past you walked according to the course of this world, according to the prince of the power of the air, the spirit that now worketh in the children of disobedience'. So the sky and the air beneath it formed a dangerous region ruled over by a prince who could be, and was, identified with the Devil, and in which evil spirits existed and fought. Was this their natural dwelling-place rather than Hell? If we understand 'natural' in its proper sense, 'pertaining to Nature and the created scheme of things', the answer will be, Yes; and if they inhabit the sky and the air when they are not in Hell, it is no big matter for them to descend to earth and continue their mischief there in whatever form they can manage to assume. The third-century AD philosopher Porphyry emphasised the association of evil spirits and air. 'They are not clothed in a solid body', he wrote, 'nor do they all have a single shape. They take many forms, and the shapes which imprint and are stamped on their aerial body [*pneuma*] are sometimes visible and sometimes invisible. The worse ones sometimes change their shape'. Spirits both good and bad, he says, 'administer large parts of the regions beneath the moon'. Good spirits bring fine weather, moderate rain, and balance of the seasons: evil spirits 'are responsible for the sufferings which happen round the earth, such as plagues, crop failures, earthquakes, and droughts'. Hence spirits find their natural place in the air and on the earth and thus exist cheek-by-jowl, as it were, with human beings.[15]

A compelling impetus working towards the acceptance of this conclusion was the common tendency of early Christians to identify the numerous pantheons of deities worshipped by their pagan ancestors and contemporaries as no more than demons posing as gods and goddesses. As an early sixth-century inscription on the martyrdom of St George in Zorava says, 'The abode of pagan spirits [*daimones*] has become the house of God. The light of salvation shines where darkness used to cause concealment. Where sacrifices to idols used to happen, now there are choirs of angels. Where God used to be provoked, now He is propitiated'. But frequently the intellectual-philosophical-religious opposition between pagans and Christians in a given area concealed, or half-concealed, a continuing pagan worship on the one hand and burgeoning Christian hegemony on the other. In Menonthis, a village not far from Alexandria in Egypt, for example, the local temple of Isis was closed and partly dismantled in 392. While monks took over the temple-estates, however, the temple itself continued to be used as it always had been for sacrifices and incubation under the guidance of a pagan priest. Uneasy co-existence spanned the generations, too. An Egyptian monk, the son of a pagan priest, recalled how he used to watch his father making sacrifices to Satan, (as he expressed it), and his army, while demons reported the damage they had done on land and sea. In Asia Minor, paganism lingered in some of the remoter districts as late as the tenth century, so the experience of a Bithynian monk, Hypatius, in the fifth will come as no surprise. After establishing what turned out to be a flourishing monastery, he would make tours of inspection through some of the further-flung country parts, and on one of these made during the fifty-day festival of the Basket of Artemis, he met the goddess – 'a woman as tall as ten men' – walking about and tending pigs. But Hypatius stood firm and crossed himself; the goddess disappeared and her pigs ran away with a loud whistling noise. (One is reminded of St Antony's advice to make the sign of the cross if one is faced by a demon.) Hypatius was also told about an abandoned pagan temple where forty men were living and offering sacrifices to the old gods, and so he set about threatening divine destruction upon it, a fulmination which seems to have been successful, as the squatters died off or abandoned the temple for other, less dangerous places.

By and large, however, Christians did not so much actively fight to destroy the older religions whose deities and spirits they successfully demonised – although, to be sure, there are many and enough examples of this happening over time – as absorb the cultures around them and, by a combination of steadfast adherence to their own *mores* and exorcism of traditional methods of placating and pleasing the local non-human entities, they provided a more effective alternative to their pagan counterparts' religious discourse and practice, and thus gradually became both dominant and acceptable. As David Frankfurter puts it, '[they] performed the Christian worldview and scheme of authority *within* the traditional landscape', and an ascetic such as St Antony who 'stands between two worldviews, two frameworks for experience ... thus represents both uniqueness ... and the possibility of *synthesis*', and in consequence can 'inspire people to begin the process of *embracing* that synthesis whose very possibility he represents'. Cyril Mango has suggested that 'the system of demonology adopted by the Church was specifically a response to the situation of the second- to fourth-centuries', by which he means that this was the crucial period in which Christianity adapted the failing pagan religions to its own specific theology.[16]

It was an adaptation which turned into a flood of awareness of demons in everyday life, but which was not so acutely sensitive to the presence of Satan. This, perhaps, is partly because there was no real equivalent in the Greek or Roman pantheon with which he could be identified, and partly because he tended to be identified not, as his demons were, with temporal illness, loss, or disaster, but with the Final Days and Armageddon, the ultimate battle between Good and Evil. When he does appear to individuals, however, he acts largely as a tempter – his New Testament role – endeavouring to distract monks from their prayers or virgins from their chastity. 'Seedy' is how Mango describes him at this juncture, and one cannot help noticing the frequent incompatibility between the Devil's dominant, terrifying, and apocalyptic associations, and the comparative triviality of what he actually does in many instances, and the ease with which he can be dismissed by a psalm or a sign of the cross. It is a disjunction between role and action we shall have cause to note frequently as we review his later history.

CHAPTER 3

Planting his Seat in the North

The fall of Satan-Lucifer-the Devil from Heaven because of overweening pride was accompanied, as we have seen, by that of myriads of angels who joined his rebellion against God and fell with him. The links between this cosmic event and the constant presence of impulses to do evil deeds among human beings are explored in a wide variety of religious literature of Jewish origin. The *Book of Enoch*, written in about the second century BC, reveals that a number of angels known as 'Watchers' had been given charge of supervising humanity but, through lust for human women, abandoned their duties and thus turned into evil beings. As the angel Uriel says to Enoch, 'Here shall stand in many different appearances the spirits of the angels which have united themselves with women. They have defiled the people and will lead them into error so that they will offer sacrifices to the demons as to gods, until the great day of judgement on which they shall be judged till they are finished', (1 *Enoch* 19.1-2). The Watchers are also accused of teaching humans the arts of magic and other occult knowledge: 'Amasras taught incantation and the cutting of roots; and Armaros the resolving of incantations; and Baraqiyal astrology, and Kokarer'el [the knowledge of] the signs, and Tam'el taught the seeing of the stars, and Asder'el taught the course of the moon as well as the deception of humankind', (1 *Enoch* 8.3). *Jubilees*, composed at about the same time as *Enoch*, goes further and has Noah complaining to God about the offspring of these angels (now demons), whom he wants God to remove from the ambit of his grandchildren, a petition resisted by Mastema, prince of the spirits. It is clear from this passage (*Jubilees* 10.1-11) that Mastema is, in fact, Satan and what follows indicates that Mastema-Satan and these spirits bring illness and hunger to humans, while at the same time encouraging them to commit idolatry and practise divination.

These themes were picked up by early Christian writers: by St Justin Martyr who emphasised the way illicit sex and the worship of demons served not only to indicate most clearly the difference between Christians and pagans, but also the demon-inspired origin of pagan religions and the wickedness perpetrated by impious human beings of all kinds; by Tertullian (c.160 to post-220) who stressed the importance of women's behaviour in the light of these narratives of angelic lust; while the third-century *Homilies* attributed to St Clement make it clear that the spirits concerned, who live in the lower celestial regions close to earth, originally acted as they did by permission of God, with the aim of causing humans to be punished for their ingratitude towards their divine Father. Contact with humans, however, brought about their downfall:

> Having become in all respects men, they also partook of human lust, and being brought under its subjection they fell into cohabitation with women; and being involved with them, and sunk in defilement and altogether emptied of their first power were unable to turn back to the first purity of their proper nature, their members turned away from their fiery substance: for the fire itself, being extinguished by the weight of lust, and changed into flesh, they trod the impious path downward. For they themselves, being fettered with the bonds of flesh, were constrained and strongly bound; wherefore they have no more been able to ascend into the heavens. For after the intercourse, being asked to show what they were before, and being no longer able to do so, on account of their being unable to do aught else after their defilement, yet wishing to please their mistresses instead of themselves, they ... imparted the discovery of magic, and taught astronomy, and the powers of roots, and whatever was impossible to be found out by the human mind; also the melting of gold and silver, and the like, and the various dyeing of garments. And all things, in short, which are for the adornment and delight of women, are the discoveries of these demons bound in flesh ... But by the shedding of much blood, the pure air being defiled with impure vapour, and sickening those who breathed it, rendered them liable to diseases, so that thenceforth men died prematurely. But the earth being by these means greatly defiled, these first teemed with poison-darting and deadly creatures. All things, therefore, going from bad to worse, on account of these brutal demons, God wished to cast them away like an evil leaven, lest each generation from a wicked seed, being like to that before it, and equally impious, should empty the world to come of saved men.[17]

This was an interpretative tradition, which lasted until the early fourth century, gradually petering out thereafter as *Enoch* became firmly regarded as uncanonical. Nevertheless, it did not die out completely, and we shall find elements of its aetiology of evil appearing in later Mediaeval demonological treatises and several subsequent discussions of the origins and workings of witchcraft. What is more, the constant perception by Christians that the pagan deities who surrounded them were no more than demonic entities of a kind identical with or, if not identical, similar to those fallen angels of Enochic narrative, meant that one of the principal aims of Christian missionary work was to challenge these demons openly wherever they were to be found and, by defeating them, to demonstrate the superior power of the one true God.

Thus, for example, the fifth-century Bishop of Cyrrhus, Theodoret, recorded in one of his sermons, 'Their temples have been destroyed in such a way that not even a semblance of their outline survives, and the people of this century have no knowledge of what their altars looked like. What is more, the material from which they were built has been devoted to shrines of the martyrs. For our Lord God has installed His dead in the temples instead of your gods and has rendered those [gods] insignificant and meaningless. Instead of the Pandia, Diasia, Dionysia, and your other festivals, the Masses of Peter, Paul, Thomas, Sergius, Marcellus, Leontius, Antoninus, Mauricius, and other martyrs are celebrated; and instead of the ancient procession with its disgusting obscenity in deed and word, seemly festivities are observed without any display of drunkenness, jokes, and mocking laughter, but with chants in praise of God, listening to holy sermons, and prayers enhanced by praiseworthy tears'.

Theodoret was discussing the conversion of Arabs in the Syrian countryside, and records of this kind of contact reveal something of the polytheism which used to inform that region – not that these native religious traditions remained isolated or unchallenged until orthodox Christianity ventured into their ambit, for in Bedouin territory there is evidence of Jewish religious influence as well as of Monophysite and Nestorian Christianity. But more to our purpose is the widespread belief that *jinn* – spirits of Nature hostile to human beings, who haunted the desert – exercised such influence over the people who lived there that they took pains to propitiate and honour these spirits by ritual sacrifices, as Charles Doughty recorded as late as 1886:

This sheyk – and in general they of el-Hayât are such – was a man of the Arabian hospitality; so that it was commonly said of him, in Kheybar, "He will sacrifice a sheep if but a (strange) child come there". The good man brought us clotted dates, and sat down with much goodwill to make his guests kahwa. I asked wherefore the corner of his new building had been sprinkled with gore? They wondered to hear me question them thus (and felt in their hearts that I was an alien!) They thought I should have known that it was the blood of a goat which had been sacrificed (to the jân) for the safety of the workmen, "lest, as they said, any one should be wounded".

These spirits, like Christian demons, were seen in both bestial and human shape. 'The *ghrôl* or *ghrûl*', wrote Doughty:

> Is a monster of the desert in which children and women believe and men also. And since no man, but Philemon, lived a day fewer by laughing have here the portraiture of this creature of the Creator, limned by a nomad. [*A picture follows in Doughty's text. See here, fig. 29*] A Cyclops' eye set in the midst of her human-like head, long beak of jaws, in the ends one or two great sharp tushes, long neck; her arms like chickens' fledgling wings, the fingers of her hands not divided; the body big as a camel's, but in shape as the ostrich; the sex is only feminine, she has a foot as the ass's hoof, and a foot as an ostrich. She entices passengers, calling to them over the waste by their names, so that they think it is their own mother's or their sister's voice. He had seen this beast, "which is of a Jin kind, lie dead upon the land upon a time when he rode with a foray in the *Jeheyna* marches'; but there was none of them durst touch her". He swore me, with a great oath, his tale was truth.

Later folklore attributed to *jinn* many of the powers we find in the demons of Christian tradition. They knew secrets; especially those connected with magic, and were capable of changing shape and appearing in many guises. Iblīs, the post-Koranic equivalent of Satan, the Adversary, was said to have been one of them. One of the names applied to these *jinn* is *shayātīn*, 'satans'. These were supposed to be non-human entities in the service of King Solomon, but over time this plural turned into a singular proper noun, al-*shaytan*, a rebel against God and a manifest enemy of humankind, as Qur'ān 19.44 and 17.53 say. There is thus a clear parallel with the development of the Hebrew *ha-satan* into 'Satan'. This Satan figure in the Qur'ān mirrors the Jewish and Christian Satan in other ways, too. He causes fear, envy, and hatred, leads people astray, and tempts them, is able to communicate with humans by calling out, speaking, and whispering, and makes promises which are not to be trusted. As Iblīs, indeed, not only is he the great tempter of humankind (and will remain so until the resurrection), but the embodiment of an overweening pride, which led to his disobedience and fall. For God commanded His angels to bow down before Adam in the garden of Eden; but Iblīs refused, saying that Adam was lesser than the angels, and younger, to which God replied, 'It is not for thee to wax proud here, so go thou forth. Surely thou art among the humbled ... Go thou forth from [Eden], despised and banished. Those of them that follow thee, I shall assuredly fill Gehenna with all of you', (Qur'ān 7.11, 16).

This version of Satan's/Iblīs's fall is not peculiar to Islam. It can be found in the early Christian apocryphal *Life of Adam and Eve*, which exists in several versions and in several languages. After their expulsion from Eden, Adam and Eve wander unhappily upon the earth, and after sixteen days Eve asks Adam how she can express her repentance for offending God and bringing down Adam with her. He suggests they stand in a river up to their necks in silence for forty days, (we have seen a type of this penance inflicted on certain souls in Hell), and so they do, she in the Tigris, he in the Jordan. But after a further eighteen days, Satan disguises himself as an angel, possibly the archangel Michael, and goes to Eve and successfully tempts her yet again, persuading her to break her term of repentance and come out of the river. Triumphantly Satan leads her to Adam who reproaches her. Whereupon she and Adam ask Satan why it is he feels such malice towards them:

The Devil sighed and said, "O Adam, all my enmity and envy and sorrow concern you, since because of you I am expelled and deprived of my glory which I had in the heavens in the midst of angels, and because of you I was cast out on to the earth ... When you were created, I was cast out from the presence of God and was sent out from the fellowship of the angels. When God blew into you the breath of life and your countenance and likeness were made in the image of God, Michael brought you and made [us] worship you in the sight of God, and the Lord God said, "Behold Adam! I have made you in Our image and likeness". And Michael went out and called all the angels, saying, "Worship the image of the Lord God, as the Lord God has instructed". And Michael himself worshipped first, and called me and said, "Worship the image of God". And I answered, "I do not worship Adam". And when Michael kept forcing me to worship, I said to him, "Why do you compel me? I will not worship one inferior and subsequent to me. I am prior to him in creation; before he was made, I was already made. He ought to worship me". When they heard this, other angels who were under me refused to worship him ... And the Lord God was angry with me and sent me with my angels out from our glory; and because of you, we were expelled into this world from our dwellings and have been cast on to the earth.[18]

The stage is thus set for Satan to develop his persona and reveal in how many ways he can visit his spite and resentment on humanity. In the *Hadīth*, sayings attributed to Muhammad and edited by a ninth-century Persian scholar, Muhammad Isma'il al-Bukhārī, Satan is mentioned about 200 times and appears as a personality distinct in many ways from Iblīs who has yet to be merged with him into a single Devil. As Peter Awn describes them, 'Iblīs is ascetic, devoted worshipper, master of the heavens, guardian of Paradise, defender of the Throne,

arrogant, prideful, impetuous ... The title Ash-Shaytān, as employed in the
hadīth, views the Muslim devil from a substantially different perspective. We are
confronted more with a malevolent force than with a highly nuanced personality
... Ash Shaytān is more often than not one-dimensional; he is evil, cunning,
and wily; his delight is to lead mankind astray'. That Satan is a spirit, but is still
capable of entering the world of matter and meddling with it in various ways
presents the same problem of explanation for Muslims as it did for Christians,
but in these early years, at any rate, neither tradition seems to have concentrated
upon it. Rather, they described the phenomena and left explanation on one side.
Thus we learn that Satan-Iblīs contacts human beings in sleep, in dreams, and in
visions. He disrupts their prayers and interferes with their bodies in remarkably
physical fashion:

> A person was mentioned before the prophet and he was told that he had kept
> on sleeping until morning and had not got up for the prayer. The prophet
> said, "Satan urinated in his ear"', (*Hadīth Bukhārī* 2.245). 'The prophet said,
> "If any of you rouses from sleep and performs the ablution, he should wash
> his nose by putting water in it and then blowing it out three times, because
> Satan has stayed in the upper part of his nose all night", (*Ibid.*, 4.516).

Iblīs also has the power to change his shape and appear in different forms to
different people, even that of an angel (as he did to Eve), or an apparently godly
man. He is especially dangerous at night – there is an interesting Islamic tradition
which says that angels are made from *nūr*, 'the cold light of the night', that is,
the moon – and during the two threshold periods of twilight and dawn; and
there is also an *hadīth* which rings a small bell in the ears of historians familiar
with the witchcraft Sabbats of late Mediaeval and Early Modern Europe. '[The
prophet said], "Iblīs places his throne upon the waters. Then he sends forth his
flying columns. To those who are best at sowing discord, he has granted a place
close to him. One of them comes and says, "I have done such and such". Then
he replies, "You have not accomplished anything" ... Then another of them
comes and says, "I did not leave him until I had caused division between him
and his wife" ... Then [Iblīs] brings him close to himself and says, "You have
done well"'. In Christian witchcraft tradition, too, Satan commends those who
have done harm and reproves or beats those who have not done enough to please
him. Nevertheless, like the Christian saints, a number of holy men, according to
Sufi tradition, have the ability to resist Satan-Iblīs and even to inflict harm on
his person. One such holy man, we are told, happened upon Iblīs in a group of
people, and proceeded to seize him and tie him up, refusing to let him go until

he testified to the unity of God; and Muhammad himself once grew so tired of Iblīs's pestering him that he grabbed him by the throat and choked him until the demon's saliva ran down on his hands.

In Jewish, Christian, and Islamic tradition, then, the emergence of a personification of evil, a rebel against the one true God's authority, a spirit eaten up by pride and envy, who was punished for his presumption and cast out from the presence of God, follows a very similar pattern. Cross-cultural and religious themes produced a composite picture. Satan, a creation of God just as much as Adam or Eve or anything else in the universe, would henceforth seek to assuage his personal torment in the world of matter, directing his malice against that part of creation which had been fashioned in God's image and, by seeking to corrupt and destroy that image, strike back at God Himself.

So far we have been discussing the various conceptions and roles of Satan in the Middle Eastern world and Byzantium. Neither Christianity nor Islam, however, confined itself to the geographical area of its origins and quickly spread to the rest of the Mediterranean and thence to more northerly regions. In consequence, Satan migrated with both and rapidly established his presence in the consciousness of those burgeoning hundreds and thousands who converted from their native paganisms, which by and large, seem to have had no equivalent to him in their own pantheons and theogonies. Deities to be feared and propitiated there certainly were – those presiding over death, those bringing disease, those inflicting storms or drought or famine. The Sámi god Ruto, for example, required sacrifice to keep him away from communities lest he bring illness and misfortune; and Loki was a notorious liar, trickster, and shape-shifter, his mischievousness at last resulting in the death of Baldr the Beautiful, a deed for which he was punished by the other gods who bound him and put him in a cave. (The parallels with Satan are interesting and Christianity may, of course, have influenced this part of the story.) The deities who presided over the dead were especially uncomfortable, for ghosts were more likely than not to be hostile to the living, and spirits associated with them could be extremely dangerous. One such was Stallo, an evil entity with iron teeth who had a great desire to eat the flesh of the living. Hence we find that the dead needed to be kept under constant guard, and in one of the *Eddas* we are told that the god Odinn threw Hel into Niflheim and gave her authority over the regions of the dead. 'Niflheim' was a world of mists, and Hel seems to have given her name to that part of the Germanic Christian afterlife in which unregenerate sinners are tormented and ruled by the Devil.

But none of these could really be regarded as a personification of evil, none was perceived as a rebel against the supreme divine monarch, none was a spirit being created by that monarch, and none interacted with humans in order to involve them in a downfall and torment owed entirely to wilful pride and disobedience. It had taken time for this version of evil to emerge in Christianity and in Islam, but once it had done so, it proved persuasive and convincing. Indeed, it even achieved a geographical dimension, for St Augustine associated Satan with the north, observing that, whereas he did not remember that the south signified anything bad anywhere in Scripture, in spite of its being oppressive to human flesh, the north never signified anything good, and in his paraphrase of *Isaiah* 14.14, putting words, as it were, in Satan's mouth – 'I shall plant my seat in the north and I shall be like the Most High'. Christian architecture may have contributed to or reinforced this perception, too, for, as Jeffrey Russell points out, churches are built facing east, so the north is always on one's left as one enters, left being the 'sinister' side where the Devil lurks and where people are reluctant to bury their dead.

In consequence, of course, the north represented a particular challenge for Christian missionaries and during the eighth and ninth centuries they made especially vigorous efforts to convert the peoples there. Pope Gregory I issued advice anent their endeavours to the English mission in 601:

> The idol temples of that race should by no means be destroyed, but only the idols in them. Take holy water and sprinkle it in these shrines, build altars and place relics in them ... When this people sees that their shrines are not destroyed, they will be able to banish error from their hearts and be more ready to come to the places they are familiar with, but now recognising and worshipping the true God. And because they are in the habit of slaughtering many cattle as sacrifices to devils, some solemnity ought to be given them in exchange for this. So on the day of the dedication or the festivals of the holy martyrs whose relics are deposited there, let them make themselves huts from the branches of trees around the churches which have been converted out of shrines, and let them celebrate the solemnity with religious feasts. Do not let them sacrifice animals to the Devil, but let them slaughter animals for their own food to the praise of God, and let them give thanks to the Giver of all things for His bountiful provision. This while some outward rejoicings are preserved, they will be able more easily to share in inward rejoicings. It is doubtless impossible to cut out everything at once from their stubborn minds: just as the man who is attempting to climb to the highest place rises by steps and degrees, and not by leaps.

Advocating the use of pagan religious sites for Christian purposes is a shrewd piece of psychology, and such a tactic would probably have put an end to the practice of paganism in a number of places although not, to be sure, in all. In 1251, for example, Mindaugas, King of Lithuania, appeared to convert to Christianity but continued to worship his native deities in both clandestine and open defiance. 'Secretly', says the Galician-Livonian Chronicle:

> He made sacrifices to the gods – to Nenadey [god of ill fortune], Telyavel [protector of the dead], Diveriks the hare-god [sky-god], and Meidein [forest-goddess]. When Mindaugas rode out into the field, and a hare ran across his path, then he would not go into the grove, nor dared he break a twig. He made sacrifices to his god, burnt corpses and conducted pagan rites in public.

Effecting changes of use to pagan temples and sacred sites, however, was by no means the first thing a missionary tried or was able to do. Such changes cannot really get under way until the process of conversion has started, and this raises a crucial question. When missionaries went to convert, how did they overcome the language barriers between them and their pagan targets; and even if they used interpreters or learned the local languages themselves, how could they be sure that the Christian concepts they were trying to convey were actually transferable accurately from one language to another? *Heliand*, for example, a ninth-century Old Saxon verse epic of the life of Christ, renders 'Lord, teach us to pray' as 'reveal to us the runes', a quite different request, and one of which in fact the Church would not have approved, since the runes were employed at least in part for divination and 'pray' has nothing to do with attempts to reveal the future. There are many examples of similar attempts to reformulate even the simplest expressions in terms a northern audience will have understood. The Virgin Mary is 'a woman of noble lineage'; St Peter, 'the sword thegn' of Jesus; and the desert in which Jesus was tempted becomes a forest. So how was a missionary to explain 'God' (as opposed to 'gods'), or 'sin', or 'redemption'? How could he make clear the Christian concept 'Satan' to people who had no such entity among their gods or demons; and how was he to be sure his potential converts would understand that their gods and goddesses and spirits and ghosts were 'demons' in the Christian sense of that word? Constant repetition would help, of course, as would the miracles so often described as attendant upon the lives of these missionaries, thereby showing that the 'magic' of the Christians was superior to that of the local priests or shamans; while a willingness on the part of the Christians to accommodate to some extent, to adapt within limits – which is what Pope Gregory was suggesting – would encourage good will, and allow the passage of time to create a technical native vocabulary which would gradually lose its pagan meaning and turn into Christian terminology. Thus, *Geist*, 'possession by a non-human entity' became 'spirit'; *Heil*, 'material well-being' became 'holiness' or 'salvation'; and *Truhtin*, 'military leader' narrowed itself into 'Lord'.

The body of hagiographic literature which followed found itself obliged even more urgently to provide terms for specifically Christian concepts, and so we find Old Norse, for example, casting about for words to apply to Satan: *fjándi*, 'enemy', *andskoti*, 'one who shoots from the opposite ranks', and *úvinr*, 'enemy' and also 'unnatural monster'. Words referring to demons cover the same range of meaning, but add other connotations, such as *púki*, which may be related to Irish *púca*, 'fairy', while *blámadr*, 'a black person' clearly reflects the association of black individuals with devilish spirits we have already seen in the Egyptian Fathers' use of 'Ethiopian'. Even the Old English *aelf*, whatever its original connotation, came to mean 'demon', and Christian parents sought to protect their children against demonic envy or interference by giving them such names as *Aelfraed*, 'demon-counsel', or *Aelfric*, 'demon king', while an eighth-century prayer book shows the process making its way into Latin with the phrase *Satanae diabolus aelfae*, 'the devil of the demon Satan'.[19]

Talking was one thing, miracles another, and hagiographies regularly tell how a saint reveals the true nature of pagan idols and exposes the demons lurking within. Thus, in the late sixth-century *Historia certaminis apostolici*, the Apostle Bartholomew fights against demons who deliberately inflict wounds on people and then, in the guise of pagan deities, pretend to cure them. The hero of the late tenth- or early eleventh-century *Vita Martialis* does the same, and pseudo-Deodatus's *Vita Taurini* has Taurinus banishing a demon from the image of a goddess – 'an Ethiopian, black as soot, having a wild beard and emitting fiery sparks from his mouth'. So by explaining to pagans that Satan and his demons were the real causes of sickness both physical and mental, and by identifying the pagan deities they met with these evil spirits, Christian preachers were able to suggest that they, the new-comers, had answers to so many ills which plagued the communities they had come to address and convert. But then the missionaries had to prove their superior power. One such demonstration brought about the conversion of the Danish King, Harald Bluetooth, in c.965. During a feast at which the King was present, a Christian priest, Poppo, and some Danes were arguing about whether Christ was a greater or lesser god than others. Poppo offered to prove that there was only one true God and that pagan idols were merely demons. 'As a result, the next day the King had a large piece of iron heated and ordered Poppo to carry the glowing iron for the sake of the Catholic faith. Poppo took the iron and carried it as far as the King determined. He then showed his undamaged hand and demonstrated to all the truth of the Catholic faith. Consequently the King converted, resolved that Christ alone should be worshipped as God, ordered all people subject to him to reject idols, and thereafter gave due honour to priests and God's servants'.

But perhaps most direct of all the different ways whereby pagans might be helped to grasp a part of the new religion was the proliferation of multifarious likenesses to the Devil. These were both literary and artistic; but while literature showed him in remarkably protean guises – animal, insect, reptile, as well as old man, young woman, fisherman, student, priest, pilgrim, doctor, and theologian – in art he and his demons were frequently depicted in shapes which may have been grotesque and ugly, but were still recognisably human. Thus, in the eighth-century *Life of Saint Guthlac* we are told:

> They were ferocious in appearance, terrible in shape with great heads, long necks, thin faces, yellow complexions, filthy beards, shaggy ears, wild foreheads, fierce eyes, foul mouths, horses' teeth, throats vomiting flames, twisted jaws, thick lips, strident voices, singed hair, fat cheeks, pigeon breasts, scabby thighs, knotty knees, crooked legs, swollen ankles, splay feet, spreading mouths, raucous cries. For they grew so terrible to hear with their mighty shriekings that they filled almost the whole intervening space between earth and heaven with their discordant bellowings.

In the Valenciennes *Apocalypse* (first quarter ninth century) Satan is shown as a naked human figure chained by the neck to a huge snake, which may be there to represent his evil nature. Flames issue from Satan's mouth, as a symbol of destruction. Nearly two centuries later, the Bamberg *Apocalypse* presents us with a very similar picture, Satan entirely human, naked, yoked to a giant horned snake, his wrists bound, but now with his hair sticking up in flame-like spikes, a feature which is often to be seen in portraits of him. But if we look at him in the twelfth-century *Liber Floridus*, we see a number of changes. Satan is still roughly speaking humanoid, but his hands have turned to talons and his feet to animal's paws with their claws extended. He now has a tail and ass's ears, while his face, seen in profile, is distorted, pulled out, as it were, into a sharp nose and elongated lips, which are parted over clamped, snarling teeth. Transfer Satan to Hell, as he appears in the twelfth-century *Hortus Deliciarum*, and we have an extraordinary figure, labelled 'Lucifer as Satan', emaciated in limb but fat in torso, chained by the neck to the cell or cave which holds him, his face a mask with beard and flaming hair. This hair is a reminder of the permanent fiery condition in which the Devil and his spirits lived. 'Whenever they fly in the air or wander on earth or are held prisoner beneath it', wrote Bede:

They always carry with them the torments of their flames. They are like someone who has a fever, who cannot avoid the heat or the cold of the sickness, which has been grafted upon him, even if he is put in beds made of ivory or in places warmed by sunshine. Thus, therefore, demons always burn with the fire of Hell even if they are worshipped in temples made of gold or if they run around in the air.

At first, then, it looks as though painters, glassmakers, and sculptors had free range and could represent Satan and evil spirits according to free flights of fancy. But in fact the ugliness of their depiction seems at basis to have had a certain uniformity. If, for example, we take the theme of the temptations of Christ, a stained-glass panel from Troyes, c.1170-80 shows a composite humanoid figure covered in thick hair, with two hissing serpents instead of horns issuing from its temples, wings sprouting from its buttocks, a beak-like nose, claw-like fingers, and winged or feathered animal's feet. His head is painted brown, his body green – as the fourteenth-century Benedictine, Pierre Bersuire, noted, 'The Devil, a hunter, (that is to say, a hypocrite), usually wears green clothes' – and he appears against a background of aggressive red. In the Huntingfield Psalter (c.1215), the Devil is shown three times, once for each of the three temptations of Christ. In the first he has ass's ears, goat hoofs, and a lion-like face covering his groin; in the second, horns have replaced the ears, spikes have grown from his knees, small wings form his elbows, two wide eyes stare from his chest just below the shoulders, and his feet have changed into the talons of a bird of prey; in the third, the head horns are longer and better-defined, his feet have altered yet again to those of some kind of land animal, and there is a hook-nosed face on his belly. In the Psalter of Amesbury Abbey, c.1250-55, Satan's head is painted red, the rest of his body a shaggy brown. He has large curved thorn-like spikes poking out of his shoulder, elbows, and knees, and his nose is unnaturally elongated and drooping, like an anteater's proboscis. An illustrated life of Christ, c.1350-60, has the Devil similarly bestial, but with antlers instead of horns, and webbed feet instead of unguiform. Remove the extraneous changing features, and what we have is a human figure depicted as bestial with horns, body hair, and animal hands and feet, the closest model of which is the Classical satyr.

Nevertheless, as Luther Link points out, a great number of sculptures and paintings throughout the Middle Ages show Satan without body-hair or wings, sometimes naked and sometimes with a kind of short feathery loincloth, (as in the Amesbury Abbey Psalter), and he suggests that one of the principal influences on painters and sculptors was the mystery play. Illustrations in the twelfth-century Winchester Psalter, for example, clearly show actors wearing costume – a horned animal mask and loincloth – and this can be paralleled from French works of the fourteenth and fifteenth centuries. But presentations of the Devil vary somewhat not only according to the theme of the scene in which he appears – ruler of Hell, tempter of Christ, adversary of God in the last days – but also at different times, when diverse conventions come to dominate. Thus, from the ninth century until the twelfth, the ruler of Hell looks like a satyr or wild man in loincloth; from the twelfth to the fifteenth, he has horns and hoofs and a tail; and when he is shown with wings these are feathered, like those of an angel, until the fourteenth century when he is depicted with those of a bat. From the fifteenth century, he starts to look more angelic except in some scenes of witchcraft and the Last Judgement. So if there is to be a common theme running throughout these concepts, it is that of the Devil as a human figure overlaid by a wide variety of grotesque and animal features, most of which are there to indicate to the onlooker his fallen and sinful nature. In other words, the grotesqueries are to a large extent artistic or theatrical convention, acting as guides to enable onlookers to comprehend both who and what he is. For, as we have noted already, the common experience of people seeing the Devil was to mistake him, at least initially, for one of themselves, an experience which could not have been possible had he betrayed himself from the first in his artistic or theatrical guise, and this is what we see in the late tenth- or eleventh-century manuscript of poems entitled *Genesis, Exodus, Daniel,* and *Christ and Satan,* with drawings which date to the second quarter of the eleventh century. One illustration shows Satan bound in Hell, and apart from his tail and animal's feet, there is no indication that he is not simply a human being prepared for torment. Indeed, a second and third drawing show him as a shackled figure with no outward mark of his status at all except, perhaps, for his wild, unkempt hair, while a fourth likewise depicts him as entirely human except for angelic wings which fly from his shoulders; and the two drawings which show the temptation, first of Eve and then of Eve and Adam, present him as a clothed human figure with bare human feet, and long hair held in place by a wreath or circlet. Again, the only indications of his non-human status are his wings.[20]

It must be asked, therefore, whether any of these likenesses, grotesque or otherwise, can be detected in personal accounts of Satanic or demonic visitation. When a demon appeared to Cecilia Ferrazzi, for example, he did so in human shape and under the guise of a holy man, a guise he maintained for quite a while; and even when he revealed his true nature and turned violent, there is no indication he changed his shape from human to bestial. But is this true of earlier accounts from the Middle Ages? Rudolf Glaber (c.985-c.1046) who lived in various Benedictine monasteries in what was then the semi-independent Duchy of Burgundy, saw the Devil on three separate occasions, according to his account, and in three different places. The first happened in the middle of the night, just before Matins, and Rudolf describes it in detail:

> A mannikin-like being of terrible aspect appeared before me from the direction of the foot of the bed. As far as I could judge, he was of middling stature with a thin neck, skinny face, jet-black eyes, and a lined and wrinkled forehead. His nostrils were pinched and he had a wide mouth and blubbery lips. His goat-like beard covered a receding and pointed chin, while his ears were covered in hair and pointed. His hair was a disordered mop, and he had dog-like teeth. He had a pointed head, a swollen chest, a hunchback, and mobile haunches. Clad in dirty clothes, his whole body seemed to quiver with effort as he leaned forward, seized the head of the bed, gave it a mighty blow, and said, "You will not remain longer in this place". I woke in terror and, as happens when we are suddenly woken, such an apparition as I have described was still in front of me. He gnashed his teeth and said time after time, "You will not remain longer in this place".

The sighting was thus not a dream, or at least not entirely, since it continued after Rudolf awoke. We may note that the apparition was able to speak aloud and coherently, and that it was able to interact with the world of matter in as much as it seized hold of the bed-head and struck it hard. But perhaps the most notable thing about this apparition is that, by and large, it looked human. To be sure, it was very ugly, with one or two unusual features such as pointed ears, a pointed head, and dog-like teeth; but none of these is so grotesque as to render entirely non-human the entity Rudolf was seeing, and when Rudolf saw it a second time he says it was *non dispar*, 'not dissimilar' to the first. The third time, like the other two, happened around about the hour of Matins. Rudolf says he felt tired and did not get out of bed as quickly as he should have done. But then:

> This same devil emerged and came puffing and blowing up the stairs after the last of the brethren had gone. Leaning against the wall, with his hands behind his back, he repeated two or three times, "I am he, I am he who stays with those who hang behind". Stirred by these words, I raised my head and recognised him as the being I had seen twice before.

Why was the Devil puffing and blowing as he came up the stairs? If he was the same entity Rudolf had seen before, he was of medium build, not fat. Putting his hands behind his back as he leaned against the wall also strikes one as a somewhat odd gesture. Both actions, in fact, are a touch theatrical and seem to be calculated to draw Rudolf's attention to him. Now, if he was dressed as a monk, and wore a cowl as the brothers would on their way to Matins, perhaps these oddities would be necessary, and indeed it is not until the Devil has spoken, once again in a way more ritualistic than natural, that Rudolf realises who he is. The implication must be that there was nothing particular about his appearance to make Rudolf look at him. Even if very ugly, he is at least human or human-like.

Another monk, who recorded Satanic and demonic visitations to himself and others, principally monks too, was Guibert de Nogent. His largely autobiographical work, *Monodiae*, was written in c.1115. For thirty-eight years Guibert lived in the Abbey of St Germer-de-Fly. He recalls the experience of one of his fellow monks, Otmund, who was opening the church doors one evening, and found himself brutally threatened by the Devil disguised as a poor man he had roughly expelled from the church the previous day. Another monk was confronted by the Devil dressed as a Scotsman who demanded alms and, when he was refused, picked up a stone and threw it at the monk, striking him in the chest so violently that the poor man suffered agonising pain for the next forty days; and that was not the end of it, for not long after the Devil troubled him again, this time dressed as a cowled monk, while his victim sat on the lavatory. Likewise, a third monk was lying in bed, half asleep, when two demons in monastic habits came and sat on a small bench next to his bed. He did not recognise them, but noted that one had red hair, (a bad sign, since red hair was associated with both Judas Iscariot and with Satan), and bare feet with dried mud in between the toes. The other was almost hidden inside a long cloak and a black hood. Not realising at first that these were evil spirits in disguise, the monk had an increasingly irritated conversation with them before leaving his cell and going to speak to other monks by the front door. These told him that no one had passed them to go into the monastic house, and so they all quickly recognised what had been the true nature of his visitors.

Whatever we may think of these anecdotes, and however we may care to interpret them, one notable feature is common to all of them. The monks see, or think they see, demons or the Devil in entirely human shape. There are no vestiges of bestiality in their accounts. The only suspicious trait in one is his red hair, and that cannot have been an unknown natural phenomenon in northern France, so there would have been no reason to interpret it as demonic straight away. Even when the demons or the Devil are invisible to all but the individual they are targeting, there is no indication they look anything but human. Guibert tells us that when his mother's chaplain lay dying, he 'began to cast wild glances all about him. Those who really knew him asked him what he was looking at. He replied, "I see a house full of barbarous men!" They understood that the creatures appearing to him were nothing other than demons hovering over him'. Now, admittedly the chaplain's remark could be regarded as ambiguous – was he looking at the people around his deathbed and calling them 'barbarous'? – but from our point of view it makes no difference. If *he* thought he was seeing demons, he designated them 'men', which means they were appearing in human form. 'Barbarous' simply means they looked foreign, and that could have referred to peculiarities in their attire, as in the case of the Scotsman-demon we noted earlier.

Guibert's mother's experience was odd. She was worrying about her husband who had been taken prisoner by Guillaume of Normandy, and was lying in bed, sick with anxiety and unable to sleep. Suddenly, 'the Adversary himself appeared ... And lay upon her, crushing her with his tremendous weight until she was almost dead. The pressure began to suffocate her, she was completely deprived of bodily movement, and her voice could not utter a single sound'. We may, if we wish, interpret this as an episode of sleep apnoea, the phenomenon also known as 'the night hag', but clearly neither Guibert nor his mother did so, because the experience continues with a battle between two spirits, the one oppressing her and the other a benevolent entity. 'She suddenly felt that this spirit had violently hurled himself against the foe who then rose up. The other spirit faced him, took hold of him, and threw him to the floor with a fierce noise. Their impact shook the room violently, and the servants who were usually plunged into a deep sleep were unexpectedly wakened'. One has the impression that both spirits were invisible; but their actions made an impact in the physical world, and the good spirit was able to speak, since we are told he invoked the Virgin Mary and, after his conflict was over, addressed Guibert's mother and urged her to make sure she was virtuous. This was by no means the only time Guibert's mother had experience of the spirit world. She also had visions of the Blessed Virgin, of ghosts (including that of her dead husband), and of 'two very black demons' who were carrying away the shadowy figure of an old woman. In this last case, her concept of the demons appears to have conformed to their conventional depiction in art, but this is the only one in which such a close correlation is clear.

Guibert's own experience was just as disconcerting. One night he woke with a feeling of panic and heard 'the clamour of what seemed to me many voices coming out of the dark of the night, voices without words'. Guibert then says he became unconscious, 'as if in sleep' (does he mean he fainted, or slipped into a trance, or merely fell asleep?) and saw a dead man who, someone shouted, had died in the baths. Now, according to Guibert's account, this frightening sight made him jump out of bed, screaming, at which time a lamp burning close by suddenly went out. 'Then', he goes on, 'I discerned in the darkness an enormous shadow, the very contour of the Devil standing near me'. How did he know this was the Devil? Was it by instinct, or was there something about the contour which reminded him of a picture of the Devil he may have seen, let us say, in the Abbey church? He gives no further details, so we are left with a very hazy impression. The Devil was huge and dark and in some way recognisable.

These personal as opposed to second-hand experiences, then, were vague in impression but overwhelming in emotional impact, and it may be significant that both took place at night. Neither is able to tell us the same kind of detail as appears in the other anecdotes. Those others strongly suggest that the demons involved were human in appearance, but it may be that since both Guibert and his mother were convinced their visitant was the Devil himself, their experiences were different in kind from those of the other parties. This certainly seems to be true if we take into account Guibert's anecdote about a man who was lying awake at night and suddenly saw 'the Great Deceiver', 'the Adversary', with a small head and very broad shoulders, tiptoeing through the room before making his way to the lavatories. Here once again the Devil appears in human shape, not some inchoate form, so it looks as though distance from immediate involvement by the reporter lends him some degree of ability to see detail and describe it.

It will now be informative to turn to a second account of personal encounters with evil spirits. Christina of Stommeln was a beguine in Köln, who left a series of letters, drafted for her in 1272 by a Dominican who had first met her five years earlier. In these she recounts a number of frightening and painful experiences of demonic activity aimed largely at her, but also at other people. Like Cecilia Ferrazzi, Christina was very devout, like Cecilia, she found herself under a certain amount of suspicion because of the intensity of her devotional behaviour and her brushes with the non-material world, and like Cecilia, she wrote down her experiences in an attempt to clarify and explain them to Church authorities:

(i) Between late June and mid August 1271, she suffered from sores on her mouth and face, produced by a demon who had burned her with a hot iron.

(ii) After May 1272, she was molested again by what her confessor called 'that nasty old perpetrator of evil'. The demon appeared to her 'in a terrible way, menacing and threatening her with lances and knives'. (Does the 'terrible way' refer to his dreadful appearance or his hostile manner?) When Christina tried to pray, the demon stuck a lance in her mouth and made it bleed copiously.

(iii) Christina records that she was in fear of the demon's burning iron and that her face was badly burned, so much so that white pustules broke out round her chin. Then her eyes and brow were burned. 'Last night', she says, 'I was locked in a terrible battle with a demon who pierced my ears with a hot iron'. He held the iron there and asked Christina whether she wanted to deny God. 'He wanted to kill me immediately, since he had the power to do so'.

(iv) This was not her only trial that night, because four more demons appeared, 'standing before me like an apparition'. One of them told her his name - a remarkable thing to do, as it happens, since knowing a demon's name gives an exorcist immediate power over him, and Christina could therefore have used the name to her advantage had she known how. But Christina refused to be diverted from prayer, and the demons disappeared with a great roar, leaving her burned all over her head and face.

(v) One demon came to her disguised as a beghard, the male equivalent of a beguine, and they entered into conversation, Christina asking what he wanted and the demon explaining he was trying to provoke her to sin, but that God was protecting her.

(vi) In September 1272, the same demon disguised himself as her brother, apparently wounded and covered in blood. He asked for her help, but Christina knew he was a demon and so he disappeared.

(vii) In October that year, Christina was confused. She thought she was praying in the name of a demon instead of the name of God. (Perhaps the name of the demon who had told her what it was had lodged, unwelcome but persistent, in her mind.) The she saw a demon instead of the consecrated Host during Mass.

(viii) Just before the Feast of All Saints (1 November) a demon came to her in church and boasted he had stolen money from a beguine Christina describes as 'my rival'. Rival in or for what is not explained, but clearly the demon's intention was to make Christina feel glad at her 'rival's' misfortune.

(ix) That night Christina remained in church with her father and friends. The demon then indulged himself in acts of violence. 'He broke all my limbs and removed a shoe from my foot, which he afterwards threw at a servant's head in my father's house. He broke a window so frightfully in the house that my brother almost went insane', and then he wounded Christina in the nose with an iron and made it bleed. (Again, what does 'so frightfully' mean here? Since the episode terrified her brother, did the demon appear in bestial, frightening shape, or did he smash the window in so violent or unexpected a manner that Christina's brother was badly frightened?)

(x) On the vigil of All Saints (31 October), he fouled the beguine hermitage and some people heard him use his name, 'Berlabam'.

(xi) On All Saints day itself, he threw a stone at Christina's father and inflicted two wounds on his arm. He also badly injured the priest's sister in the face, and threw a big stone at the head of a Jewish woman.[21]

The majority of these incidents conform to an expected pattern. A demon appeared to Christina and by various means tried to lead her into sin. The experiences left their mark in painful skin disorders of the face and head, but Christina seems to have persisted with her devotions in spite of them, and it is perhaps noteworthy that although she clearly sees the demons, her distress is caused by the pains they inflict on her, not by the sight of some dreadful composite creature. The implication is that the demons appeared – when they were not in disguise as a beghard or her brother – in more or less human form. Indeed, when the four demons appeared together, they stood in front of her 'like an apparition', that is to say looking rather like ghosts, and ghosts in the Middle Ages tended to be solid, human shapes, not the grey wispy figures we tend to imagine now. Ghosts, too, are what one thinks of in connection with the apparitions and incidents from the Vigil and Feast of All Saints. In these, the behaviour of the demon – and only one demon seems to be involved – is different. He no longer tries to frighten or tempt Christina, but indulges in violence almost, one might think, for its own sake. This behaviour is much closer to that of a poltergeist, since throwing stones and breaking things is typical of that kind of ghostly activity. Poltergeists also speak from time to time – hence some people heard this 'demon' pronounce his name – but they rarely become visible, and we may note that there is no evidence of any of his victims' catching sight of their destructive visitant. The likelihood is, therefore, that in Christina's letters we have a record of two types of experience – one demonic, the other spectral – and that during Christina's encounters with demons, she saw figures sufficiently human-like in appearance and behaviour to warrant her not feeling obliged to describe them, although instinct if nothing else clearly told her they were spirits, not human beings.

The experiences of these people – Rudolf, Guibert, and Christina – seem to suggest that their brushes with the demonic world did not reflect what they saw in paintings and sculptures, but were closer to home and more familiar in the way they looked and sounded, a familiarity which, for that very reason, appears to have made the experience memorable, highly disturbing and filled with menace. They also make us aware that encounters between the spirit world and the material plane were taken for granted by inhabitants of the latter: that is to say, their fear was caused, not by the fact that their world had been penetrated by non-human entities, but partly by the realisation that this had happened and was now presenting them with an unnerving situation, and partly by the unexpectedness of that intrusion, which took them aback, just as they would have been thrown off balance by other humans (such as footpads or burglars) whom they were not expecting to see and whom they realised were likely to have hostile intent. But painting and sculpture did not seem to play a significant role in expressing people's personal encounters with Satan or demons. They did, however, very forcefully express the emotional understanding of theological concepts, and for this reason formed an integral part of the exterior and interior furniture of churches, revealing in paint and glass and stone a complex symbolism which acted as a kind of distorting mirror whose twisted and monstrous shapes gave any who looked therein a physically contorted but emotionally accurate notion of what the various embodiments of evil were actually like.

CHAPTER 4

Satan's Release from Bondage

If art had a special way of reflecting the Satanic and demonic realms, so too did theatre. Opportunities to represent Biblical episodes in theatrical form were gradually taken up by the Church and workmen's guilds, using church porches and steps and the area in front of both as interconnected stages, or wagons with painted scenery to indicate different locales. With acting came costumes, and with both there developed conventions, especially when it came to the Devil and his demons. Inventories for mystery plays and masques, for example, record 'the Devil in his feathers', (a reference to bird-like wings worn also, of course, by angels), 'a black robe, hair, wreath, and wings black', woollen and black garments, gloves, staffs, and forks, and above all, masks. In 1372, Philippe de Mézières required that Lucifer 'be decked out with those ornaments which themselves befit what is most shameful and abominable, with horrible horns, teeth, and face' – a picture reminiscent of the early fifteenth-century *Castle of Perseverance* in which Belial, (calling himself 'Satan'), tells the audience, 'Now I sit ... in filth, like a dragon ... as Belial the Black'. Over and over again we find indications of features that can refer only to masks, such as 'crooked snout' and 'bottle nose', and there are even instructions on how to make a mask which will let the actor seem to breathe out fire. It was to contain a burning coal across which the wearer would blow a sulphurous, inflammable liquid contained in goose quills. Double-faced masks also existed, as did costumes with faces painted on elbows, knees, stomachs, or backsides.

Why were such devices worn? They enabled the audience to distinguish immediately between good and bad characters, of course, and visually emphasised their differences. Sometimes all the participants in a play concealed their faces, as happened in liturgical plays presented in Toledo, when even the clergy wore veils to heighten the drama's ritualistic effect and hide their personal identities. Masks, however, were ambiguous. They could indeed distinguish between the good and the bad, but they also enabled the bad to disguise themselves as the good. As Wycliffe put it, 'Therefore they [worldly prelates] become the Devil's jugglers to blind men's ghostly eyes ... and are Satans transfigured into an angel of light ... and thus instead of Christ's Apostles, [they] become masked devils to deceive men in good life, and bring them to Satan, their master'. Even in illustrated romances, such as that of *Maugis d'Aigremont* (mid fifteenth century), we find evidence that one of the leading characters dresses as a devil – dark, hairy body-suit with animal's feet and hands, and a mask with teeth, horns, and flame-like hair – in order to achieve a particularly difficult quest.

Nevertheless, the mask may not always have been de rigueur for playing such a part. In the twelfth-century Anglo-Norman *Ordo Repraesentationis Adae*, for example, after the Devil has failed to tempt Adam to sin, the rubric says, 'Then sadly and with face downcast, he will withdraw from Adam and go to the gates of Hell and hold conference with the other demons. Thereafter he will run about among the people. Then he will draw near the paradise, on the side where Eve is, and with a cheerful expression will coax her as follows'. Conveying 'downcast' and 'cheerful' could always have been done by a stylised gesture, of course, but the likelihood is that here the Devil had applied black make-up, (such as grease and soot), to his face so that his own features thus altered might achieve the desired expressions. The effect would have been unnerving. As Twycross and Carpenter point out, 'On a European face the blackening intensifies the whites (or yellows) and reds of the eyes, the red of the inside of the mouth and nostrils, and the white of the teeth by contrast, so that they become more vivid than normal. It also upsets the balance of colour and texture between face and hair, so that the hair, paradoxically, looks false'.

Now, it is easy to assume that wearing a mask would have affected the actor's delivery – hence Hildegard von Bingen's description of the Devil's way of speaking as *strepitus*, ('loud noise, din, uproar'), and other German plays' rubrics telling him to speak either in a loud sonorous voice, in a way which makes people's hair stand on end, or in the manner of a lunatic. (One instruction, however, tells the actor to speak in a normal voice, but perhaps in this instance the actor was blacked up rather than wearing a mask.) But such differences in delivery could equally well have been dictated by the requirements of the immediate episode in which the Devil was appearing. 'It is wrong', says C.W. Marshall anent Roman theatre, 'to assume that masks imposed a limitation on the actors, preventing them from representing such features as a character blushing ... It is precisely the power of the mask to appear to come to life and move and convey emotion, when properly animated by a trained actor', or, as Jacques Lecoq puts it, 'A good theatre mask must be able to change its expression according to the movements of the actor's body'.[22]

Satan and his demons were thus distinctively portrayed in Mediaeval plays, and their frequent intrusions into the audience from the acting-space would have been done with the intention of being not so much amusing as disturbing. Hence, in the *Ordo Repraesentationis Adae*, stage directions say more than once that demons or Satan or both should run about in the *platea*, the open area at the bottom of the church steps, and also run *per populum*, through the spectators, and, as Twycross and Carpenter observe:

> With the masked person clearly defined within a Christian framework as a devil, the relationship [between him and the members of the audience] becomes more decisively that of tormentor and victim. The mask and costume, with the bestial teeth and claws, emphasise the predatory intent and the alien unpredictability of the creature ... The devil's freedom to indulge in the forbidden, the grotesque, the excessive, and the trivial in language and action generates delight and laughter: but the laughter is always uneasy ... [and] if the devil moves from the sphere of the dramatic narrative to play directly at you, you may laugh, but the laughter will remain nervous, as there is no longer a barrier between you.

Imagine, therefore, the effect on spectators when (or perhaps if) the stage directions following Adam and Eve's expulsion from Eden were carried out:

> The Devil will come, and three or four devils with him, carrying in their hands chains and iron fetters, which they will put on the necks of Adam and Eve. And certain ones will push them, others drag them to "Hell"; still other devils will be close beside "Hell", waiting for them as they come, and among themselves they will make a great dancing and jubilation over their damnation; and each of these other devils will point at them as they come, and will take them and put them into "Hell". And therein they will cause a great smoke to arise, and they will shout to one another in "Hell", rejoicing and they will bang together their cauldrons and kettles, so that they may be heard outside. And after a short interval, the devils will issue forth, running in different directions through the open spaces; certain of them, however, will remain in Hell".

But if there were opportunities for horseplay and nervous laughter in the behaviour of attendant demons, Satan himself remained and was presented as a serious character with deadly aims and seductive methods. Sometimes he might be used as the mouthpiece for social satire, as in the N-Town *Passion Play* which opens with the rubric, 'Satan, gorgeously attired as a gallant, boasts to the audience'; and sometimes he turns to violence against his own kind, demons or personified vices, in conflicts which John Cox describes as 'undoubtedly comic', but which are more likely, depending, of course, on the way they were presented, to have elicited a combination of satisfaction at seeing evil turn upon itself prior to the restoration of moral order, and a recognition of contemporary *mores* derived from warfare or brawling. Again and again, however, plays emphasise the Devil's pride, that essential arrogance which caused his fall from Heaven. 'Behold me', says Belial in *The Conversion of St Paul*, 'the mighty Prince of the parts infernal. Next to Lucifer I am in majesty, by name I am nominate the god Belial'. (Now, although the author appears to distinguish between Belial and Lucifer, it is clear that the distinction is of little real consequence and that, to all intents and purposes, this Belial is the Devil himself. The common equation of these various names with a single personification of evil is shown in the N-Town *Passion Play* when he says, 'I am your lord Lucifer that came out of Hell, the Prince of this world and the great Duke of Hell. Wherefore I am called Sir Satan'.) In *Mary Magdalene*, there can be no mistaking the Devil's pride. 'Now I, a prince elaborately dressed, attired in pride, I Satan your sovereign, take advantage of every circumstance. For I am fitted out in my tower to tempt you this season. As a royal king I sit at my pleasure, with Wrath and Envy in my royal retinue'; while in *The Creation and the Fall of the Angels*, the Devil in his prelapsarian persona of Lucifer boasts to the audience of his own brilliance - 'I am a thousandfold brighter than the sun' - and issues an order, 'my will is this. "Master" ye shall me call', before reaching the pinnacle of his arrogance in an act of blasphemy. 'Ye shall see full soon anon how that it suits me to sit on a throne as king of bliss. I am so seemly, blood and bone, my seat shall be where His was' - whereupon he sits down on the throne of God. The thrust of this portrayal is to underline the complete unmitigated evil of the instrument which precipitated the fall of humanity from Paradise, the impulse behind original sin, and a hatred which, while spilling over in its excess to include human beings, originated in envy of God Himself before human beings were ever created.[23]

Popular literature, in the sense of sermons, poems and anecdotes aimed at the entertainment or instruction of the unlettered, tended to show that demons were ubiquitous, that Satan was ever ready to appear in various forms and tempt people into sin, but that both demons and Satan could be resisted and overcome by simple reliance on the prayers and ritual gestures of Christianity. Thus, in Jacobus de Voragine's collection of edifying narratives, known as the *Legenda Aurea* (c.1260):

When Lucifer wanted to be equal to God, the archangel Michael, standard-bearer of the celestial host, marched up and expelled Lucifer and his followers out of Heaven, and shut them up in this dark air until the Day of Judgement. They are not allowed to live in Heaven, or in the upper part of the air, because that is a bright and pleasant place, nor on the earth with us, lest they do us too much harm. They are in the air between Heaven and earth, so that when they look up and see the glory they have lost, they grieve for it, and when they look down and see men ascending to the place from which they fell, they are often tormented with envy. However, by God's design they come down upon us to test us, and, as has been shown to some holy men, they fly around us like flies. They are innumerable, and, like flies, they fill the whole air.

Likewise, Anatole de Montaiglon (1373) tells the story of a priest celebrating Mass, who noticed that the congregation was not paying any attention, and that 'near to their ears [were] dark and horrible demons laughing at their jangling, and writing down each word they heard. These demons were leaping on their hair which was done up like horns, on their rich attire, and on their finery, like little birds hopping from branch to branch'. A woodcut of 1490 illustrates this. It shows a priest at the altar and a fashionably dressed woman with her back both to him and the altar. A small horned black demon is playing on the long train of her cloak, (fig. 10). Sometimes while St Francis of Assisi was praying, he heard demons running around on the roof of his house, but when he ran outside, made the sign of the cross, and challenged them, they fled; and the same powerful gesture was sufficient to repulse a demon who tried unsuccessfully several times in different guises to seduce St Justina, as he explained to the magician who had summoned him for that purpose. 'That young woman made the sign of the cross, and at once all my strength ebbed away. I could do nothing and, like wax melting at a fire, I melted away'.

But demons could be controlled in other ways, too. A great magician such as King Solomon could confine them in a vase; a broadsheet issued in Augsburg in c.1475 told its readers about an old woman who dispersed an army of demons, armed only with a wooden spoon; and women were also able to bind the Devil to a tasselled cushion, as is shown, for example, in an armrest on the stalls at Hoogstraeten and in misericords at Aarschot, Dordrecht, and L'Isle-Adam. Demons might thus be seen as mischievous and relatively easy to disperse or conquer, but their mischief was always dangerous and often painful, so that, as with the laughter which might be aroused by their tumbling and japing in the theatre, reaction to their presence was always tainted by fear. Thomas of Cantimpré tells the story of a deacon who was summoned to the bedside of a dying rich man:

Standing on the threshold, he saw black cats running around the bed of the rich man who, seeing them and knowing them to be bitter enemies, bellowed loudly: "Take the cats away, take them away; help a miserable man!" Finally, a black man threatened him, and with a dreadful look plunged a hook, which he was carrying in his hand, into his throat. The unhappy soul, finding in his conduct no comfort for his conscience, was in fear and trembling, and death little by little seized upon the poor wretch. Then the black man in a rage drew out his hook from his quivering throat, and uttering a dreadful cry, the sick man gave up his unhappy soul. Rushing on the sinning soul, the rest of those confederates in malice wounded it with their scourges and plunged it into the place of gloom and the lake of eternal death.

This black man was probably the Devil. He is certainly identified as such by Rudolf von Schlettstadt in his *Historiae Memorabiles*. A woman, intent upon summoning demons to help her get something she wanted, was working in company with her godmother on a magic brew, when the door to the house suddenly blew open three times. On the third occasion, 'in walked a black man [*ethiops*], tall and thin. He grabbed the woman working the magic by the neck, twisted it round to her back, and wretchedly killed her. In the meantime, her godmother, who was sitting near her, fainted, terror-stricken. The black man, who was the Devil, ignored her'. Similarly, Anne Marie de Georgel was washing clothes one morning when she saw a huge man coming towards her. 'He was dark-skinned and his eyes burned like living coals. He was dressed in the hides of beasts'.

Were these descriptions of demons and of Satan himself influenced by the way these entities were depicted on the stage, in stained glass, and in sculpture? The likelihood is that they were, and that such literature as we have been reviewing reinforced both the general concept and its details. We must not, however, make the mistake of thinking that there was one culture for the common people and another for the educated. Liturgical drama, mysteries, and morality plays took place under the patronage of the Church and, in many instances, as we have seen, were played on and around the steps of the church itself; the majority of anecdotes involving demons and Satan were embedded in sermons and edifying stories intended to warn, instruct, and advise; and most artistic representations of evil were highly visible in churches round the pillars, in the windows, and on the vividly painted walls. A single culture relating to non-human entities of all kinds, therefore, embraced all classes of people and was accessible to all.

When conception of a persona of evil entered the realm of literature, however, did it become different? Did the figure of Satan, for example, change in its essentials from that perceived and feared by the unlettered? His portrait in Dante's *Divina Commedia* (1290s-1310s) is well known:

The Emperor of that dire empire
was stuck chest deep in the ice;
and I'd come nearer to a giant
than a giant would to his arm,
so you see how enormous he was
with all of him on this scale.
If he's as ugly as he was lovely
when he stood up to his Maker,
all pain indeed derives from him.
Oh, what a marvel followed then,
when I saw he had three faces!
One vermilion, looking forwards,
and another two joining this one
above the middle of each shoulder,
all three uniting at the crown –
the right a sort of yellowy-white,
the left coloured like the people
who live where Nile descends.
Two huge wings beneath each face
stuck out, big as everything else,
bigger than the sails on a ship,
not feathered, more like a bat's;
these he was flapping around him
and so giving rise to three winds:
this is what makes Cocytus freeze.
His six eyes weep, his three chins
drip with tears and gory slaver.
In each mouth, his teeth grind away
at a sinner; as you'd rake flax
with a scutch.

T.S. Eliot was disappointed. 'The vision of Satan may seem grotesque', he wrote, 'especially if we have fixed in our minds the curly-haired Byronic hero of Milton; it is too like a Satan in a fresco in Siena ... I can only say that Dante made the best of a bad job'. Thinking of Milton's version at this juncture is, of course, the last thing we should be doing, and remembering a Sianese fresco the first. Dante's Satan is ugly in contrast to what he was. He is given three heads in parodic reference to the Trinity, as a late thirteenth-century illustration of Abraham kneeling before a single divine figure with three heads illustrates, and as Matteo Chiromono, a fourteenth-century commentator on Dante, points out. The three colours of those Satanic heads – vermilion, yellowish-white, and black – were not only the colours of the horses in the *Apocalypse* (6.2-5), but also, according to Chiromono, of impotence, envy, and ignorance. These colours, however, also carried many other associations. The yellowish tinge to the white indicated the corruption of a natural innocence by sorrow, covetousness, hunger, and death; and yellow was the recognised sign of an outsider, frequently associated in the Middle Ages with Jews and Muslims. It also typified ugliness, untrustworthiness, and betrayal. Red, on the other hand, was associated with kingship and with blood, although it also had a negative association with lust; while black, as we have seen, had been one of the Devil's colours from the earliest times. But it is worth noting that Dante limits these colours to the Devil's three faces. Facial colour, or complexion, was one of the primary indications of both illness and temperament in Mediaeval medicine, and so the red, yellowish-white, and black present us with a diagnostic tool whereby we may gauge Satan's emotional and physiological state. The red face indicates an excess of the humour blood; the yellow-white, of the humour bile; and the black, of the humour bile tainted with blood. Consequently, he is being portrayed as irascible, passionate, sullen, dejected, bad-tempered, and lustful. The missing humour (phlegm) would make him cold, dull, apathetic, and calm, none of which is in the least suited to his character.

The bat-wings Dante attributes to his Devil may have come from his memory of seeing frescoes by or attributed to Giotto in the basilica at Assisi. Scene 10 illustrates an episode from the life of St Francis, described in the *Legenda Maior* of St Bonaventure:

> It once happened that he arrived at Arezzo at a time when the whole city was shaken by a civil war which threatened its impending destruction. Indeed, while he was lodging in one of the suburbs, he saw demons leaping about above the city and inflaming the turbulent citizens into slaughtering each other. Thereupon, in order to put to flight those rebellious powers in the air, he sent forth as his herald Brother Silvester, a man of dove-like simplicity, saying, "Go in front of the gate of the city and in the name of Almighty God command the demons, in virtue of the obedience [they owe to God], to leave quickly". The honest [Silvester] did as he was told and hurried to carry out his father's commands, and engaging in his praises before the divine presence, began to cry with a loud voice in front of the city gate, "In the name of Almighty God and by command of His servant Francis, go far away from here, all demons!" At once the city returned to peace, and all the citizens, in complete accord, undertook revision of their civil laws, (6.9).

The fresco shows Silvester extending his hand towards the walled town of Arezzo, which has seven demons flying above it. Four of these demons are black, one is brown, and the other two are blue. All have bodies covered with shaggy hair, humanoid hands, bird-like talons, 'flaming' hair, in the sense that it streams upwards in stiff plumes, like flames from a blazing fire, human though distorted faces, and immense bat-wings which actually look incongruous beside their hairy, bestial bodies. This species appears in another fresco, too, the Confession of the Woman of Benevento, in which an angel with feathered wings chases away a brown-coloured, beast-like demon with bat's wings. 'The Devil has bat's wings', says Chiromono:

> Because of the similarity between them. A bat hates the light, just as the Devil hates God who is the highest light and those who walk in the light, too. Just as a bat flies only at night, so the Devil strikes in secret. Just as a bat has forsaken other birds, so the Devil has betrayed other angels through his wicked prompting. Finally, just as a bat is driven away by others who hate it, so also the Demon is driven off by other angel.[24]

The Biblical, apocryphal, and pseudepigraphical traditions lying behind these artistic, theatrical, and literary interpretations also provided the basis for theological interpretations which, in their turn, fed into the art and literature: and we can begin by reviewing the relevant work of St Anselm (1033-1109). He addressed himself to two important questions: what is evil and whence does it come? To look for answers, he concentrated on the Devil's fall from Heaven. Lucifer, like all angels and, ultimately, humankind was given the grace of free will, and since this gift came from God, the free will itself could not be evil. Free will means what it says: it is a will which is genuinely free to choose and act as it wishes. So when Lucifer chose to sin, to be like God in as much as he wanted to obtain something through his own will without subjecting himself to God's will and superior authority, he elected to seek his own advantage and interest (*commodum*) rather than subordinate that egocentric impulse to the balance and harmony (*justitia*) God has ordained for His creation. He sinned because he chose to sin, and the result of this unhappy choice was to introduce sin into that same creation. Adam and Eve sinned by failing to render God His just due of honour which was to obey His command not to eat the fruit of a particular tree. The Devil links these two events – his own unhappy choice and that of Eve and Adam – by tempting our first parents to misuse their free will in the same kind of way he had misused his; and as a result of this original sin by which everyone is tainted at his or her origin, God granted the Devil limited powers to tempt and punish human beings. Nevertheless, in St Anselm's theology, the Devil is relegated to a subsidiary role in the cosmic drama of humanity's fall and redemption, and this tendency to play down Satan to some extent can be seen in later schools of thought which pursued the questions of how God's harmonious creation came to be polluted and how its restoration was to be achieved.

Other questions, too, continued to perplex theologians. How much genuine power did Satan have over human beings? If his decreed place of existence was Hell, how did he manage to leave it and appear in the world of matter; or were such appearances merely illusion, and if so, was the illusion created by him or did it spring from the repository of images, ('imagination' in its technical sense), which every human carried in his or her head? What about demons, too? Were they constrained in the same way as the Devil, or did they have greater freedom to come and go from Hell either at his bidding or in accordance with their own evil impulses? Indeed, did demons inhabit Hell as their natural destined state, or had they fallen short of it when they fell from Heaven and lodged in the sublunary air, as earlier speculation had suggested? These were not trivial or empty questions. Scholastic theologians had an immense desire for exact knowledge. They wanted to pin down details so that their understanding of a topic would be comprehensive, and these questions about the Devil and evil spirits, as we have seen, sprang from the immediacy of one of the great inquiries at the very frontiers of contemporary research: what is the relationship between matter and apparent non-matter, how does that relationship work, and what, if any, are its limitations?

One attempt to provide answers to these questions came from the revival of an old idea: that there are, in effect, two deities rather than one, God and the Devil. This dualistic heresy stretches back to the Manichaeism of the third century, and although adherents of this sect had been subject to fierce persecution, the notion of an antithesis to Christ, of whom Satan-Lucifer-the Devil provided the perfect embodiment, proved seductively long-lasting. Apocalyptic fears bursting forth in the years leading up to the year 1000 saw signs of Antichrist – Satan unchained – and therefore the approach of the Final Times increase to an alarming extent. Perhaps the most influential expression of those fears was a letter written by a French monk, Adso, not long after 950, to Queen Gerberga, a document which was copied over and over again, ascribed to writers much more noteworthy than Adso himself, and translated into several vernaculars:

> Since you wish to know about Antichrist, learn first why he has this name. This is because he will be the contrary to Christ in all things ... He will destroy the law of the Gospel, bring back the worship of demons in the world, seek personal glory and call himself the almighty god. Furthermore, Antichrist has many servants of his evil here, many of whom have already

preceded him in the world, such as Antiochus, Nero, and Domitian. In our own time also we know there are many Antichrists. For whatever person – lay, cleric, or monk – lives contrary to justice and opposes the rule of his station in life and blasphemes the good, he is Antichrist and the servant of Satan ... Antichrist will have magicians, criminals, soothsayers, and wizards who, with the Devil's inspiration, will bring him up and instruct him in every iniquity, trickery, and wicked art; and evil spirits will be his guides and eternal friends and inseparable comrades.

Signs pointed to Antichrist's arrival. In 989 Halley's Comet swept through the heavens, indicating that there was not much time left; and it was thought appropriate in 996 to embroider the coronation robe of the Holy Roman Emperor, Otto III, with scenes of the Apocalypse. Others therefore followed Adso's lead in seeing their own times as a period in which Satan was particularly active – as Rudolf Glaber said, '[It] accords with the prophecy of the Apostle John, in which he said that Satan would be released when a thousand years had passed' – and the apparent rise in demonic activity and the burgeoning of heresy were increasingly understood to be two sides of the same coin. Magic was a symptom of heresy, heresy the outcome of surrendering to the temptations of magic.

Hence, although it took quite a time to get going, the relatively quiet attempts of the eleventh century to persuade miscreants of their errors gave way to more aggressive methods of extirpating error and imposing orthodoxy; and in consequence dualist heretics in particular, since they were seen as demoting the ones of God and promoting the importance of Satan, became the targets for concerted action by the Church. Similarities can be noticed between Bogomilism, a dualist heresy of the East, and Catharism, by this time a dualist heresy of the West, for both believed that the Devil was to be identified with the God of the Old Testament, and both despised and rejected the official Church. Indeed, Cathars called the Catholic Church 'the Church of Satan'. Cathars, (so called because they believed themselves to be 'pure'), spread rapidly throughout northern Italy and the Languedoc, and it is not surprising to find a Church Council, held at Rheims in 1157, decreeing life imprisonment for Cathar leaders and branding for the rest if they were caught.

A statement of Catharist belief in relation to the Devil was communicated to Pope Gregory IX in 1229 by two repentant Cathars, one known simply as 'Andreas', the other, Pietro Garcias from Toulouse. The early statements are sometimes interrupted either by an explanatory addition from the recording clerk, or an aside from the speaker himself:

First of all, we, Andreas and Pietro, say and affirm that this is the creed of the Paterini [Cathars], which until now we believed was Catholic.

First, there were two primary causes, (*that's to say, of good and evil*), and these were gods from before time, (*that's to say, of light and darkness*). The god of light made everything which is light, and the class of spirits, while the god of darkness, (*that's to say, the Devil*), made everything which is evil, the whole of darkness, and certain angels; and the said Devil, along with his angels, went and deceived Lucifer and *his* angels who fell with him. These belonged to the host of light.

Item: The Devil and Lucifer along with their angels fell from Heaven.

Item: A certain good angel, (*that's to say, of the god of light*), along with some of his comrades, came to that darkness to ransom Lucifer and *his* comrades who fell from Heaven.

Item: The Devil, (*that's to say, a large snake*), and Lucifer constructed this world in six days in harmonious alliance with each other. At the same time, they seized hold of that [good] angel and his comrades, and removed from him the crown and brilliance that he had.

Item: With the permission of the god of light, the Devil and Lucifer constructed this world in six days in harmonious alliance with each other.

Item: Lucifer repented of the deception which was done to the god of light. He agreed with the snake that they make a human being from earth. The snake wanted the human to be immortal, and Lucifer wanted him to be mortal, and he was made mortal. They put in the body of the human, (*that's to say, Adam*), that angel who came to ransom Lucifer and his angels, [namely, the angel] from whom they removed the crown from which they made the lights which are in the sky, and made for Adam a companion, a woman; and in the shape of these humans, after they were in a body, they [Adam and Eve] forgot everything which was good and clung to the makers of their bodies as gods. Lucifer ordered them not to eat from the tree of knowledge of what is good, (*that's to say, they were not to have sex with each other*), and the snake made them sin, (*that's to say, have sex with each other*).

Item: When the snake saw that the human was mortal, he repented of making a human, and so, with the permission of the god of light, he sent a flood over the earth; and Lucifer, with the permission of the god of light, saved Noah and his comrades.

Item: The snake made the Tower of Babel and there made many kinds of languages so that if it turned out that anyone came from the heavenly kingdom to preach, people would not understand him.

Item: Lucifer began to speak to Abraham, Isaac, and Jacob, revealing that he was the god of light; and to this person he gave the Law of Moses, and they are saved.[25]

Item: The god of light began to speak through prophets, announcing the coming of the Son of God; and he says that John was sent by the god of light.[26]

Item: He says that the Son of God came into the Blessed Virgin Mary who was made from higher elements; and from her He took flesh, but not from these elements, and came down from the heavens with 147,000 angels; and after death, He went down to Hell and brought back with Him the holy fathers and prophets and those who had obeyed the prophets.

Item: On the Day of Pentecost, He sent the Holy Spirit and taught the Apostles every language, quite the opposite of the one who jumbled the languages together; and he believes that through the Holy Spirit he has salvation which he says he and no one else has.[27]

Item: He believes that no one is saved without the imposition of hands; and he says that no confession of sin is necessary in [the case of] any individual who comes to their [Cathar] faith for the first time.

Item: He says no good is done or given in relation to salvation by a wicked minister or priest.

Item: He says that the Roman Church does not have the Catholic faith, that there is no salvation in her, and that no one can be saved by her. They detest all the decrees of the Roman Church.

Item: They condemn marriage; they condemn [the eating of] flesh, cheese, and eggs; and he says that [swearing] an oath is utterly prohibited.

Item: He believes that the Roman Church has nothing of use to say about the body of Christ and baptism.

But the said Pietro said he understood nothing about any of the many headings, which are contained in this document. Andreas, on the other hand, affirmed without reserve that this is the life of the Paterini [Cathars].[28]

It is clear from this catalogue of creedal points that, according to Andreas – Pietro seems to have been puzzled by a number of things Andreas was telling their interrogators, either because he was poorly instructed in his creed or because Andreas's beliefs were more singular than those of other Cathars – there were two gods of equal status and equal eternity, and that one of them, the Devil, is constantly distinguished from a persona called 'Lucifer'. Even though both share a history which was recounted by orthodox Catholic theology as that of a single entity, they act partly as though they were confederates on a number of enterprises – the creation of the world, the creation of Adam and Eve – and partly as though they were separate and individual powers. The Devil wanted Adam to be immortal, Lucifer did not, and Lucifer got his own way. The Devil sent the Flood; Lucifer rescued Noah and his family. The Devil created Babel and a cacophony of languages; Lucifer began to pretend he was the good god and issued laws and prophecies via Moses and the prophets. In other words, we are presented with two personifications of evil, one the equivalent of God and the creator of evil and darkness, the other a fallen angel who repents of his sin and begins to intervene in human history in a number of ways not altogether wicked.

So unorthodox are these views that, even if Cathars apart from Andreas did not necessarily subscribe to every jot or tittle of theirs, we can scarcely be surprised they were condemned as heretical, as indeed happened at the Fourth Lateran Council in 1215, which made it clear that the Devil was not a co-equal with God, but a creation of His, which turned bad of its own free will. 'There is no doubt that the Devil and the other demons were created by God with a good character, but became wicked through their own actions. Humankind [*literally, 'the Man', i.e. Adam*] sinned at the Devil's prompting ... Let them receive according to what they have done, whether this be good or evil - those who keep company with the Devil, everlasting punishment: those who keep company with Christ, eternal glory'. Increasing episodes of this kind of heresy and of a variety of others throughout the twelfth and thirteenth centuries, thus caused the Church not only to address herself to those criticisms of clerical behaviour which provided fodder for many of these deviations, but also to return to the central problem of evil and its manifestations in the world.

St Thomas Aquinas (1225-74), a Dominican theologian and one of the most significant in the Church's history, pressed home the view that the Devil's sin was pride which he indulged, willingly and knowingly, even though he was perfectly aware that he could never be God's equal, nor achieve his own beatitude by his own endeavours without reference to or dependence on God. The Devil's function, he said, was to be ruler of all those who fell with him and to incorporate all evil beings and sinners into his mystical body, just as all good beings and the faithful are members of Christ's mystical body. This oppositional existence also means that, just as the good are motivated by love and enjoy its blessings in perpetuity, so the wicked are governed by hatred and know only the pangs of envy and malice. Hence the attacks which demons make on humans in a constant effort to impede the advance of the kingdom of God, and because they, like human beings, are part of creation (*natura*), they operate through Nature by manufacturing tempting illusions causing distress through violation of natural processes, or actually occupying human bodies to perpetrate acts of destruction and cruelty in their name.

Who were these human agents who, either willingly or perforce, assisted Satan in his constant work of malice? The twelfth and thirteenth centuries saw not only a burgeoning of heresies within Christendom, but a growing awareness, fostered in part by the experience of the Crusades, of 'The Other', in the form of Muslims (Saracens), Africans (Ethiopians), Mongols (Tartars), and Jews. Saracens, for example, were idolaters and therefore worked hand-in-hand with the Devil. Eulogius of Cordoba called Muhammad an angel of Satan and precursor of Antichrist; the mosque outwith Antioch was labelled a house of the Devil by an anonymous chronicler; and a picture in the *Grands Chroniques de France* (1370s) shows Saracens with horned demons' heads, (looking remarkably like theatrical masks), threatening Charles V, the French King, and some of his knights on horseback. Moreover, Saracens were dark-skinned, as were demons, and it took only a step to represent them as demonic in other ways, such as in a fifteenth-century bench-end in a Norfolk church, which shows a figure with unmistakably Saracen attributes, a body covered in hair like an animal, and a loincloth round his middle. Books of marvels, travellers' tales, and illustrations, wood carvings, sculptures, and stained-glass pictures by artists created a remarkable other world peopled by grotesques and monsters whose geography could be made to encompass not merely lands far away, but communities on one's doorstep. As for the Jews – 'I have absolutely no idea whether a Jew is human', wrote Peter the Venerable in the first half of the twelfth century. 'He doesn't respond to human reason, nor does he trust authoritative utterances whether they come from God or his own people'. Of uncertain humanity, then, Jews could be and were likened to demons, both being shown with hooked noses and beards reminiscent of those of goats. Indeed, like demons, Jews were friends of Satan, as their association with the crucifixion on the one hand and magic on the other served to illustrate. The early thirteenth-century Spanish Dominican, Raimund Martini, for example, asserted that the Magog and Gog of *Ezekiel* 38.2-3 were to be identified with the Devil and the multitudes of the impious respectively, as St Augustine had said, or that 'Gog is some great devil whom they [*the Jews*] call Bentamalion ... The said devil Bentamalion, through some devilish piece of wonder-working, got back and restored to them circumcision, the Sabbath, the ability to offer solemn prayers and study the Law; and because the Jews had been stripped of this kind of religious practice by God at the hands of the Romans ... this devil, (as his Talmud bears witness), restored their impiousness to them once again under the cover of this sort of religious practice'. Distinctive marks of Jewish religious life were thus of demonic origin.

As for magic, the view that Jews were magicians or at least had intimate knowledge of the art meant that Guibert de Nogent felt free to tell a long anecdote about a monk who was foolish enough to make friends with a Jew, question him about magic, and insist on being 'initiated' into the practice of it, as though magic were some kind of cult. Sure enough, the Jew agrees and introduces the monk to the Devil who consents to initiate provided he renounces his baptism, and masturbates as a sacrifice of his purity. Naturally, he comes to a bad end, but it is noteworthy that his go-between or pander with Satan is said to be a Jew. Popular legends, plays, and (no doubt) genuine magical practitioners in the Jewish community fed the common perception that they were masters of the various esoteric arts. Special clothing, too, marked them out. A decree issued by the Council of Vienna in 1267 said that Jews must wear a horned cap. The origin of this may actually have been the two beams of light supposedly protruding from Moses's forehead (*Exodus* 34.29: 'When Moses came down form Mount Sinai ... he did not realise that his face had developed horns'), but an immediate association between 'horns' and 'Satan' was almost inevitable, and quickly made by writers and artists alike, even though the Jewish cap had only one horn, not two.[29]

But if Satan's human agents included Saracens and Jews and other beings perceived as monstrous, who lived round the margins of the Christian world, the worst and most dangerous by far were the enemies within, the heretics who, by their own deliberate act and choice, had rejected the tradition of truth handed down to them by the Church, and gone whoring after false gods and chimaeras of their own imagining. Among the more notable of these were the Waldensians, a sect apparently founded in c.1170, according to the inquisitor Bernard Gui, by a Lyonnais called Valdès or Vaudès:

> He was rich but, having given up all his worldly goods, he set about observ-
> ing a life of poverty and evangelical perfection, following in the steps of
> the Apostles. He had the Holy Scriptures and other books of the Bible
> translated for his own use into the vernacular, along with a collection of
> maxims of St Augustine, St Jerome, St Ambrose and St Gregory, which were
> distributed, bearing titles he and his followers called *sententiae*. They read
> them frequently, but barely understood them. They were infatuated with
> themselves, although they had little education, and usurped the function of
> Apostles, and dared to preach the Gospel in the streets and in town squares.
> The above-mentioned Valdesius or Valdensis encouraged a number of
> accomplices of both sexes in this presumption, sending them out to preach
> as disciples.

Their beliefs clustered around literalist interpretations of certain passages in Scripture, resulting in such practices as refusing to tell falsehoods or swear an oath, and rejection of aspects of Catholic doctrine, as in their denial of Purgatory and transubstantiation, the cult of saints, and the power of the Pope to canonise. Like the Jews, they wore a badge to distinguish themselves from the rest of society, a kind of buckle on their shoe, although this practice may have ceased once they began to be prosecuted for heresy, and unlike the Jews they chose to wear this sign and could therefore choose to discard it. On one point concerning the Devil, however, they were orthodox enough. In his treatise against the Cathars, one of Vaudès's companions, Durand de Huesca, produced a summary of Waldensian faith, which included the article, 'We believe that the Devil became wicked, not because of his situation but through an act of will'.

But by the beginning of the fifteenth century, a number of disparate events, movements, perceptions, and linguistic usages had begun to coalesce. Pope Alexander V (1409-10), for example, noted in 1409 that 'several Christians and treacherous Jews have set up new sects [*in the Dauphiné and south-eastern France*], and invent forbidden rituals, hostile to the Faith, which they formulate, teach, preach, and assert in secret', an observation repeated by two of his successors in 1418 and 1434. Next, Pope Eugenius IV (1431-47) issued a decree to all inquisitors in 1437:

It has come to Our attention, (and We are gravely disturbed by what We hear), that with his crafty tricks the Prince of Darkness has so bewitched (*infascinavit*) large numbers of those bought by the blood of Christ that he makes them participants in their own damnation and fall, and that they, following the detestable persuasions and illusions of him and his followers with a delinquent blindness, sacrifice to evil spirits, worship them, await and receive responses from them, do them homage, and, what is more, hand over a written document or something else as a sign [of submission] when they inflict on or remove from whomsoever they want, simply by a word, touch, or gesture, the acts of harmful magic they have obligated themselves to the spirits [to carry out]. [We hear] that they cure the sick, summon a lack of temperateness in the air and, in addition to other acts of sacrilege, ratify pacts or arrogantly claim to have produced such things; that they set up images, and have them set up so that the evil spirits may be confined therein when they perform their acts of harmful magic by means of invocations; that they are not afraid to misuse items used in baptism and the Eucharist, as well as [misusing] other sacraments and some of the items connected with them in their divinations [*sortilegiis*] and acts of harmful magic [*maleficiis*]; that they baptise images made from wax or from something else with invocations of this kind, too, or arrange for them to be baptised. [We also hear] in addition to this that some of them, having no reverence for the symbol of the most holy cross on which the Shepherd hung for us all, inflict on carvings and, on some occasions, the image of the foresaid cross various acts of shame by abhorrent movements of the body; and when it comes to the sacraments, which they should not perform under any circumstances, they take it upon themselves to perform them with acts of superstitious and unwarranted presumption.

Here apostasy, idolatry, blasphemy, forbidden magic, and (by clear implication), heresy are all mixed together; and it was only three years later that Pope Eugenius followed this by another decree, this time directed against the former Duke of Savoy who had been elected anti-Pope by the Council of Basel:

The leader and principal force [of this Council] and the architect of the whole impious business was that first-born of Satan, the most disastrous Duke Amadeus of Savoy, who had had his mind set on these things for some time already and, as is alleged by a very large number of people, was seduced many years ago by the conjuring-tricks, prophecies, and fantasies of several wretched men and silly little women who, having abandoned their Saviour and apostatized to follow Satan, are led astray by the illusions of evil spirits. These people are called "witchikins" in the vernacular, or "witches", or "Waldensians", and it is said there is a huge number of them in his home country.

Wolfgang Behringer concludes that it was no accident Waldensianism became identified with witchcraft. Some Waldensians claimed that magic was taught during their meetings, and that their instructors (*magistri*) had remarkable abilities, including those of travelling to spiritual realms. Add to this the topsy-turvydom of their allowing women to play an important part in their organisation, and it is easy to see that the ill-disposed or suspicious could easily begin to elide what Waldensians themselves claimed as fact, and the well-known, indeed traditional, slanders spread about religious deviants, which depicted them as devoted to magic and self-indulgence and secret blasphemies, and so produce an amalgamation of truth, half-truth, and falsehood which would prove both irresistible and lethal in the not too distant future. It helped give rise, in fact, to the notion that there existed a sect of Devil-worshippers, actively hostile to the Church and her flock, which needed to be rooted out of the body of Christ and destroyed, like an alien growth, before it could do more damage. Satan, it seemed, had indeed been released from bondage as the *Apocalypse* had foretold.[30]

CHAPTER 5

Meeting the Devil in Public

Since it appeared that the Devil had either, been released from bondage in preparation for the Last Days, or was being allowed to rampage within the world to prosecute his war against Christian souls, the likelihood that human beings would come face to face with him at some point in their lives was considerably increased. The *Chronica de Mailros*, to give only one example, records that in 1165, 'there was a great storm in the province of York. The Old Enemy was seen by many people, going in front of that storm in the shape of a very big black horse constantly hurrying towards the sea in its flight and pressed hard by lightning and thunder, with dreadful roaring sounds, and hail which laid waste to everything. The hoof-prints of this horse were found to be of an abnormally immense size, most especially on the hill of Scarborough whence it leaped towards the sea. There, each hoof-print was as deep as a stinking sunken ditch'.[31] Apart from such group experiences, however, one of the most likely ways an individual had of seeing and meeting Satan was either to be taken by surprise and find that a chance encounter with a strange man was actually a meeting with the Devil whose blandishments and promises were then frequently effective in recruiting the human individual to be his servant and follower, or to attend a meeting of his actual or would-be agents – heretics of various kinds and those workers of magic generally known as 'witches' – during which Satan would appear to the concourse under one or more of his several guises.

Conventions of witches, known as 'synagogues' and then more commonly as 'Sabbats', (a reflection of the anti-Jewish atmosphere in which official formulation of these notions was conceived), are perhaps the best-known public manifestations of the acute witch-consciousness of the later sixteenth and early seventeenth centuries, and vivid, indeed often lurid, accounts of them can be found in a number of treatises dealing with the subject. But for all their notoriety, Sabbats were not an everyday occurrence, nor were they the usual means whereby a human might come into the presence of Satan; and yet in spite of their dramatic form and content, they represent a more interesting concept of interaction between spirit and corporeal worlds than histrionic descriptions of them might suggest. The idea of such a meeting has complex origins. Carlo Ginzburg has offered an account of them, which ranges through European fertility rites, shamanistic trances, and the spreading notions of a conspiracy between Jews and Satan to overthrow the kingdom of God on earth by spreading plague; and he points to the first half of the fourteenth century as a period in which specific persecutions of Jews, in answer to these ideas of a conspiracy, broke out in the Dauphiné and Savoy. Images of incest, cannibalism, and the worship of some bestial divinity had a long history, of course, and can be found in the work of first-century AD Roman historian Tacitus when he is speaking of Christians, and in other early anti-Christian literature refuted by such apologists as the third-century Minucius Felix and Tertullian; and since it contains several of those accusations which would be used against Jews, heretics, and witches in future centuries, it is worthwhile looking at the relevant passage from Minucius Felix. It comes from his dialogue *Octavius*. One of the speakers, Quintus Caecilius Natalis, addresses Minucius on the subject of charges currently being circulated in Rome against what he calls 'an impious conspiracy':

> Root and branch it must be exterminated and accursed. They recognise one another by secret signs and marks; they love almost before they have become acquainted; everywhere they have sex with each other as though they belonged to a religion of lust, and they call each other "brother" and "sister" indiscriminately, so that ordinary lewdness, under cover of a sacred name, becomes incest. Thus their vain, mad superstition boasts of its crimes ... I am told that, from what tasteless and absurd belief I do not know, they regard the head of a really disgusting beast, the ass, as sacred, and worship it – a religion worthy of the morals which gave it birth! Some say these people actually reverence the genitals of their overseer and priest, and reverence his penis as if it belonged to their father. I don't know whether this is true or not, but there can be no doubt that the suspicion is appropriate [in light of] their secret, nocturnal rituals ... What is reported about the initiation of their recruits is as abhorrent as it is well-known. A small child, covered in dough to deceive the unsuspecting, is placed next to the person who is to be initiated. The recruit is summoned [to strike] apparently harmless blows on the surface of the dough, and the child is killed by injuries randomly inflicted and hidden from view. Thirstily (oh horror!) they lap up the child's blood, compete with one another in sharing out parts of its body, ratify

their covenant by means of this sacrificial victim, and by their awareness of this crime bind themselves to mutual silence ... On the day set aside for the feast, people of both sexes and every age meet, together with all their children, sisters, and mothers. There, after they have eaten a great deal, when the party has heated up and a fever of incestuous lust has burst into flame in the drunken [participants], they throw a small piece of meat to a dog that has been tethered to a lamp-stand. [It goes] further than the length of the cord by which the dog is tied, [and so] he is excited and rushes forward and jumps in the air. Thus the light which shares their guilt is overturned and extinguished and, in the shameless dark, they roll around in the embraces of an unspeakable, indiscriminate lust. [9.2-7]

The Christian conspiracy is thus distinguished as a religious sect by the use of such terms as 'worship', 'priest', 'initiation', and 'sacrificial victim'; and it involves the murder of newborn or very young children, the swearing of an oath and the making of a pact, and illicit, indiscriminate sex. Bearing these points in mind, let us turn to a decretal letter issued by Pope Gregory IX on 1 June 1233. It is addressed to the Archbishop of Mainz, the Bishop of Hildesheim, and Konrad von Marburg, a Papal inquisitor with a special commission from the Archbishop to seek out heretics in the Rhineland. Once again, the language is that of religion – to be expected, of course, since Pope Gregory is describing the activities of an heretical sect – and three basic horrors are similar to those in Minucius Felix's text: the reverence bordering on worship paid to an animal, the shameful killing and illicit sex in the dark. But elaborate developments upon these themes provide a particular pattern, which later authors on witchcraft tended to follow, so it is worth our looking further at some of those details:

The initiatory rites of this plague are carried out as follows. When any novice is received into it and enters the ranks of the damned for the first time, there appears a kind of frog to which a few people used to give the name 'toad'. Some [of the participants], risking damnation, kiss it on its hindquarters. Others kiss it on its mouth and allow the creature's tongue and saliva to come into their mouths. Sometimes this [frog] appears unduly large – occasionally it takes on the size of a goose or a duck, and frequently that of a young fallow deer.[32]

The ranks of the damned are the *scholas perditorum*. The word *schola* refers to a body of soldiers such as a royal guard, a craft guild, a choir, and a retinue of clerics attendant on a bishop. We have, then, both military and ecclesiastical associations to attach to the assembly right from the start, but we are probably meant to think principally of the ecclesiastical. 'Novice' is a monastic term, and 'schools' (another meaning of *scholas*) were attached to cathedrals; so the initiation of the novice into the ranks of Satan's clerics who will instruct him in the ways of evil paints the picture of an organisation aping the Church herself, while at the same time running counter to everything she stands for and wishes to achieve, and having the Devil as her 'bishop'. This notion of a counter-Church will be one heavily emphasised in certain later accounts of the witches' Sabbat. (One says 'him' because this is the assumption of the Latin text, although there is no reason to suppose that female initiates were not received in the same way). At the entry of the frog, we learn that a few people 'were accustomed' to call it a toad. The tense of the Latin verb implies that they did so on a single occasion, so here we may have an echo of Konrad von Marburg's report to the Archbishop: 'I was told that a few people were in the habit of calling it a toad'. The association of frogs with the Devil goes back to *Apocalypse* 16.13-14: 'I saw three unclean spirits like frogs come out of the mouth of the dragon, and out of the mouth of the beast, and out of the mouth of the false prophet. For they are the spirits of demons'. Reverence is paid to the frog, not because it is the Devil himself, but because it is his representative, and in Coppo di Marcovaldo's mosaic of the Last Judgement in the Baptistery in Florence, for example, we can see a huge frog or toad lunging out from between Satan's feet to begin devouring a damned human whom the Devil has pinned to the ground. Toads were alleged to be venomous. Therefore, by kissing the frog/toad on its mouth and receiving its saliva, participants of this occasion are symbolically feeding upon that which will make them fatal to other people. This creature is called a *species ranae*, which may mean 'a kind of frog', but may also mean 'the semblance of a frog', thereby implying that the assembly is honouring a demon disguised in this fashion:

> After all this, while the novice is stepping forward to present himself, he is met by a human being with an extraordinarily pale complexion and jet-black eyes. [This person] is thin and emaciated to the point where his flesh has been destroyed and only the skin drawn over his bones has been left behind. The novice kisses him and has the sensation that he is cold, like ice; and after this kiss, memory of the Catholic faith vanishes entirely from his heart.

The next stage in the novice's initiation now begins. We are not told directly that he kissed the frog or, indeed, if he did so, which of the alternatives, buttocks or mouth, he may have chosen. But his encounter with the frog-demon is succeeded by what appears to be a meeting with Death in the form of a skeleton. The heyday of death-skeletons in art would not come until the burst of *danses macabres* during the fourteenth and fifteenth centuries, but there are thirteenth-century frescoes in the hospital church of Wismar, which show three gentlemen out riding who encounter the skeletal remains of three of their ancestors, and a thirteenth-century manuscript in the library of the University of Louvain illustrates a Burgundian execution with attendant skeletons in a kind of *danse macabre*. Kissing Death will, naturally, produce a sensation of icy coldness, and the resulting disappearance of the Catholic faith from the novice's 'heart' may perhaps be taken as a preliminary step to demonic possession. 'Dominant opinion in the Middle Ages', as Nancy Caciola says, 'held that spirit possession – whether by an unclean or the Holy spirit – involved a literal entry into the body. Once inside, this foreign spirit interacted with the body's internal physiology, including the organs, pathways of sense apprehension, the mind, and the indigenous human spirit of an individual'. Pope Gregory's reference to the heart, therefore, may perhaps be taken more literally than we would be inclined to do at first reading:

> Presently, they sit down to a formal meal (*convivium*). Once it is over, they rise to their feet, and a black cat, as large as a medium-sized dog, comes down backwards, with its tail twisted back on itself, past a certain statue which is usually found in assemblies (*scholas*) of this kind. First the novice, then the master of ceremonies, then one by one, according to rank, those who are "worthy" and "perfected" kiss [the cat] on its hindquarters. The "unperfected", on the other hand, who do not consider themselves deserving [of this honour], receive the kiss of peace from the master of ceremonies. Then each takes up his or her place, chants certain magical utterances, and inclines his or her head towards the cat. "Be merciful to us", says the master of ceremonies, and the person next to him enjoins [the rest to do likewise]. A third person replies, saying, "We know, Master", and a fourth says, "And we must obey".

Sitting down to a formal meal is described here as 'reclining'. Pictures of witches' Sabbats, which illustrate such an occasion, show the participants sitting at a table in the expected way; so Pope Gregory's language here may reflect his training in Classical Latin which does have people reclining on their left side on couches at dinner parties. The appearance of the black cat signifies either that the Devil had joined the assembly in one of his bestial guises, or that a demon had done so on his behalf. In his description of a Cathar meeting, Walter Map in 1182 had already confirmed that Satan might be pleased to show himself thus:

About the first watch of the night, when gates, doors, and windows have been closed, the groups sit waiting in silence in their respective synagogues, and a black cat of amazing size climbs down a rope which hangs in their midst. On seeing him, they put out the lights. The do not sing hymns or repeat them distinctly, but hum through clenched teeth and, breathing heavily, feel their way towards the place where they saw their lord. When they have found him they kiss him, each more humbly as he becomes more inflamed with frenzy – some the feet, more under the tail, most the private parts.

More or less contemporary with Pope Gregory, a treatise against the Waldensians of Leiden, attributed to David of Augsburg, noted that it was said these heretics met secretly at night, kissed cats and frogs, invoked the Devil, and indulged in sexual orgies in the dark. Interestingly enough, however, 'David' observed that this kind of thing was usually said of Cathars and not of other heretics, so one wonders if Konrad von Marburg's report to the Archbishop of Mainz, and Pope Gregory's decretal letter had not made current, or at any rate helped to spread, the lurid details the Pope's letter describes. Certainly the details were circulated and open to variation. Information provided by a heretic called Lepzet during the 1250s or 60s said that an initiate into this sect would formally renounce the sacraments of the Church, after which a pale-faced man in black and a large frog would appear in succession to be kissed by the initiate. At meetings of the sect, participants would kiss the buttocks of two of their leaders, after which an enormous cat appeared and climbed to the top of a pillar on which a lighted lamp had been placed, and there it clung, lifting its tail so that people could kiss its anus. This done, an orgy followed in the dark. The manuscript calls these people 'Cathars', so David of Augsburg may have been right in suggesting that what was said of Cathar initiations had details, or at least a flavour, peculiar to them.

Pope Gregory's letter says that when the cat appeared, its tail was twisted backwards (*retorta*). This is not the same as 'erect', and I think we should picture the tail curled back on itself like a Cumberland sausage. This backward contortion and movement is a simple reversal of movements in orthodox society. Alien groups might be expected to behave in a counter-fashion, an expectation which almost certainly lies behind the notion, for example, that Jewish ghosts walked backwards; and it is possible, too, that it is illustrated in the engraving by Jan Ziarnko for the second edition of Pierre de Lancre's *Tableau de l'inconstance des mauvais anges et demons* (1613) in which the naked dancers are moving in a circle, hand in hand, but facing outwards and bending back in a way which strikes one as rather uncomfortable. The cat's peculiar entry takes it past a statue. What or

whom the statue represents is not explained, but one is left with the impression
- possibly intended - that it will be honoured or worshipped at some point in the
proceedings and thus provide the focus for Cathar idolatry. Lepzet's pillar with
a lamp on top, for example, may have been intended to represent Lucifer, the
'bearer of light', himself.

The person who seems to be directing proceedings is called *magister*. This is a
word with a large number of possible meanings: foreman, manorial officer, major
domo, master craftsman, provost, administrator, captain of troops, teacher. Given
the context of this particular Cathar assembly in which he plays an important
directorial role, it seems appropriate to refer to him as the master of ceremonies,
especially since some of what he does is meant to remind us of the Mass.
The kiss of peace which he gives to the majority of those present, originally a
gesture confined to the celebrating clergy, had recently been extended to all the
faithful by Pope Innocent III, and we have this situation reflected here, with the
'perfected' - the spiritual élite of the Cathars - having the privilege of kissing the
cat's buttocks while the *magister* passes it on to the rest. In other Cathar contexts,
however, *magister* seems to refer to the person who instructs everyone else in the
beliefs and practices of Cathar, and not always a man, for we find *magistra*, the
feminine form of the title, used as well. But it is perfectly possible for one person
to fulfil more than one role, of course, so the *magister* in Pope Gregory's account
may well have been meant to act as captain, teacher, and master of ceremonies
according to the demands of the moment. Having received the kiss of peace from
him, the participants take up their allotted or customary positions (*loca sua*) and
recite a number of *carmina*. A *carmen* is a solemn ritual utterance which may be
said, sung, or chanted. It may also mean 'song', 'poem', or 'magical incantation'.
The verb *dico* usually refers to speaking, although it may on occasion mean 'sing'
or 'recite'. This context, however, clearly suggests that Pope Gregory is thinking
of antiphonal responses sung during Mass or the Divine Office by one section
of the choir in answer to another, and although 'hymns' might be another way
of translating *carmina*, the suggestion of the whole passage that we are dealing
with a counter-Church leads us to look for a less ecclesiastical, more 'demonic'
interpretation of what is going on: hence chanting magical utterances or spells.

The pseudo-Catholic flavour is continued with 'Be merciful to us', which
comes from the Litany, ('Lamb of God, who takes away the sins of the world, be
merciful to us, o Lord'), and 'We know, Master' is a significant phrase from three
of the Gospels, occurring just before the Pharisees' trick question to Jesus about
whether it is lawful or not to give tribute to Caesar. 'Master, we know that you tell
the truth and teach the way of God in truth, and that you have no anxiety about
anyone because you don't pay heed to people's outward appearance', (*Matthew*

22.16; *Mark* 12.14; *Luke* 20.21). So a combination of sacrilege and deliberate blasphemy characterises this part of the ceremony:

> Once this part of the proceedings is finished, the candles are put out and they go on to practise lust of the most polluting kind, making no distinction between strangers and relatives. In connection with this point, if by chance there are more men present than women, they give themselves over to the passions of degradation, inflamed in their desires for each other, males engaging themselves in depravity with males. Likewise, the women also change natural intercourse into that which is contrary to Nature, doing this with each other at the risk of their damnation.

So far the initiate has shown himself willing to revere evil, and has passed through a symbolic death by kissing the skeletal figure and forgetting his Catholic faith. He is then admitted to a participation in the new counter-Church by dining with his new companions and then taking part in blasphemous parodies of communal worship. It remains to seal this new relationship by yet another blasphemous parody. Mediaeval and Early Modern marriage was made indissoluble and legally binding by the act of sexual intercourse. Betrothal, wedding, and wedding feast were preliminaries, solemn enough in themselves but not quite the very last word, which would unite the couple as one in the eyes of God and of their own community. Here in these acts of indiscriminate sex, the initiates as it were consummate their 'marriage' to Satan in ways that deliberately break all Biblical and ecclesiastical laws, and once again Pope Gregory seems to have chosen his language carefully. For in addition to the words of disgust, which characterise his description of the orgy in darkness, he writes of 'the passions of degradation' (*passiones ignominiae*), which convey rather more in Latin than their English equivalents. *Passio* is 'emotion' or 'passion', but it is derived from a verb meaning 'I suffer' – hence the Passion of Christ refers to His suffering – and *ignominia* means 'loss of good name', 'loss of rank or status', 'disqualification', and 'disgrace'. In describing the men's surrender to their lusts, therefore, the Pope also passes judgement on them and indicates that these passions will bring them suffering and loss of face in their community:

> When they have finished committing this utterly disgraceful crime, the candles have been lit again, and each person is stationed in his or her place, from a dark corner of the assembly, [a corner] which is not devoid of the most morally depraved of people, there comes forward a certain human being. From his loins upwards he shines – more brightly than the sun, so

they say – while [from his loins] downwards he is covered with hair, like a cat. His brilliance lights up the whole place. Then the master of ceremonies takes something from the novice's clothing and says to the shining man, "Master, this, which has been given to me, I give to you", and the shining man replies, "You have served me well. You will serve me more often and better. I entrust what you have given me to your safe-keeping"; and with these words he disappears at once.

The orgy is a chaotic episode in the midst of order. Each person has an allotted rank and place within the assembly, and each person assumes that place for the kiss of peace, for the antiphonal responses, and for the appearance of the shining man. Only while the lights are out and the orgy is happening does this order dissolve and the pseudo-liturgy give way to confusion. Once a kind of propriety is restored, the Devil makes his second appearance, this time in half-human, half-bestial guise. The shining upper half signifies that he is Lucifer, 'the light bearer'. The hairy legs refer to his previous appearance as a cat associated with the pillar and lighted lamp, which symbolised his nature as Lucifer. This manifestation now conducts a formal exchange with the master of ceremonies. It is worth noting, perhaps, that the novice remains silent and plays no part in these proceedings. Something, (we are not told what), is taken from his clothing by the master of ceremonies and presented to Lucifer. We know that amulets were frequently worn and that sometimes these were hidden below the uppermost layer of what a person was wearing. The *Malleus Maleficarum*, for example, advises judges to make sure that someone being prepared for torture is stripped. In the case of a woman, the reason for this is 'that she may have sewn into her clothes some kind of magical apparatus, such as they often make from the body-parts of an unbaptized child (under instruction from evil spirits), with the intention of depriving the children of the Beatific Vision'; and the *Malleus* also notes another occasion on which it proved impossible to execute some heretics either by fire or by drowning until 'someone found out that [the condemned] had a magical amulet sewn between the skin and the flesh in a particular part of the body, namely, under one arm', (Book 3, questions 14 & 15). Amulets were also worn to assist the witch in case of arrest and torture, and were meant to make her or him invulnerable to pain and thus able to maintain silence in the face of a judge's questions. But all these are more likely to have been devices made by the witch her or himself post-initiation rather than before. Nicolas Rémy, on the other hand, records that witches were obliged to give Satan a present, no matter how small: 'Some pluck the hair from their heads, or present a straw or a little bird or some such small gift, it may be coins made from ox-hide'. Now, this may be significant, for we know that,

according to the rules of sympathetic magic, if a witch could obtain an object –
no matter what – belonging to someone, she or he would be able to exercise power
over that person, set up a magical connection, because something essential to the
object's owner had transferred itself to the object by virtue of his or her owning it
and handling or using it. It is possible, therefore, that the object removed from the
novice was a protective amulet, but it is more likely that it was something else, more
personal and not magically charged, which could be used to keep magical control
over him in future. The master of ceremonies, it seems, will exercise this control,
since it is to him that Lucifer gives the object in turn. Lucifer then congratulates
the master on serving him well – the Latin verb carries the sense of acting in the
capacity of a slave or serf – and suddenly disappears.[33]

What we have here, then, is a detailed account purporting to describe the
initiation of an individual into a sect of heretics who worship Lucifer. The
information came to Pope Gregory from Konrad von Marburg who had a
distinguished but stormy career as a Papal inquisitor, so stormy, in fact, that he
ended it as the victim of a murder. Waldensianism and Catharism were spreading
in many of the German states, the dangers to the Faith were thus highly evident,
and Konrad pursued heresy within his jurisdiction unremittingly and with a degree
of harshness which evoked adverse criticism from a number of his contemporaries.
'He thought he could arrest a cursed daughter of the Manichaean heresy, who
had been very well hidden for some time past', the Archbishop of Mainz wrote to
the Pope by way of example:

> Provided [the testimony of] witnesses who were beginning to confess they
> had some slight knowledge of the Manichaean crime and had played some
> slight role in it could be counted as admissible without their being present
> [in court]; so the result was that the accused had a choice – either confess of
> his own free will and stay alive, or swear he was innocent and be burned on
> the spot.

Now although the period of its principal flourishing was the fourteenth century,
a sect known as the Luciferians fits Konrad's description in many respects. But
were these Luciferians really worshippers of the Devil or not? Norman Cohn
notes that the German and Italian sources which describe them and their activities
are 'wholly unreliable' on two grounds: first, their accounts are accompanied by
details (such as the toad, the cat, and the incestuous orgy) which are too fantastic
to be believable; and secondly, just because a sect was dualist does not mean its
members necessarily worshipped Satan. Indeed, Cohn observes of the Cathars, 'so
far from worshipping the Devil, they were passionately concerned to escape from

his clutches. That aspiration was the very heart of their religion'. This is a perfectly reasonable point, but appearance of reality rather than reality itself is often more important in creating and sustaining a common conviction, and the fact is there were so many accounts of Devil-worshipping heretics circulating in Europe during the thirteenth and fourteenth centuries in particular that it would have taken a scepticism of more or less foolhardy proportions to have dismissed them all as unreliable. Moreover, as Cohn also points out, acceptance that a cult of Satan existed also involved acceptance of at least some of the astonishing details attributed to it. So, if there was indeed such a figure as Satan, there was no reason one should not believe he was capable of changing shape or appearing and disappearing as he chose; and, in the light of the extraordinarily widespread and frequent accusations of adultery and incest which kept on reaching church courts, we ourselves would be foolish to treat accounts of incestuous orgies as unbelievable in themselves, in connection with which, it is worth bearing in mind what John of Reading had to say about the moral laxity attendant upon the Black Death:

> Widows, forgetting the love they had borne towards their first husbands, rushed into the arms of foreigners or, in many cases, of kinsmen, and shamelessly gave birth to bastards conceived in adultery. It was even claimed that in many places brothers took their sisters to wife ... [They] no longer worried about sexual lapses. Now fornication, incest, and adultery were a game rather than a sin.

Some accounts of Luciferian meetings, however, are less lurid than others. The chronicler of the *Annales Matseenses*, for example, writes anent the year 1315 a detailed exposition of Luciferian beliefs and practices. 'They were paying for Masses [to be offered] to Lucifer, believing that with their help he must do battle with Michael, the good angels, and all the faithful, and triumph in a manner worthy to be praised' – a remarkable comment on the willingness of certain priests to say Mass for unorthodox ends. This we know they were prepared to do, as we have plenty of evidence that Mass was celebrated over amulets and other magical instruments concealed under the altar cloth; so the notion that Masses could be and were offered to Satan is by no means beyond the bounds of possibility. The chronicler then lists the various beliefs of these heretics, quoting the German of their hymns and peculiar terminology, but adds that they surrender themselves to debauchery and incestuous sex, giving the example of one Ulrich Wollar who copulated with his siblings on an Ash Wednesday, and invited fellow heretics to his house where they spent the whole night in drunken lust. Finally, the chronicler tells us that a man known as the 'New Master', who was burned in Vienna, confessed he had been bishop and master (*magister*) of the sect for fifty years, and that there were more than 80,000 of them in Austria and even more in Bohemia and Moravia. Cohn lumps this statement together with others about demons vanishing into thin air, and gigantic toads and demonic cats, but there need not be anything implausible about a very large number of heretics, (we do not need to accept 80,000 at face value), in a country as big as Austria. Moreover, given the highly individual and often peculiar beliefs we know people were capable of holding, the notion that dualist, anti-Catholic groups of one kind or another could be found all over the German states and surrounding areas is scarcely a stretch too far for the imagination.

Still, it is one thing to say that such dualistic groups may well have existed in fact, and another to gauge the reliability of many of the detailed behaviours attached to them. Cohn, as we have seen, dismisses the Luciferians out of hand. Richard Cavendish is inclined to give the description in Pope Gregory's letter a cautious nod. 'This account of an initiation carries a certain conviction, and it could have been stage managed without too much difficulty'. Now, if one looks again at what Pope Gregory says, one can see that his narrative contains many of the elements we have noted in Minucius Felix's text – the language of religion designating the group a sect, reverence paid to an animal, the making of a pact, (in the Luciferians' case a covenant made implicitly rather than explicitly), and illicit, indiscriminate sex in the dark. The fact that some of this is cast in pseudo-liturgical language is the kind of detail one might expect from clerics seeking to reduce to some kind of coherent order the answers of heretics to their questions. This is not to say that the clerics necessarily fabricated parts of the narrative: merely to suggest that, in the face of information shocking to both their theological certainties and their ecclesiastical sensibilities, they may have sought to formulate the material in such a way as to make sense of it both to themselves and to their ecclesiastical superiors. That leaves us with Cavendish's reference to theatre. It is doubtful whether the performance as we have it described actually took place in reality, stage managed or not, since it does not resemble anything in the theatrical experience of either the laity or the clergy of the time. But the more vivid details may have been influenced by people's visual memories of how Satan-Lucifer and his demons were portrayed in the decorative arts of their local church or cathedral. If Death was to appear in a gathering, he would surely look like a skeleton; if a demon came thither, he might look like a frog or a cat; and if Lucifer revealed himself – and these people were, after all, specifically 'Luciferians' – he would shine, would he not, because that is what his name implies; and he would also appear bestial in part because his nature is demonic and therefore he should not look entirely human. It is thus possible that the Papal account of such a meeting is not completely remote from truth, although where the *precise* boundary between true details and false may have been is not altogether easy to gauge at this distance of time.

Nearly a hundred years later, says Alain Boureau, 'demons seemed ready to swoop down on humans'. He explains this by reference to three fundamental changes which had taken place by the early years of the fourteenth century: the theory of the pact, which altered relationships between humans and the demonic world; the perceived expansion of co-operative activity between humans and demons from a relatively small group of magical practitioners to embrace, potentially, the whole of humanity; and the pressure of millenarianist ideas which signalled the imminence of the Last Days. These three together, along with the proliferation of heresies, the stubbornness of Jews in refusing to convert, and the constant threat of Islam on Christendom's borders, irresistibly suggested that Satan was creating a network of conspiracies across Europe in particular, ready to strike at the Faith wherever and whenever he could; and the growing equivalency between heresy and the practice of magic meant that sooner or later official attempts to eradicate heresy would begin to include similar efforts to deal with magic.

As it happens, it would be later. It is a complete mistake to think that there was universal agreement on these matters, or that people did not debate aspects of such theories as they arose and while they were developing. As early as the tenth century, a document mistakenly believed to come from the Council of Ancyra in 314, and known as the *Canon Episcopi*, described in the most sceptical terms the foolish belief of some women that they rode through the air at night in company with the goddess Diana. Priests, it said, should explain to their congregations that this was merely a delusion wrought by Satan in the minds of the credulous, a point of view which was repeated by figures both ecclesiastical and lay for the next several centuries. Bartholomew Iscanus, Bishop of Exeter (mid twelfth century), enjoined one year's penance on anyone misguided enough to maintain he or she took part in such a ride; Jean de Meun (c.1270) called it an illusion; Boccaccio (c.1350) had great fun describing a secret society which met twice a month for feasting and sex – clearly versions of a dualists' 'Sabbat' were current in Italy – and the appearance of a small, black, horned creature which, it was said, would come to carry the gull of the story to his initiation into a 'society of rovers'; while a medical treatise, *Illnesses of the Head*, written by Antonio Guaineri, a lecturer in medicine at the University of Pavia during the early 1400s, suggested that certain illusions were caused by vapours rising in the body rather than from interference by a demon.

Nevertheless, 'scepticism' did not mean that these writers dismissed human interaction with the preternatural or supernatural worlds, merely that they raised questions and doubts about certain popular aspects of it. The evidence everywhere of increased demonic and Satanic activity was too great to be anything other than convincing; and so when treatises dealing with witches began to appear during the first half of the fifteenth century, describing their Sabbats in terms often remarkably similar to those which had described the nocturnal, blasphemous, and idolatrous conventions of dualist heretics, there was a widespread inclination to accept them as true. In c.1430, for example, there appeared a short anonymous tract, *Errores Gazariorum*, 'The Errors of the Cathars', with the subtitle, 'or of those people who are regarded as riding on a broom or a fork-handle' – a clear reference to witches, and a development of the ride with Diana, condemned as a fantasy by the *Canon Episcopi*. Once the participants have assembled in the place of the 'synagogue', as the Sabbat is called, 'the Enemy appears, sometimes in the likeness of a black cat, sometimes in the likeness of a human being – not a "perfect" human, though – or under a resemblance to some other animal'. (What does 'perfect' mean here? Does it imply there is something lacking complete humanity in his appearance, such as excessive body hair or a cloven foot? If so, one would expect to be told directly. It is perhaps more likely to be an echo of the term 'perfected' that was applied to the Cathar spiritual élite.) The initiate, who has been seduced by the Devil into coming to the Sabbat in the first place, tells Satan he wants to be a member of that society and swears an oath of fidelity, after which he pays homage by means of a kiss on the Devil's anus. A feast of roast and boiled children follows, and then, on the Devil's command, 'Meslet, meslet', which seems to mean something like, 'Have sex, have sex', (Latin *miscete*), everyone engages in indiscriminate copulation in the dark.[34]

Six or seven years later, Claude Tholosan, a senior judge in the Dauphiné, who tried more than a hundred cases of witchcraft during his career, wrote a brief treatise containing a description of the Sabbat, whose details he said came from witches themselves and from those who had suffered from their magic. It takes its clumsy title from a quotation originating in St Augustine's *City of God*, 'Ut errores magorum et maleficorum: so that the errors of magicians and workers of harmful magic', a sentence which goes on to say that the saint had decided to reveal what these dreadful people actually did and believed, so that the general public would not remain in ignorance about them. Many of Tholosan's details are familiar. At meetings of the sect, initiates renounce their faith, commit sacrilege by spitting and trampling on the cross and making obscene gestures three times towards God and the east, and sacrifice small children. The Devil is present throughout the proceedings, and receives their kiss of homage, although Tholosan says they kiss him on the mouth, not on the anus. He is seen in the shape the participant wants him to assume. So if, for example, says Tholosan, the participant is young and lustful, the Devil makes himself look handsome. But this does not happen invariably, for from the records of a trial over which Tholosan presided in or just after 1436, we are given a quite different version of the Devil's appearance. 'He had big, dull eyes, like those of a cow, and they sent out fiery sparks. He had a long tongue protruding from [his mouth]. It hung towards the ground ... and he had bowed legs and black toes'.

One detail of these proceedings, however, is new, a blasphemous parody of taking communion wine. Near the start of the meeting, just after the initiates have renounced God, 'they upturn a vessel and put it in a circle they have drawn on the ground. The Devil then pees in it and the initiates take a drink. Finally, they bury it[35] in order to signify that thus they dissociate themselves from the faith of Christ'.[36] Johannes Nider, a Dominican who fulfilled important offices at the Council of Basel (1431-4), wrote a lengthy treatise arguing for reform within the Church, and included a somewhat similar detail in his chapter on witchcraft in the diocese of Autun, a chapter which proved to be both popular and influential, judging by the large number of manuscripts and early printed copies which were produced. A local judge who had tried and executed many witches in the territory of Bern told him that a witch confessed that she and her companions would kill young children, boil their flesh, and preserve the liquid in a glass bottle; and a young man, subsequently executed as a witch, said that his initiation consisted of going to church, renouncing his faith, doing homage to the Devil (whom he calls *magisterulus*, 'little master'), and then drinking from the bottle, an action which immediately confirmed him as a member of the sect. *Magisterulus*, which is not often used of the Devil, is the Latin diminutive of *magister*. Latin uses diminutives to indicate shortness, smallness, affection, or patronising condescension; so unless we are to suppose that on this occasion the Devil appeared as a dwarf, we should think of this form of address as an affectionate greeting – an interesting comment not only on the relationship the initiate feels he has with Satan, but also perhaps an indication that the Devil has not appeared in frightening or grotesque form, since it is difficult to imagine some of his guises producing anything like affection and claim of intimacy from the onlooker.

In c.1440, Martin le Franc, a clerk in the household of the Duke of Savoy who had been so scathingly condemned by Pope Eugenius IV only three years earlier as someone susceptible to the tricks and blandishments of witches, wrote a long poem in French, *Le Champion des Dames*, whose slightly ambiguous attitude towards witches may have come from Le Franc's years of service with the Duke. Only a short section deals with witchcraft, but it contains one or two small variants upon the description of the Sabbat. Thousands, according to the speaker Le Franc uses for his poetic dialogue, turn up in the shape of cats or goats. The

Devil is present and receives their kiss on his backside, after which there is dancing and feasting and drink. Then comes a course of instruction in hostile magic from the Devil in his role as teacher (*magister*), followed by praise and punishment according to the participants' deserts. Finally, the Devil takes the shape of a cat, listens to people's requests, and accepts their further homage. What makes Le Franc's manuscripts particularly interesting are the accompanying illustrations in the margin. One shows two witches flying through the air, one on a broomstick, and the other on a long pole – the first such pictures we have. Both witches are women. They are labelled *vaudoises*, 'Waldensians', although by this time the word had ceased to refer exclusively to that group of heretics and had become a loose term for witches. Another illustration from a later manuscript copy shows Satan as a large grey striped cat seated upon a rock, instructing a group of women who are kneeling round him, their hands pressed together in the customary attitude of prayer. A third depicts four men and women, two young and fashionably dressed, two older and more staid, grouped round the Devil who is in one of his grotesque forms: very tall, with horns and what appears to be reptilian, scaly ears protruding on each side of a face which is completely blank – no features of any kind. His torso and arms are those of a human, but he has a grinning human face covering his belly, and his legs and feet are those of a hirsute animal. This version of him does not correspond to anything in the poem, so here we have an artist appealing to conventional artistic forms to achieve his effect – a rather lazy piece of shorthand, in fact.

These details, however, become rather pale beside an extraordinary collection of information from Arras, (*Recollectio*), based on trial documents of 1460. It deals with what it calls 'Waldensian idolaters', and describes at length how 'Waldensians', (that is, witches), attend their Sabbats, are initiated into the sect, and learn how to operate hostile magic. The Sabbat is presided over by a demon who sits in a chair raised high above the heads of the congregation. An initiate is usually introduced into the sect by a human rather than by a demon, and when he or she arrives, the standard formula of initiation is observed: renunciation of the Faith and the Church, trampling and spitting on the cross, and homage to the demon. This last is done by kissing his hand and foot, and then offering him a lighted black candle, which is then doused. The initiate performs the *osculum infame*, the kiss on the buttocks, and enters into a pact whereby she or he becomes a full member of the sect. He or she then gives the demon a part of his or her body – hair, nail-cuttings, or quite frequently blood, (is this an explanation of the unspecified object mentioned in Pope Gregory's letter?) – in return for which the demon gives the novice a physical sign of his or her initiation, a gold, copper, or silver ring, or a thread, or a roll of paper with strange letters on it. A female initiate is then obliged to undergo anal sex with the presiding demon whose penis, like his whole body, is cold and soft, and emits semen which is rotten and saffron-yellow, rather like pus. There follows the usual banquet and orgy. It is not made altogether clear whether this demon is Lucifer himself – we are told he always takes the form of a man during these proceedings, but that is modified in a later passage by the phrase, 'whatever form he takes' – but no name is attached to him, not even *magister*, for instruction in the teachings and practices of the sect is usually done by human beings. Nevertheless, we may assume, and it seems we are meant to assume, that this presiding demon is probably the Devil in person, for manuscripts of Johannes Tinctor's *Tractatus de secta Valdensium* from the same year, 1460, show Satan as a large goat surrounded by kneeling men and women, some of whom are carrying a candle, with one person lifting his tail so that another can kiss the creature's anus. A second picture has a demon urging worshippers to kiss Satan in the form of a cat, and a third has Satan as a monkey, a reference to a widespread concept of him as *simia Dei*, 'God's ape'.[37]

In the light of so much scholarly and official interest in the Sabbat, however, it is worth noting that the best-known witch treatise, the *Malleus Maleficarum* of Heinrich Institoris, published in 1486, makes very little mention of it and relies almost entirely on Nider for the few details it gives. Indeed, as far as Institoris is concerned, it makes no difference to the efficacy of the novice's initiation whether the Devil is present at the Sabbat or not. So in fact, in his view, the whole apparatus of the Sabbat is more or less unnecessary to the process of becoming and acting as a witch. This lack of interest in the Sabbat among learned writers coincides with a period of nearly a century during which intense preoccupation with and fear of satanic conspiracies seems to have abated. It was revived, however, in the 1580s, one of the principal impetuses being the rupture between the Catholic Church and a burgeoning number of Protestant groups influenced in part by religion, in part by politics, and thenceforth for several decades it raged anew, bringing in its wake fierce episodes of witch prosecution in certain areas, especially some of the southern German states where a variety of circumstances once again produced concerted attempts to eradicate Satan's human agents. With this apparent resurgence in spiritual terrorism came writings to describe its origins and workings, and advice on how best to remove it.

Jean Bodin (1529/30 - 96), a remarkable writer who impressed his contemporaries with his treatises on history, politics, economics, and religion, wrote also on witches in 1580, and noted that according to the many accounts and trial records he had read, Sabbats were often held in woods or near local crosses, usually on Monday nights, and took the form of an abjuration, worshipping the Devil, dancing, feasting, and kissing Satan's anus. Satan frequently appeared there as an animal, but might also take the form of a very black, hideous man. In Poitiers, however, the proceedings included a curious variant. A very large black goat with the gift of human speech stood in the midst of the witches while they danced around it. Then each person, holding a lighted candle, kissed its backside, after which they burned the goat on a fire and used its ashes to work hostile magic against both animals and people. Was this goat the Devil? It is presented in Bodin's text as though it were something apart, a real goat merely symbolic of Satan himself. But in a later treatise by Henri Boguet, there is no doubt that Satan and the goat are one, so perhaps this is how the Poitiers goat should be interpreted too. Another French jurist, Nicolas Rémy (1580-1616) gave further information in his *Démonolatrie* ('The Worship of the Demon'), published in Lyon in 1595 and running through several reprints after that. It contains a remarkable number of vivid details drawn from witches' confessions. For example, according to Nicolette Lang-Bernhard, while she was walking in the countryside on 25 July 1590 in the blaze of noon, 'she saw in a field nearby a band of men and women dancing round in a ring. But because they were doing so with their backs turned towards each other in a manner contrary to the usual practice, she looked more closely and also saw them dancing around with the others, some whose feet were deformed and like those of goats or oxen'. Rémy records many equally vivid details about preparations for the Sabbat and what participants did once they got there, and he makes it clear that it was not necessarily Satan himself who occupied the high throne set above people's heads, which was a frequent feature of these meetings. He says merely that 'a demon' presided 'with a proud and haughty manner'. However, after receiving the *osculum infame*, 'to the terror of the beholders, he changes to some huge monster, in size and shape not unlike a mighty wine vat, ceaselessly breathing out fire and smoke from his enormous mouth, in order to inspire fear into his subjects'. This information came from Jeanne Gransaint who had been arrested and questioned in July 1582. What was this shape like a wine-vat expelling fire and smoke from its mouth? One is reminded of a very common representation of the entrance to Hell, a monstrous animal with a great gaping mouth open to swallow the souls of the damned. These hell-mouths were found all over Europe in paintings, and as enormous props in religious plays, large enough for actors to pass through; so it is possible that Jeanne's highly unusual description of the demon was influenced by memories of a picture in her local church of Condé-sur-Meuse, or of an elaborate piece of stage-machinery which had made an impression on her imagination.

After that of Rémy, we find a somewhat unusual description of the Sabbat, relating to 1594. A young French girl from Aquitaine had been corrupted by an unnamed Italian who, in the middle of the night before the Feast of St John the Baptist, took her to a field where he traced a circle on the ground with a beech twig, muttering some words out of a black book:

Suddenly there appeared a large and perfectly black goat, well horned, and accompanied by two women, and soon there came up a man clothed and vested like a priest. The goat asked the Italian what girl that was; and he answered that she had been brought by him to be enrolled among the goat's subjects. Hearing this, the goat ordered her to make the sign of the cross with her left hand, and all who were present to approach and perform their act of veneration. Thereupon they all kissed him with their lips under his tail. Between the goat's horns a black candle gave a horrid light, and from this they all lit the candles they were holding; and as they worshipped the goat, they dropped money in a bowl.

What makes this unusual is the way the meeting happens. According to convention, witches flew to the Sabbat, or were conveyed thither in some fashion, from their own homes. Here the Sabbat is conjured by an act of ritual magic, and contains a number of distinctive features: the presence of a vested priest; the sign of the cross, (usually a way of dispersing evil spirits, although this sign is made with the left rather than the right hand); an act of veneration, which would require the participants to bend low or approach the goat-demon on their knees; the carrying of candles; and the offering of money dropped into a bowl. This, apart from the candles, is reminiscent of the old-style 'creeping to the cross' on Good Friday, a ceremony in which a vested priest slowly uncovered a crucifix and members of the congregation made their way towards it on their knees, kissed it, and then often made an offering of coins which they dropped into a nearby bowl. So it is possible that here, as appears to happen quite frequently, an echo of genuine Catholic ritual has made its way in some distorted form into the account given by or attributed to an accused witch. This is a thought to which we shall return later.

But if we think of descriptions of the Sabbat, one of the most notable appears in a résumé given by one of the outstanding scholars of the late sixteenth century, Martín Del Rio, whose magisterial survey of the magical arts, *Disquisitiones Magicae*, ('Investigations Into Magic'), was first published in 1599-1600. For some of this, he uses Rémy, a French inquisitor, Nicolas Jacquier, whose *Flagellum haereticorum fascinariorum*, ('The Scourge of Heretics who cast Spells'), though written in 1458, had been published only in 1581, and Peter Binsfeld (c.1545/6 - 98), the Jesuit Bishop of Trier, whose treatise on the confessions of those who worked harmful magic had appeared in 1589. Del Rio's account, however, does not depend on these except for one or two small details. Witches fly to the Sabbat in a variety of ways – his examples are drawn from Rémy – their meeting being called 'a *ludus* of good fellowship'. The word *ludus* means 'a game' or 'an entertainment' or 'a bit of frivolity'. It also means 'a place of instruction, especially an elementary school', so whenever the writers of these treatises call the Sabbat a *ludus*, they are relying on both senses of the word to convey how participants viewed the occasion. 'There', Del Rio says:

> On most occasions, once a foul, disgusting fire has been lit, an evil spirit sits on a throne as president of the assembly. His appearance is terrifying, almost always that of a male goat or a dog. The witches come forward to worship him in different ways. Sometimes they supplicate him on bended knee; sometimes they stand with their back turned to him; sometimes they even throw their legs in the air and hold their head, not forwards but tilted right back so that their chin points up to the sky. They offer candles made of pitch or a child's umbilical cord, and kiss him on the anal orifice as a sign of homage ... Once they have committed these and similar atrocious and execrable abominations, they sit down at table and start to enjoy food supplied by the evil spirit or brought by themselves. Sometimes they perform a ritual dance before the feast, sometimes after. Usually, there are various tables – three or four of them – loaded with food which is sometimes very dainty and sometimes quite tasteless and unsalted. Each witch has his or her place allotted according to station or wealth. The evil spirit attached to each of these workers of harmful magic (*malefici*) sits near him; sometimes on one side of him, sometimes opposite. Nor do they omit to use a grace worthy of such a gathering, using words that are always openly blasphemous and in which Beelzebub himself is declared to be the creator, giver, and preserver of all things. (This information comes from a list of graces, which they stick underneath the tables placed at their disposal. I have read a copy of these formulae written in the hand of a very famous worker of evil magic).
>
> Sometimes they take part in this feast with their faces covered by a mask, a linen cloth, or some other veil of facial representation. Usually they are masked. After the feast, each evil spirit takes by the hand the disciple of whom he has charge, and so that they may do everything with the most absurd kind of ritual, each person bends backwards, joins hands in a circle, and tosses his head as frenzied fanatics do. Then they begin to dance. Sometimes they hold lighted candles in their hands, with which they worship the evil spirit, and exchange kisses in his presence. They sing very obscene songs in his honour, or jump up and down to a drum or a pipe, which is played by someone sitting in the fork of a tree. They behave ridiculously in every way, and in every way contrary to accepted custom. Then their demon-lovers copulate with them in the most repulsive fashion.

When they sacrifice, they usually start with an act of adoration; but they often make sacrifices outwith the Sabbat. Finally, we are told, each person gives an account of the wicked deeds he has done since the last meeting. The more serious these are and the more detestable, the more they are praised with ever-greater fulsomeness. But if they have done nothing, or if their deeds are not dreadful enough, the sluggish witches are given an appalling beating by the evil spirit or by some senior worker of harmful magic (*maleficus*). Finally, they receive powders – which some writers say are the ashes of the he-goat whose shape had been taken by the evil spirit whom they worship, and which has suddenly been consumed by fire in front of their eyes – or else they receive some other poisonous substances.

Virtually all these details have appeared in earlier sources, despite occasional differences. The contorted variants upon the witches' supplicatory postures in front of Satan remind one of those into which the bodies of hysterics or possessed individuals were frequently thrown; the use of a child's umbilical cord as a candle is unusual; the blasphemous grace before the meal is interesting for Del Rio's claim to have read a copy of it; and the wearing of masks is a feature noted by quite a number of other authors. Henri Boguet, for example, offers an interesting explanation for the witches' habit of dancing back to back, which may have a bearing on having their faces covered. 'The witches dance back to back', he says, 'so that they won't be recognised, and they hold their meetings at night for the same reason ... Etienne Poicheux, alias "The Hoe", said that some women she had seen at the Sabbat wore veils, and this is why Lombards call them *mascas* ('masked women', i.e. witches) in their laws'. If we were to accept that meetings of witches actually took place, considering these were illegal and would bring down a possible death sentence on anyone found or confessing to have attended, the notion of some participants' wishing to remain anonymous, especially if they were rich, or important in their community, is well understandable. But mask-wearing also brings us back to the theatre in which the Devil and demons, as opposed to the other characters in the play, regularly wore masks; and so it may be that a memory of this convention is responsible for the appearance of masks in the remembered spiritual or psychological theatre of the Sabbat, with the human participants demonising themselves or demonising others by claiming to have seen instances of this distinctive theatrical behaviour among those who were willing or wishing to play a demonic figure in a Luciferian drama of their own.

Henri Boguet (c.1550-1619) was a near contemporary of Jean Bodin, and a senior judge in the southern Franche-Comté. In 1602 he decided to publish a warning account, based on what was then his limited experience of trying witches, *Discours des Sorciers*, which went into a second edition the following year, and a third in 1610, by which time he had accumulated further experiences. Boguet's description of the Sabbat rests largely upon the evidence of Françoise Secretain, a woman aged between thirty and forty, who spent three days in prison protesting her innocence, but failed to shed tears, (a mark of a witch), and had a broken cross attached to her rosary, (a suspicious point). But when her head was shaved to see if she carried the Devil's mark there, she began to tremble, even though no mark was found, and started to confess that she was indeed a witch. The details she gave of the Sabbat are as follows, and it is instructive to compare them with those in Del Rio's account. The witches present begin, she said, by worshipping Satan who appears there sometimes in the shape of a tall, black man, or sometimes that of a goat. They offer him candles, which burn with a blue flame, lit from one he carried between his horns, and kiss his backside in homage. 'The others', says Boguet, 'kiss him on the shoulder'. Presumably we are here meant to understand that the company is divided into grades or ranks, as Pope Gregory's letter indicated; but it is also possible that 'the others' were novices, waiting to be initiated. Then comes dancing, the participants moving in a circle, back to back. Some people, even at this early stage of the proceedings, are drunk, and the drunks urge the dancers to jump and dance more vigorously while demons, in the shape of goats or sheep, join in the round. Oboes provide the music and Satan very often plays the flute. When these instruments are not available, however, the witches sing, although they sing very fast and their notes are all over the place because no one listens to anyone else.

After dancing, the orgy; and after the orgy, there is a feast. Eating is preceded by a grace full of blasphemous expressions, and then the participants enjoy all sorts of meat 'according to people's place and rank'. So the customary social order is restored once the mêlée of indiscriminate sex is over and done. There is wine to drink, and water, but the Devil strictly forbids the use of salt – salt, of course, being used in Catholic baptism as an apotropaic. 'I exorcise you, creature of salt', says the priest in the rite of infant baptism in the *Rituale Romanum*, 'so that in the name of the Holy Trinity you may act as a redeeming sacrament to put the Enemy to flight'. Once the meal is over, the witches tell the Devil how much harm they have done since the last Sabbat, and if they have not done enough, the Devil beats them to the scornful laughter of all the others. At some point – it is not clear when – a counter-Mass is celebrated, one which mocks and inverts the genuine liturgy; and finally, Satan takes on the form of a goat and burns away in a fire, leaving behind only ashes which the witches then collect and use for harmful magic.[38]

The general format of these two accounts as one can see, is more or less the same, but Del Rio, the priest, includes the detail of the blasphemous grace and mentions some kind of sacrifice, while Boguet, the layman, tells us that some of the participants were drunk and behaved as inebriates do. These are subtle variations, but they throw emphases in the directions one expects the narrator to take: religious misbehaviour from the priest, social rowdiness from the layman. Both note that Satan takes the form of a goat for at least part of these proceedings, and although this identification had appeared in writers well before their time, the increasing number of instances of it which one can find during the sixteenth century raises the question of whether the artistic stereotype of a witch riding a goat, increasingly popular during the first two decades of the 1500s through the work of Dürer, Altdorfer, Schäuffelein, and Baldung Grien, may not have contributed, perhaps subliminally, to the consciousness of officials, ecclesiastical and lay, who at some time in their careers had cause to deal with or write about witches and therefore, perhaps, the Sabbat.[39]

It would be useful, of course, to have illustrations of the Sabbat itself, in order to see how it was visualised by those who recorded its details, and we are fortunate, in fact, in possessing just such a series of pictures. It consists of woodcuts which were added to the *Compendium Maleficarum*, ('A Condensed Account of Witches), by Francesco Maria Guazzo, a monk of the Order of St Ambrose. Each chapter in his book consists of a brief summary of its subject matter, followed by illustrative examples drawn from a wide variety of sources. Eight initial relevant woodcuts show some of the stages of entry into the sect, as listed by Guazzo: (1) denial of faith, (2) mock baptism, (3) novice re-named, (not illustrated), (4) denial of Christian godparents and assignment of new diabolical ones, (not illustrated), (5) gift of clothing to the Devil, (6) oath of allegiance, (7) writing the novice's name in the book of death, (8) promise to sacrifice a child, (9) promise of an annual gift to the Devil, (not illustrated), (10) novice marked by the Devil, (11) vows to abandon the Church and her sacraments. In each of these pictures, the witches consist of both men and women, the novice is a man, and the Devil is shown as a humanoid animal with a brutish face and horns, a long tail, hands and feet like those of a bird of prey with long talons, and bat's wings – an entirely conventional and easily recognisable portrait.

A further woodcut in a later chapter shows the Devil seated upon a throne, teaching or at least addressing assembled witches, two of whom appear to be asking a question or trying to make a point; and a second illustrates the witches' feast. Here they sit two by two - a man and a woman - at separate tables, accompanied by two demons, and served by demon waiters, some of which come fresh from the fires of Hell. There are also woodcuts illustrating the *osculum infame*, with the witches holding lighted black candles, and a dance with two men, a woman, and two demons, (one of whom may be the Devil, since he is shown with bat's wings, like the demon on the throne), while a man seated in the fork of a tree plays a violin. One or two of these pictures appear more than once in the text, including a scene of homage to the Devil by a group of men, in which one of them looks as though he is preparing to dance. His hands are raised in the air, so is one leg, and he seems to embody a sentence in the text which says, 'It is sufficiently clear from our own experience that the desire of men for wanton dancing and treading light measures nearly always leads by evil example to more lust and sin'.

Why do we find pictures in a book written in Latin and obviously composed for learned readers? The notion that they have been included for the benefit of the unlettered clearly does not apply in this case, although we should not be too precious in assuming that learned readers would not welcome a visual diversion from solid print or manuscript. We must also bear in mind the practical point that the printer may have found it convenient to fill blanks in his proposed layout with relevant or near-relevant pictures, so as to present an aesthetically pleasing page to the eye. This may explain why, for example, some woodcuts in Guazzo's book appear more than once in the text, an unnecessary repetition unless their message is to be regarded as especially significant. Nevertheless, when all this is said, it still remains true that Guazzo's woodcuts, (as those in other texts), were there for a purpose and the purpose here seems to be to alert the reader to specific points which he thought were of particular importance. In Book 3, for example, which deals with 'the divine remedies for those who are bewitched, and ... certain other matters', pictures are placed at the head of a number of chapters or divisions within the chapters, and are quite clearly intended to draw the reader's attention to their content, acting, as it were, as signposts or markers for his or her benefit. Similarly, repeated pictures in Book 1 connected with the Sabbat, (apart from those we have mentioned already), as well as illustrating points made by Guazzo's supporting anecdotes, lay a particular emphasis on certain aspects of the witches' activities: worship of the Devil (3 pictures), feasting with demons (2 pictures), and dancing with demons (3 pictures).[40] The thread which binds them is, of course, human association with and subordination to the malevolent spirit-world, an observation which echoes Guazzo's remark that the Devil and his minions were let loose and creating havoc in the world with the help of his human agents, male and female witches, magicians, and foretellers of the future – a cliché, perhaps, since everyone who wrote about witchcraft said much the same thing, but an article of deep conviction, nevertheless, for each of them and most of their contemporaries.

Deep conviction, however, did not necessarily extend to every aspect of the Sabbat, including its preliminaries such as anointing the body or broomstick, thereby enabling flight through the air to take place, or the actual possibility of flight itself. Plenty of writers especially ecclesiastics, expressed doubt on both individual details and on the whole experience itself; so it is instructive to note briefly two opposite reactions to very similar and, indeed, contemporary outbreaks of Sabbat-attending and worshipping the Devil, which took place among the Basques of south-west France in the region of the Labourd in 1608-9, and just over the border in Spain during the same years. The former was investigated by a French lawyer, Pierre de Lancre, sent there by the government in Paris to deal with the problem and submit an official report: the latter came under the scrutiny of the Spanish Inquisition under the leadership of Venegas de Figueroa and Alonso de Salazar Frías, the latter producing a detailed report for his superiors. The lay lawyer found what he investigated entirely credible, the Inquisitor did not.

Pierre de Lancre was labouring under difficulties when he went to the Labourd at the instance of King Henri IV. He despised the people of the region and its culture, he did not speak the Basque language and had to rely on interpreters, and because a majority of the male population was absent at sea for long periods, he was forced to rely for testimony and evidence upon women, children, and old men. None of this, however, means that we should prejudge his opinions and immediately start to formulate explanatory theories based on that prejudgement. De Lancre was not a fool, and the reason we know about his difficulties is that he himself tells us about them. What we should also bear in mind is that the witchcraft and Sabbat-attending described for him came from a highly distinctive region, and should therefore not be taken as precisely detailed evidence applicable in its entirety to other regions in Europe. One detail, for example, is the Satanic Mass, which was celebrated frequently at these Labourdin Sabbats:

[Witnesses] asserted one after the other that the one who said this Mass was assisted by two others, all three dressed as they are in church. There was some kind of elevation of a black Host which was not round ... but in the shape of a triangle ... Jeanne d'Abadie said that she had heard the Mass performed several times by priests whom she named ... and she said that she was taught at the Sabbat always to say "Black crow, black crow" the moment the chalice was held up.

The apparent involvement of several parish priests in these blasphemous meetings, which shocked De Lancre tremendously, is a notable feature of this Labourdin witchcraft, but by no means unusual elsewhere; and indeed over the border in Spain, Salazar Frías was told that on Sabbat nights, the Devil himself would put on a priest's vestments and celebrate Mass during the course of the convention. These Spanish Basque Masses, however, are referred to in evidence that is heavily influenced by its French counterpart, because refugees from De Lancre's investigation poured over the border and acted as a stimulus to further outbreaks of witchcraft there. Diabolical Masses are thus not unique to the Labourdin, but we do not find them commonly testified to in other places in Europe, and what De Lancre saw as a virtual wholesale involvement of parish priests in the Sabbat is certainly unusual.

The standard activities of a Sabbat, however, are all present in De Lancre's account, although they tend to be scattered throughout his narrative rather than being clumped together, so that the effect is to produce a description of witches and their practices in which the details are almost like beads threaded upon a string, the string being the Sabbat itself; and the details being that which make the treatise especially interesting.

Sometimes, said eleven year old Catharine de Naguille, she and her friends would attend the Sabbat at noon, particularly after staying awake many hours in church the previous night and then going home to sleep. Meeting-places, it appeared from other testimony, might be a cemetery, a place on the coast, crossroads, the church square, or a deserted heath, but always near water of some kind. Satan did not always attend his Sabbats, but when he did, he usually changed his appearance more than once during the course of the meeting. The form he took might be most unexpected. Marie d'Aguerre (aged thirteen) and others said that a jug would be put in the middle of the assembly, and Satan would come out of it in the form of a goat. Others said he looked like a great dark tree trunk without arms or legs, reminding them for some reason of a large, horrible man. For the most part, however, he appeared as an enormous goat:

> Others say that he seems to be a big billy-goat, with two horns in front and two at the back. Those in front point upwards like a woman's coiffure. But the general opinion is that he has only three horns, and that the one in the middle has some kind of light which serves to illuminate the Sabbat, giving off fire and light, even illuminating the witches who carry lit candles to the ceremony as if to Mass, which they want to imitate. Sometimes people see a kind of bonnet or hat above his horns. In front he has an erect member, which he shows fully extended, and at the back he has a long tail, with some kind of face below it. From this face come no words; rather, he presents it to be kissed by those whom he deems worthy, honouring in this way certain special witches, male and female, more than others.
>
> Marie d'Aspilcouëtte, from Hendaye, aged nineteen, testifies that the first time she was presented to him she kissed the face on the rear underneath a large tail, that she kissed him there three times, and that he also had a face in the form of a billy-goat's snout.

Others say that he looks like a large man dressed in black, who does not wish to be detected. Others say that he is covered in flames and has a face as red as an iron which comes out of a furnace.

Corneille Brolic, aged twelve, says that when he was introduced to him he appeared as a man, with four horns on his head and without arms, seated on a chair with some of his favourite women always near him. Everyone agrees that it is a large throne, which appears to be gilded and very elaborate.

Jeannette d'Abadie from Ciboure, aged sixteen, says that he had one face in front and one face behind his head, as the god Janus is depicted.

Describing Satan's two front horns as similar to a woman's coiffure is highly unusual. An effect of this kind would not really have been possible without a woman's using a basis of some stiff material such as felt round which to wind or twist her hair, and the 'horns' would then have needed pins or wire to hold them in place. This hairstyle is clearly not suited to everyday wear, so it seems we are either reading a reminiscence of the coiffure worn by one of the local upper-class women, or of imitations of such a style attempted by other, lower-class women or girls on Church feast days and holidays. Carrying candles to Mass was not done every Sunday or feast day. The most obvious occasion when this did happen, however, was 2 February, the Feast of the Purification of the Blessed Virgin, popularly known as 'Candlemas', when candles were blessed by the priest and then distributed among the clergy and laity present. There followed a procession with the lighted candles, after which Mass was said, during which, according to the rubric of the *Missale Romanum*, 'a lighted candle is held by each person present during the Gospel and from the beginning of the Canon until the communion is finished'. Witches were sometimes required to repudiate the Blessed Virgin as well as their baptism. At the Sabbat, according to the *Malleus Maleficarum*, 'the evil spirit asks whether [the novice] will deny the Faith and the most Christian form of worship and "the woman who is more than a woman", which is what they call the most blessed Virgin Mary', (Part 2, question 1, chap. 2). So it seems appropriate that on the day commemorating her presentation in the Temple of 'the Light which will give revelation to the peoples [of the earth]' should be parodied by the carrying of candles often described as black. Once again, therefore, it looks as though a specific memory of something real enough has triggered a particular detail about the Sabbat.

The notion that the Devil wore a bonnet or a hat balanced on top of his horns is perhaps somewhat bizarre, not to say, comical. But his wearing a bonnet is noted very frequently in confessions about meeting him as an individual in the normal circumstances of everyday life rather than in company during the Sabbat, so it may be that two separate 'memories' have been confused or conflated here. The details about his appearing covered in flames with a bright red face, however, surely come straight from the theatre. To be sure, it was the general custom for demons of various kinds to be clothed in black and to have blackened faces or masks, but we cannot argue that this was an invariable rule in all places at all times, and since the Devil is covered in flames, he is clearly fresh from Hell or still in it and so a red face – painted or masked – would reflect this particular situation. Similarly, the horned man without arms seated on an elaborately carved and gilded chair suggests a theatrical prop. Statues do not seem to have played a part in every piece of theatre, but when they do appear – as in the statue of Our Lady in a French miracle play of 1345, *La nonne qui laissa son abbaie*, or that of the Virgin and Child in the late fifteenth-century Cornish play, *Bennans Meriasek*, or indeed that of Hermione in Shakespeare's *Winter's Tale* (first performed in 1611) – they occupy centre-stage for important episodes within the action. So it is not impossible that Corneille Brolic's version of the Satan he met might depend in part on his memory of such a statue in a play. But Jeannette d'Abadie's reference to the Devil's Janus-like faces comes straight from the classroom. Did she say that the Devil had two faces, one at the front and one at the back, and her interrogator or the recording secretary added, 'as the god Janus is depicted' – a learned side-remark emanating from them and not from the girl? Or had Jeannette picked up the information from a brother who had been reading Ovid's *Fasti* at school? ('Two headed Janus, commencement of the gliding year, you are the only one of those who live in heaven who sees his back'.)

Taken all in all, then, these details actually reduce what may seem at first glance the highly imaginative element in these young persons' narratives, and help to illuminate their possible thought-processes; and lest it be thought that the cumulative account still reads too much like the fantasies of youth, let us note the description given by eighty-year-old Marie de Zozaya:

At the Sabbat the Devil sat on a black throne and ... he was so horrible and terrifying-looking that it was impossible to describe him. On his head he wore a crown of black horns, three of which were especially big, like those of a stinking billy-goat. The other horns were somewhat smaller; there were two more around his neck, and yet another on his forehead. He used the latter to illumine and make visible everyone who attended the Sabbat, shedding a light which was brighter than the moon and just a bit less bright than the sun. It was sufficiently bright for everything that occurred at the Sabbat to be visible and to be observed clearly. He has hair like bristles and a pale angry face. His eyes are round, large, and wide-open, fiery red and hideous.

His beard resembles that of a goat; then neck and the rest of his body seem ill-proportioned: his body is in the form of a man and a billy-goat; his hands and feet appear human, except that his fingers are all of equal length; the tips of them are pointed and have sharp nails; his hands are cupped like the claws of a bird of prey, and his feet are webbed like those of a goose; his tail is long like that of an ass, and it covers his shameful parts. At the Sabbat he appears seated on a dais, often poorly dressed but in countless different guises. His voice is frightening and limited to a single tone, like a donkey getting ready to bray. His voice sounds broken; his words are badly articulated and hard to understand, because his voice always sounds sad and rough. Still, he carried himself with great gravity and pride; his countenance is that of a melancholic man, a man who seems perpetually troubled.

There is a qualitative difference between these two versions. The youngsters, as I have suggested, may have drawn upon elements of their own experience to provide their individual portraits of the Devil. Maria de Zozaya, on the other hand, appears to be fleshing out her picture as she goes along, adding carefully observed detail after carefully observed detail, as though she were following a train of thought which was delighting in the manufacture of a portrait which was becoming clearer and clearer the more she imagined it. The Devil has horns - a cliché - but then Maria adds her touch of exaggeration: six horns instead of the usual two or three. One 'horn' gives light - a cliché - but then Maria expands upon the quality of the light. The Devil looks like a humanoid goat - a cliché - but Maria adds unusual touches: his fingers are of equal length, their tips are pointed, his hands are cupped, his tail covers his penis; and when it comes to the Devil's voice, Maria enters new territory. Scarcely anyone else mentions the quality of his speaking, so it is a fascinating extra detail with which Maria provides her listeners. Notice, too, how her account slips from frightening to animal-like to incoherent to sad and rough. She has taken us from the bestial to the human kingdom in a series of thoughts and refinements, which mirror her portrait of the Devil as a whole. She began by saying he was too horrifying and dreadful to describe; she ends on a note almost of pity - 'a melancholic, man, a man who seems perpetually troubled' - as though he had brought out some motherly instinct in her.

But if Maria's impromptu variations upon a theme, (one is tempted to call them riffs), can be accepted as more or less peculiar to herself, more standard versions tend to appear in the confessions of others arrested during the outbreaks of witchcraft in the Basque regions of Spain. Miguel de Goiburu, for example, said the Devil was a dark-skinned man with dreadful glaring eyes and deformed bird-like hands and feet. He was dressed in black and appeared sometimes in

human, sometimes in animal shape. Both Miguel, and Maria de Yriarte agreed he
had horns on his head, although Miguel said that sometimes he appeared without
them. When Mass was celebrated, the Devil played his part, dressed in long, black,
filthy vestments, holding the pseudo-Host at the elevation while, according to the
Inquisition's interpreters, the assembled witches chanted, 'Up with the goat, down
with the goat!' The goat thus runs as a *leit motiv* through these Labourdin-Basque
accounts, so much so, indeed, that the Sabbats themselves were called *aquelarres*,
(from Euskara *aker* = 'goat' and *larre* = 'field'), although whether they took their
name from Satan's appearance as a goat, or whether Satan was conceived as a goat
because the meetings took place in 'the field of the goat' is obviously open to
debate.[41]

It does seems clear, however, that the extraordinarily vivid testimonies of De
Lancre's witnesses both justify and draw our attention to the title he chose for
his treatise, 'Picture of the Changeableness of Wicked Angels and Demons', the
key word being the first, *tableau*, a picture or painting. It is as though his readers
are being presented with a series of *tableaux vivants*, (actually *vivants* in this case,
not motionless), making a dramatic narrative upon which De Lancre, as *orateur*, is
offering a running commentary. For by the beginning of the seventeenth century,
the Sabbat had long ossified into a format as predictable and formal as that of a
Greek or Roman tragedy. Its 'plot' was always the same, and the separate episodes
which together made up that plot followed each other in more or less the same
sequence from outbreak to outbreak of witchcraft in the communities of western
Europe. Only the details varied according to the very specific localities and times
in which each outbreak occurred, although we must not lose sight of the fact that
by no means did every outbreak include mention of the Sabbat. When they did,
though, the 'plot' betrayed itself as an old one – what happened at the secretive
meetings of Waldensian heretics – while the details went back even further, to anti-
Christian fantasies of the third-century AD Mediterranean.

CHAPTER 6

Meeting the Devil in Private

Society as a whole during the Middle Ages and the Early Modern Period was more accustomed than we are to having access to forms of theatre in everyday life. There was the Mass, impressive enough in its simplest form, but spectacular in its most elaborate celebrations, providing a counterpoint to the dramas frozen in stone and paint and glass with which the church building surrounded it. Miracle and mystery plays enlivened the market-place and church square; saints' processions, penitents' processions, secular spectacles such as the wedding of each Doge of Venice to the Adriatic, weddings and funerals, usually more public and more elaborate than those of today, the burning of heretics, the execution of a broad range of criminals - all these, imbued to a greater or lesser extent with religious language and behaviours, meant that when people gathered together in anything other than small numbers for anything other than neighbourly reasons, be those friendly or hostile, their convention was likely to involve them, whether actively or passively, in a drama whose dialogue, sequence of actions, costume, and scenery were either prescribed or influenced in some measure by the Church. Even after the Protestant reformation, when church interiors might be whitewashed and services rendered less theatrical this strong tendency towards drama in public life continued more or less unaffected. Experience of a Sabbat, (let us leave aside for the moment the question of whether this was real, imaginary, or both), was thus very much like the experience of other public dramas. It was spectacular, satisfying on a number of levels, and highly diverting, the more so because those who attended it were active players rather than a passive audience. It was, like other public dramas, highly choreographed and had an unmistakable protagonist whose entrances were calculated to produce a sense of climax in the rest of the assembly. But the great difference between the Sabbat and other public dramas was, of course, that the Sabbat was illegal, and attendance at it carried severe penalties in this world and the next.

Why, then, would anyone confess to having attended? There are various considerations, which can be made, but before discussing these, we should be alert to some of the realities of intellectual, visual, emotional, psychological, and spiritual life which governed and directed the world in which both accused and accusers lived. It is a commonplace observation that people in the Middle Ages and Early Modern Period lived their lives surrounded by magic and the operations of occult beings and forces over which most of them had little or no control save that offered them by the Church or some local practitioner of the occult sciences. But the implications of this commonplace are not always fully appreciated. If God exists – and most people took this as much for granted as the air they breathed – then there is no reason to doubt or question the existence of Satan, angelic hierarchies, and their demonic equivalents, and the possibility, (indeed, probability), of direct interaction between humans as a group and as individuals, and any of these preternatural or supernatural entities either as a group or as individuals. The Bible alone illustrated this, from the angelic choir heralding the birth of Jesus to Satan's attempt to lead the adult Jesus into sin. Humans lived, in fact, amid a perpetual whirl of supernatural or preternatural activity which might become visible or manifest at any moment, and thus be sensed or glimpsed in signs and wonders in the sky, omens, temptations, unexplained deaths or illnesses, unforeseen onsets of erotic passion, ghostly visitants, strange lights on land or sea, crop failures, the souring of beer, the refusal of milk to turn into butter, sudden pestilential stenches, the odour of sanctity, (quite literally a particular smell), the birth of deformities in humans and animals – the list is almost endless. No part of life, no moment even, was free from potential contact with the divine, the demonic, or both; and while we must not run away with the idea that everyone lived fully conscious in each passing minute of this potentiality, it remains true that everyone's mind could slip into that mode of thinking and become aware of the possibilities in ways and with a frequency which are no longer the norm in modern Western society.

Being prepared to look for and find a non-human or non-material explanation for an astonishingly wide range of experiences both everyday and unusual was thus entirely natural to these earlier societies, and it was an inclination constantly reinforced by external influences such as the theatre, church paintings and architecture, domestic pictures, woodcuts, literature both learned and popular, and official teaching, especially that of the Church expressed in sermons. We have already glanced at late Mediaeval religious theatre. This did not suddenly disappear, of course, and in France, for example, mystery plays remained a vigorous tradition until the 1570s and 80s. Rabelais described a public show of demons, and although the passage is intended to be amusing rather than entirely factual, almost certainly gives a fairly good idea of what such street theatre may actually have been like.

Villon led a parade of his devils through the town and market, all dressed up in wolves-, calves-, and rams-skins, surmounted by sheep's heads, bulls' horns, and great kitchen hooks, with stout leather belts round their waists, hung with large cow-bells and mule-bells, which made a horrible din. Some carried black sticks full of squibs; others waved long lighted firebrands, on to which, at every street corner, they threw great handfuls of powdered resin, which produced terrible flames and smoke; all of which amused the crowd and quite terrified the small children.

The church building itself could undoubtedly have a profound effect on those who frequented it, an effect similar to the sentiment François Villon (1431- c.1463) puts into the mouth of one of the speakers in his *Ballade pour prier Notre Dame*:

I am a poor old woman
who knows nothing and cannot read.
In the church of which I am a parishioner
I see a painted Paradise where there are harps and lutes,
And a Hell where the damned are boiled.
The one makes me afraid, the other, joyful and delighted.

The walls of the church in fact constituted one entire picture, so that when someone came through the portal he or she entered into that picture and became a temporary part of it. Thus, 'looking' was not the static process to which we are accustomed when we are faced by a canvas or mural, but an active participation in a whole series of depicted events. Here, the spectator in effect becomes one of those supplementary figures, which appear in the margins of murals or in the elaborate painted capitals at the start of manuscript chapters. So, for example, in Fanefjord church on the Danish island of Møn (fig. 3), a fresco in the nave shows two women seated on a bench, talking to each other, while a tall black demon with webbed feet and ears, two long pointed horns, and a beak-like nose, writes down everything they say. It is at once both a scene from everyday life and a penetration of the physical world by the preternatural. A spectator looking up and seeing this moment experiences several things at once. He or she enters the picture as a passer-by, just as he would in 'real' life, and may pause, if he wishes, to take in what is happening. Then his vision is broadened to take in the recording demon – an extension of experience which might or might not happen in 'real' life too, for demons were everywhere and might be seen unexpectedly; and the sight of these two worlds interacting, with the spectator becoming part of that experience, if only for a moment, purveys a lesson – loose talk is dangerous because it is recorded against the Day of Judgement. Relating the picture to him or herself and his everyday experience, and to the stories he or she heard every week, every feast day, from the priest explaining the Faith in that same church, was what made the picture meaningful to Mediaeval or Early Modern spectators; and this interaction of painting and person within the context of the surrounding canvas of the church interior directed the way individual scenes or figures were seen and interpreted. The appearance of the Devil or a demon in such a scene was thus no representation of a metaphor or textual device, but an image of an entity as real, and sometimes as perceptible, as the humans who were drawn and painted along with it.

The exterior of the church, too, especially if it was one of the great cathedrals, was alive with images of Satan and demons, lurching out of the stone to instruct and warn and frighten, meant to be seen in the same fashion as the pictures within, and to elicit a similar response. At Vézelay, for example, a capital relief shows demons with flaming hair shrieking round St Antony in the desert; in the north porch of Chartres Cathedral, Job lies in the midst of his sufferings, while the Devil, hairy and grotesque, with the mask-like face of a skeleton, rejoices in his pain; a north wall relief in the church of Notre Dame in Paris embraces Theophilus who has just sold himself to the Enemy; and a capital relief in Autun cathedral shows Simon Magus plunging to earth after trying to engage St Peter in a magical trial of strength, while a horned, winged demon watches his fall with grinning amusement, (figs 8, 6 & 1).

For the rich, there were landscapes of Hell, canvasses produced for rich patrons such as the Cardinals Federico Borromeo, Francesco Maria del Monte, and Ascanio Colonna, in which Jan Breughel the Elder, among others, created extraordinary contrasts of hellish firelight and smoke which were meant to mirror the interior world of guilty consciences with horrid images of punishment for sin and the grotesque entities normally attendant upon those pains. These pictures, as Christine Göttler has pointed out, 'have an interesting parallel in contemporary Jesuit meditations on the inner faculties of the soul, in particular on one's own imagination', and thus provided their patrons with experiences at once aesthetic and devotional, underlining the horrors which awaited the soul who gave way to Satanic blandishments.

Both learned and poorly educated or unlettered could feed their image-making awareness still further by looking at woodcuts, especially since printing had made at least some literature more accessible - as Peter Matheson puts it, 'one could now buy a New Testament for the cost of a couple of rabbits for the stew'. Many of these woodcuts depicted demons or the Devil - we have already noted those in Guazzo's *Compendium Maleficarum* - some of which illustrated secular, others religious popular literature. The religious pictures contained largely traditional images. Lucas Cranach the Elder's 'Christ before Ananias' (1509) shows the Devil on top of a pillar above Ananias' head, with a human body and a distorted human face, but with horns and flaming hair; and Master I.W. presents his readers with a crucifixion scene in which the Devil in dragon-like form but curiously mixed with a skeletal torso which may or may not belong to him is chained to the foot of Christ's cross. Barthel Beham's 'Devil and a woman' (c.1532) shows a woman beating off the Devil with a stick, the Devil being like a bird of prey equal in size to herself; and Stefan Pumpernickel illustrated two broadsheets in 1609 and 1610, both entitled 'News of a naughty woman who struggled with the Devil'. The first shows him with a scaly body, a man's face, and horns; the second, more like an animal, with a hairy body, bat's wings, a tail, and an ass's ears. Ludwig Lochner's 'Devil and men' (1627) is equally traditional, his demons being horned, winged, and a mixture of beast and bird. Confessional propaganda after the Protestant reformation was quick to make use of these devices for satirical purposes. Thus, Hans Sebald Beham's 'descent of the Pope into Hell' (1524) depicts demons in the shape of pigs, grotesques, winged monkeys, and birds of prey; Matthias Gerung's satire on indulgences (before 1536) shows a winged bestial Devil with a great gaping Hell's mouth, and his 'Two devils being crowned as the Sultan and the Pope' (c.1548) has them as two grotesques, hairy, goatish, and bird-like; and the Cranach workshop's illustration of a pamphlet entitled 'The birth and origin of monks' depicts horned, humanoid demons with mask-like head-dresses and bird-of-prey feet. In England, Stephen Bateman produced *A Christall Glasse of Christian Reformation* (1569), which contains no fewer than fourteen images of Satan out of a total of forty woodcuts. One, fairly typical, shows a woman gazing into a mirror with obvious self-obsession, while Satan stands behind her, urging her on to further and further pride. He has a humanoid face, long goat's horns and an ass's ears, bird of prey talons instead of hands and feet, long crane-like legs, a tail, curious wings vaguely reminiscent of a beetle's outer casing, and a human torso; and in another of these woodcuts, a woman (whoredom) seated on a goat (lechery) is being led by an older woman (deception), while Satan hovers over them high in the air, in his usual goat-bird form.

Apart from devotional images and confessional propaganda, however, there were also woodcuts, which illustrated the kind of popular story which would today make its way into one of the tabloid newspapers. Thus, an anonymous artist produced a picture in 1569 to go with the tale of a Jesuit, who supposedly dressed up as the Devil in order to frighten an innocent Protestant girl into relinquishing her faith, but was caught in the act by her enraged father and stabbed to death. The Jesuit is shown wearing a hairy costume with the face of a bird of prey behind which his own tonsured head can be seen as he receives his fatal blow. Bartholomäus Käppeler produced something similar, with goat's horns, for 'The death of an innkeeper in Strassburg who had donned the Devil's clothes to commit crimes', 17 May 1590; Jakob Rode was less skilful in 1602 when he illustrated 'The fate of the ruthless baker' - a man who was torn to pieces by the Devil because he refused to give bread to a starving women and her three children, all four of whom then committed suicide by jumping into a well. Rode's Devil turns out to be a kind of fiery mass in the sky, in the midst of which can be discerned an insect's wings, but little that is more distinct. Then Leonard Straub the Younger illustrated a similar moral tale, 'Punishment by the Devil of a rich man who refused to help his brother', 4 May 1613, in which we see two demons, one almost entirely black (meant to represent a bestial form) but with a human head, the other entirely human in his upper half, fully clothed including a hat, his lower half black and beastly.

The stories about the Jesuit and the baker bring us back to the theatre, because their narratives make it clear the men are wearing costume, as indeed do the woodcuts. We can see the same kind of thing in Hans Moser's illustration of 'Three frivolous students and their punishment for masquerading as Death, the Devil, and an angel', 25 January 1573, in which the devil-student is wearing a hairy suit and a cockerel's face mask with goat's horns; and one cannot help but compare this with a woodcut by an anonymous artist of very similar figures, hairy monsters cavorting among a crowd during Mardi Gras in 1570. Dressing up as demons was thus clearly not confined to theatrical performances, or indeed to public feast days and holidays, but was done as a cover for crime or silly pranks. Moser's picture, in fact, is reminiscent of an anonymous fifteenth-century French work, *Repues franches*, which tells the story of two students who take their girlfriends for a midnight snack under the principal gibbet in Paris and are frightened away by two other students dressed as demons, who suddenly spring out of the darkness. Both story and woodcut illustrate the cynicism of student youth, but also the strong belief in their victims, (in the case of the story, fellow students too), that demons were not a phenomenon confined to the image-making faculty, but real and potentially dangerous existences which could manifest without warning in the material world and to whom terror was an appropriate reaction; and indeed, without this basic assumption, the use of their likenesses in crime and jest alike would have been completely ineffective. These particular illustrations, therefore, tell us how commonplace the hostile spirit-world was in the psyche of these earlier periods, and thus how prone people might be to accept that the sight of a demon or of Satan himself was a genuine, not a mistaken or hallucinatory experience.[42]

Literature, of course, added to the awareness of the circumambience of spirits. Quite apart from the learned treatises on magic and witchcraft written for a specialised readership, the tales attached to many of the woodcuts we have been reviewing provided both entertainment and information for other classes of society, as did German 'Devil-books' (*Teufelbücher*), Protestant collections of stories, which were also plundered by preachers for their sermons. They were extraordinarily popular, especially in the 1560s. Keith Roos has calculated that *Teufelbücher* accounted for 10% of the total sales of the Frankfurt publisher, Sigmund Feyerabend, at the 1568 book fair in the city, and that about quarter of a million copies all told were sold to a potential purchasing readership of one million who would then read them to small groups and lend them to individuals, thus ensuring a much bigger total readership. Their stories were varied and instructive, advocating virtue on the one hand, but on the other vividly expressing, (one might almost say revelling in), the vices encouraged by the individual devils of each story. Thus, dancing, drinking, unfaithful husbands, swearing, servants' idleness, the practice of magic, immodest trousers – all are attributed to the work of some demon; and so, despite the *Teufelbücher*'s admirable intention to warn, advise, and elevate, their lay readers were inadvertently being taught that all manifestations of human frailty, sinfulness, and vice were actually the fault of the Devil whose machinations, via co-operative demons, had caused the human to stray. Moreover, as Erik Midelfort points out:

> If every vice had not just some foolish blindness at its base but a specific Devil, then the Devil himself could begin to seem foolish, consuming his destructive energies in the effort to tempt mankind to wear large ruffled collars, pointed shoes, pleated shirts, and enormous pantaloons, or coaxing would-be Christians into un-Christian dancing, swearing, disobedience to masters, melancholy, and general laziness.

In France there was a similar situation. Hugely popular was the collection of stories, *Les Histoires Tragiques de Notre Temps*, brought out in 1614 by François de Rosset, an advocate in the *parlement* of Paris. His tales all had a moral purpose, but were full of violence, fear, death, and encounters with the Devil. One relates a famous real incident, the tale of a priest, Gaufridy, who was said to have made a pact with Satan written in his own blood, but was tricked and deprived of many years of life he expected to have, as a result of this agreement. Rosset also tells the story of three soldiers who were seduced by the Devil in the shape of an attractive young woman, a tale of sexual depravity, physical filth, death, and terrified repentance which would both attract and repel the audience for which it was written – the educated class, the nobility, and the bourgeoisie. The market indeed

was flooded with such stories. Jean-Pierre Camus, Bishop of Belley, produced no
fewer than twenty-one collections of *histoires tragiques*, amounting to 950 stories in
all, and many individual tales circulating during the last decades of the sixteenth
and the early decades of the seventeenth century emphasised the role of the Devil
in making the *histoire* 'tragique'. One such, printed in Paris, purported (as did
many) to be based on fact. Its title provides a résumé of the contents: *A Miraculous
Story, incredible and amazing, occurring at Envers, capital city of the Duchy of Brabant,
of a young Flemish girl who, through vanity and the extreme curiousness of her clothes
and ruffs, pleated in the new fashion, was strangled by the Devil, and her body, after this
divine punishment, being in the coffin, was turned into a black cat in the presence of all
the people gathered, in 1582.* This is a canard, a short piece sold in the street, probably
more to popular than to bourgeois customers, who wanted and got the Devil,
magic, bewitchment, evil manifestations, and the death or execution of those
responsible for the wickedness they describe. In Robert Muchembled's words:

> These pieces, which were usually anonymous, fell into familiar categories,
> which could be plundered to revive a theme in response to the needs of
> the moment or rumours currently circulating. Like wood engravings, they
> could be endlessly re-used, and they taught a simple moral lesson, linking
> catastrophes to the wrath of God provoked by the proliferation of sins or
> guilty passions, in particular excessive pride or lechery.

Meanwhile in England Christopher Marlowe was introducing his audience
to Mephistopheles in *Dr Faustus*, along with stock comic demons in scenes of
knockabout anti-Catholicism, and producing such an effect that as early as 1594
there were stories circulating that an extra devil had appeared in one performance
of the play, to the terror of both actors and audience. But *Dr Faustus* was simply
one among a large number of English plays which included the Devil or demons
or both in their dramatis personae, and between 1504 and 1638 there were fifty-two
such plays with six Satans, four Devils, three Lucifers, twelve demons, and eleven
characters disguised as demons. Protestant playwrights frequently used the Devil
as a stick with which to beat Catholics, identifying him with the old religion, and
so, for example, we have Barnaby Barnes's *The Devil's Charter* (1606) in which
three devils trick Pope Alexander VI over the wording of a pact he has signed with
them, poison him with his own wine, and finally use their brutal strength against
him by seizing his face and squeezing until he is brought to his knees in agony.
'Here Alexander is in extreme torment', says the stage direction, 'and groaneth
while the Devil laugheth at him'. Demons also appear in fairly traditional guise
in Thomas Goffe's *The Courageous Turk* (1619), dancing to discordant music

round Amurath the Turk on the eve of his defeat by a Christian army, in Turkish costume and with blackened faces. But as the seventeenth century proceeded, English stage demons started to take on the character of members of the lower orders. Traditionally they had been seen to get the better of the nobility which was especially associated with pride, but now, as the poor increasingly became the focus of suspicion and fearfulness, so the upper classes and the learned began to suggest that there was a distinction between their own ability to resist the primal terror which demons usually inspired in one form or another, and the inclination of the common people to succumb to that fear and so turn into agents, wittingly or unwittingly, of the powers of evil. It was, however, a distinction inspired by social and intellectual snobbery rather than by any genuine difference between the orders.

Stage demons might be resisted and turned into figures of fun. But real life was quite another matter, and for the most part the barrage of reminders of hostile spirits, which leapt out from painted walls, from carvings, from woodcuts, from stages, from stories, and from sermons, had the effect of underlining a conviction of the late sixteenth and early seventeenth centuries that the world was going wrong in some fundamental fashion. The character of the Reformation itself was in many ways destructive. Popular dreams of establishing some kind of religiously inspired Utopia, very common at this same time, began to fall apart, and it may be that lay resentment against witches during the 1590s and early 1600s was particularly strong as people saw their dreams come to nothing and looked for scapegoats among the Devil's agents who were furthering their Master's plans to thwart the establishment of any such New Jerusalem. Expectations that the apocalypse and millennium were about to arrive were also disappointed, and the feeling that Nature herself was in some measure noticeably corrupt was encouraged and, as it were, confirmed by such means as the large numbers of woodcuts from this period, showing abnormal births in both humans and animals. As Peter Matheson expressed it:

> Images of terror ... stalked the sixteenth-century mind, not unlike the masks of death, plague, or the Turk which people donned at the Lenten carnivals. The impression given by the pamphlets, the sermons, the woodcuts and the popular songs is that these images lurked just under the surface, a subterranean repertoire of horror always ready to burst up to the surface.[43]

Such, then, is the state of mind, more or less universal, which conceived, examined, and confessed attendance at witches' Sabbats and intercourse, often sexual, with the Devil. At this point I must stress once again that of course people were not in a state of heightened awareness of the Other World all the time. Like us, they lived their everyday lives largely focussed upon the immediate matter in hand, with occasional bouts of daydreaming to interrupt or accompany the focus. But, unlike us, they were able to turn quite naturally and spontaneously to the Other World to account for sights, sounds, and other experiences which took them by surprise or which seemed to them to warrant an other than natural explanation. In the words of Edward Bever, 'What we are dealing with is not just beliefs, strings of words describing ideas about reality, but lived experiences ... For these people, the Devil was not just a prop, an idea, or a symbol, a way of explaining things, but a purposive player in their situations, a manifestation of cognitive processes in their own brains perhaps, but no less real even if so. Furthermore, the stronger their emotions, the more real he became, taking on a more tangible form as visible features on a human figure, or even appearing as a walking, talking figure himself. This development, too, was not just window dressing, and its meaning was not that it symbolised something else, or related to other symbols. It was what it was ... and manifested much more power over the person's understanding of the world and his or her place in it for being full 3-D experiences rather than mere words, the fullest expression of unconscious knowing rather than the diluted messages that usually filter up'.[44] Circumstances varied, of course. Some people were more inclined than others to be sceptical on various occasions; sometimes group psychology overtook individual reaction. There is not, and cannot be, a single overarching explanation for manifestations of people's behaviour either as individuals, as small groups, or as communities. The Sabbat, however, is different from a personal meeting. As part of a crowd the individual participant in a Sabbat claimed an experience which was partly collective and partly individual, and the reactions this produced in both the individual who participated in it and those who were told about it were inevitably quite different from the reactions of people who either had or were informed of a meeting person to person with the Devil, the latter being individual in a way impossible in the former where the personal was always subsumed in the collective. It is to the personal experience, therefore, that we should now turn our attention.

Examples abound, so I shall concentrate on a few incidents from Scotland. In Lauder in 1649, the Devil appeared to Robert Grieve 'in the shape of a black man'; in c.1655 William Barton told the court that one day, while he was walking from Kirkliston to Queensferry, he met 'a young gentlewoman, as to appearance beautiful and comely' and had sex with her both then and the next night in the same place, at which time 'he became sensible that it was the Devil'. Nevertheless, he renounced his baptism, entered her service – the Devil still maintaining his guise as a woman – received the mark, and was given £15 Scots 'as a marriage settlement'. Barton's wife, however, had a different experience. One night she was going 'to a dancing upon Pentland Hills' - an interesting and perhaps significant way of describing what the court interpreted as a witches' convention - and the Devil led the way in the likeness of a rough, tawny dog playing on a pair of pipes. After the dancing was over and they were coming down the hill, he lit the way with a candle stuck in his bottom, while his tail 'played aye wig wag, wig wag'. In the 1670s, according to Annabel Stewart, the Devil came to her mother's house in the shape of a black man and Annabel, encouraged by her mother and two other women, made a ritual pact with him. He then gave her his mark by nipping her on the arm, and went to bed with her. This is the first of a series of similar episodes in which a man, now described as wearing black clothes, a blue band, white handcuffs, and 'hoggers' (coarse stockings without a foot), came to people's houses, received their submission, had sex with at least one of the women, and engaged in magic by making a clay image and sticking pins in it.[45]

There are innumerable such incidents recorded in Kirk and presbytery session books, in those of the High Court of Justiciary in Edinburgh, and in those of the circuit courts for the rest of Scotland. But they tell us little unless they receive closer scrutiny, so for this I shall turn to a set of related confessions from three women accused of being witches, who were brought before the presbytery of Stirling in May 1658 to account for their actions. They were Margaret Duchall, Margaret Taylor, and Katharine Rainie, and perhaps the first thing to note is that there is no suggestion anywhere in the relevant documents of any of them being subject to torture or deliberate maltreatment. So while we cannot say for certain that neither torture nor maltreatment were *not* used, we are certainly not entitled to assume that either torture or maltreatment *was* employed as means of eliciting the women's narratives.[46] First, then, Margaret Duchall told the presbytery that she had been in the Devil's service for the past twenty years, and in answer to the question, where had she met him, answered that it was in Isobel Jameson's little house where she (Margaret) lived by herself. The Devil came to Margaret in that house in the likeness of a man with brown clothes and a little black hat. He asked her, (perhaps because she was exhibiting some distress), 'What's the matter?' and she replied, 'I am a poor unfortunate and cannot get enough to keep me alive'. The Devil said, 'You will not want if you do as I tell you', and he gave her five shillings and told her to buy a measure of oatmeal with it. So Margaret went to the Tron, a place for weighing goods, and bought a quantity of flour made from the seeds of the pea-plant. 'It was good money', she noted, perhaps in answer to a question from the ministers, because it was well known that the Devil often gave people money, which then turned into worthless dirt or stones. She brought the flour back to the house, baked some round, flat, thickish cakes known as 'bannocks', and then, at the Devil's bidding, went out again and brought about two pints of ale: after which she and the Devil ate and drank together. After they were done, Margaret went into the cobbled street and span on her distaff until nightfall. When she returned to the house, she found that the Devil was still there. He bade her close the door, and then she went to bed. 'He came in over to me', she explained to the ministers, 'and lay with me all night. And he caused me to lie on my face, and he got on above me and had to do with me, and grunkled [*grunted*] above me like a cow'.

It is worth noting, perhaps, that up to this point there is nothing in the man's appearance, speech, or behaviour to link him with or suggest he was the Devil. He could just as easily have been someone Margaret ran into by chance, who took advantage of her poverty, paid for a meal, and repaid himself with sex, more or less as Margaret may have expected. Only after this does he apparently reveal his true nature by what he says and does, and yet even this can be interpreted as non-diabolical:

He said to me, "Maggie, will you be my servant?" and I said I would be his servant. Then he said, "You must quit God and your baptism" – which I did. And he gave me his mark on my eyebrow by a nip, and bade me, "Whenever you would have me, call upon me by my name, John, and I shall never leave you, but do anything to you that you bid me".

Whereupon at daybreak Margaret took him to a ploughed strip of land on a nearby hillside, and there he vanished from her. Nevertheless, it is still possible to see this as a relationship between two human beings. The man obviously has money and offers Margaret employment, which she accepts. His injunction to leave God and her baptism is odd in such a context, but he may have meant, in the light of the illicit sex they had just had and which he seems to promise her in future, that she will be expected to commit sin and in consequence had better be prepared to turn irreligious; while the nip on the eyebrow could be no more than an affectionate, if ill-judged, tweak. Admittedly this interpretation is not as immediately attractive as that which has the exchange an open pact between Devil and human, sealed by the Devil's mark; but the man's promise ends in an interesting way. 'I shall never leave you, but do anything to you that you bid me'. *To*, not *for*. This suggests an agreement to engage in sexual experimentation, something which would indeed offend against God's law and therefore require that Margaret be prepared to ignore her religion if she wanted to pursue such a path. As for the 'vanishing' from the hillside, it may mean no more than that he disappeared over the other side of the hill, the verb acquiring a preternatural interpretation only after the man had been recognised as the Devil.

Now, I draw attention to these non-preternatural possibilities, not because I am trying to provide a 'rationalist' explanation of Margaret's experience so far, but because they help to emphasise how very ordinary, how non-grotesque, how non-frightening that experience seems to have been, especially when it becomes clear from subsequent events that Margaret did indeed interpret her encounter as a meeting with the Devil. Of course, her apparent calm acquiescence in his demands may be the result of the way her evidence has been recorded; on the other hand, it may represent her actual behaviour, in which case we have a remarkable comment not only on the insouciance with which such an encounter could be greeted, but also on Margaret's readiness - mirrored by that of a very large number of others who confessed to somewhat similar situations - to surrender her prospects of salvation without so much as a moment of hesitancy.

Now, if we adhere to an interpretation of these events, which tries to exclude any preternatural element, we shall fail to understand what was happening from Margaret's point of view, and from that of the people who later examined her. When Margaret said the man she had met was the Devil, was she merely agreeing with the interpretation placed on her words by the examining ministers, or was it she who told them that 'John' was actually the Devil? At this distance of time and with a relative paucity of evidence, it is difficult to tell, but we have to bear in mind that very large numbers of people had similar experiences, and that everyone was aware of the Devil as a real entity who might be encountered anywhere at any time. Indeed, this is a message the clergy themselves were constantly dinning into their parishioners' heads. It seems unlikely, therefore, that Margaret (and all the others like her) remained entirely naïve about the identity of the stranger they described until they were enlightened by an official of the Church or State after they had been accused and perhaps arrested on charges of being a witch. In most cases, at least, it is rather more plausible that the accused her or himself was aware, if not at the start, certainly at some point during the experience, that the stranger was Satan. In Margaret's case, for example, that point may have been his demand that she renounce God and her baptism, a point long after they had met, eaten and drunk together, and had somewhat unorthodox sex.

Still we are faced by the question, when Margaret called the stranger 'the Devil', what did she mean? It would not be satisfactory to suggest that her experience was in effect a hallucination brought on by the stress of living alone and feeling the weight of poverty bearing down with particular force at a particular moment. Hallucinations - perceptions of persons or things which have no actual external existence - certainly may occur at such times, but Margaret's exchanges with 'John', the high level of physicality involved, and the temporary relief of pressure from stress, argue against this interpretation.[47] We may also put aside as unlikely the suggestion that the whole episode was a lie concocted by Margaret to satisfy her examiners. If we are to dismiss every confession or narrative as fiction, we shall not only suppose a remarkable uniformity of reaction over large swathes of time and geography to the charge of being a witch, or at least of practising magic, but excise entirely from the periods under discussion that essential component of people's psychology, the belief in God and the Devil as actual, living entities. Choices about what to accept at face value therefore have to be made, and in Margaret's case the strongest likelihood seems to be that events did indeed happen more or less as she described them.

Compare what Margaret says with two other experiences. In 1619, seventeen-year-old Maria Braittingen was arrested for stealing and, in reply to the constable's exasperation that she would not confess it in spite of irrefutable evidence and therefore 'appeared to be no Christian, but rather given to Satan himself', retorted that she had already had sex with him in the form of her boyfriend, realising only after the event that the man had not actually been her boyfriend but the Devil. Anna Eberlin, on this occasion in the form of a rape or at least forced sex, experienced a similar encounter, in 1660. This time the Devil was a boarder at her farm, and when Anna recounted her ordeal to the local clergyman, she mentioned his fiery glow, stinking breath, and goat's feet. Edward Bever explains that these preternaturally-inclined details were probably added by Anna later, not as 'imaginative fabrications or evidence of some sort of pathology' or as 'narrative elements in a story she constructed either in her dialogue with the preacher or in her thoughts beforehand', but as the result of a combination of cultural expectations – glow, stink, goat's feet are common diabolic features – and actual perceptions she had made during her encounter. This identification of a man with the Devil can also be seen in a woodcut by Stefan Kreutzer, dated to 1575. Here the Devil, we are told, is rewarding a priest for praying for bad weather. The Devil is depicted as an ordinary man with big moustaches and has nothing diabolic about him. Is the woodcut, then, merely a piece of anti-Catholic propaganda, or is it conveying the message that popular magic is instigated by the Devil, in which case, are we to understand that the 'man' in the picture has been taken over by the Devil in a theological sense and is thus a 'devil' in relation to this particular sin at this particular time, or that the man is in fact the Devil in human shape? The accepted fact that the Devil can change shape at will thus gives him a fluidity which is able to affect any situation, and so was Maria Braittingen really having sex with her boyfriend, or was she seduced on this occasion by Satan? Likewise, was Anna Eberlin forced into sex by her boarder or by the Devil in his shape? These were real problems for theologians and for other learned men, so it is not difficult to envisage their causing genuine distress and confusion in those who personally experienced such situations and were afterwards faced with having to make sense of what had happened.[48]

For Margaret Duchall, then, the man who seduced her turned out to be the Devil, and from the moment she made that decision her subsequent actions turned on that identification. For entry into the Devil's service involved a series of crimes, the alleged murder of three people. Margaret describes the first of these: the grudge killing of Bessie Verty:

> I went to the Devil and sought vengeance on her, and he said to me, "What will you have of her?" And I said, "Her Life"'.
> Then said he, "Go to her house in the morning and take her by the hand, and she shall never do any more good".
> Which I did, and she immediately took sickness whereof she died.

The same thing happened in the case of Janet Houston - a blow on her back was sufficient to make her fatally ill - and in the case of John Dumperstone's daughter, aged twelve and a half, a tug on the arm caused her to bleed to death. One of the examining ministers expressed disbelief. How could a tug on the arm, or a blow on the back, or shaking hands be the death of anyone? he asked; to which Margaret replied that after she got 'the word' from John her master, she would have done it to the greatest man or woman in the world. 'The word' here is significant. It does not mean 'permission' but, quite literally, a word of power whereby something beyond the normal range of human ability could be done. The word in this case acted as a vehicle, conveying the power possessed by Satan over created things to its intended object, with the witch Margaret acting as a facilitator by pronouncing the word and thus introducing it as a channel into the world of matter through which the Devil could do his work.

The minister's scepticism may seem reasonable enough, but we need to bear two things in mind: first, it was expressed in relation to Margaret's claims of killing, not to her assertion that she had had intercourse with the Devil and was now his servant - an odd type of scepticism, we may think, because if the episode with the Devil was real, there is no good reason to doubt he could give Margaret the power to kill by a word or a buffet. But as the reservation seems to have been expressed by only one minister, it may be that he also had his doubts about "John's" being the Devil. Secondly, evaluating her confession of murder is difficult, since we have no idea of her history with these three individuals; we do not know their state of health, physical or psychological; we have no detailed record of what passed between Margaret and them on the occasion of the shake, the blow, or the tug; and we do not now how Margaret viewed herself and her abilities at this stage, or what the others thought of them, either. Her manner during their conversation, the way she looked at them, the force of the physical contact between them – all are unknown, too. Yet all these factors are essential to a just and accurate assessment of what may have produced the effects that Margaret claimed. Once Margaret had acknowledged to herself, and possibly to others before her formal examination, that she was a servant of the Devil, she may have formed the impression, and given it to others, that she now had powers, or access to powers, beyond the natural. With such an assumption, relations between herself and the rest of her community would have undergone change. A degree of stress would have entered them, produced partly in Margaret as she began to lose that free amicability so important to the efficient and agreeable functioning of relations between members of a small community – although, of course, it may have also been that relations were strained already – and partly in those who had any dealings with her, since her supposed possession of powers beyond the natural rendered her different, and therefore to an extent alien, and so awkward to deal with in any normal way. Given a hostile situation, that underlying stress would have intensified, and if anyone were to add high words, fierce looks, inimical body language, a resulting chronic stress would have been quite capable of inducing all kinds of physiological reactions, any one of which might have set in train a series of consequences leading to death. Moreover, Margaret needed only one such death to convince her that the power she exercised through her relationship with Satan actually did work, and this would affect, in its turn, her future expectations and the stress levels induced in other people when they were in her presence. Success, as it were, can breed success, and one magical death can give rise to another. It is also worth bearing in mind that both Margaret and her neighbours themselves were likely to be labouring under stress imposed from the pulpit. Preaching in Calvinist Scotland aimed at constant self-examination and constant awareness of sin, and so, as David Stevenson has remarked, 'the proposition that one of the central aims of a Calvinist upbringing was to induce manic-depression has something to recommend it'. Add to this the fact that in 1658 Scotland was an occupied country, with all the tension and bitterness this implies, and it is easy to see why Margaret and members of her community should all be in a state of heightened emotion out of which such claims as sex with the Devil and magical murders might easily arise.[49]

Having been informed of Margaret's entry into witchcraft and her subsequent acts of hostile magic, the presbytery then elicited details about meetings with other witches. Yes, said Margaret, she had been present at several in the crafts of Alloway – that is, on small pieces of land adjoining houses in the neighbourhood of the town – and in the Cunningham, a fairly widespread district in the north of

Ayr. One night at midnight, she said, Elspeth Black had come to her house and taken her to the crafts where they met the Devil, and where he had had sex with them both; and on another occasion, they – meaning herself and six other women whom she named – went into the Cunningham and there danced and sang, 'with the Devil going up and down among them'. All seven also met him several times in the crafts, and there was one meeting in the Cunningham when they all turned up in the shape of cats.

Apart from this last seemingly gratuitous reference to shape-changing – one wonders whether Margaret said this in answer to a question, or whether she added it because, having confessed to being a witch and a servant of the Devil, she thought she should add a touch of verisimilitude, since shape-changing was one of the things witches were supposed to do – Margaret's accounts of the meetings are quite different from any confession of going to a Sabbat. There is no flying through the air to get there, no worship of Satan, no formal meal, no orgy, no instruction in magical arts or distribution of magical powders: just dancing and singing in the countryside not too far outwith the town. It sounds more like a party or a miniature rave. From the earliest days of the reformation in Scotland, however, dancing and music had been condemned, not so much in themselves as for the occasions on which they might be used, or the unseemly, even riotous behaviour they might provoke. The General Assembly of the Kirk was warned more than once about 'profaning of the Sabbath day with markets, gluttony, drunkenness, fighting, playing [games], dancing', and ministers were especially worried by this kind of conduct after dark. The Edinburgh Kirk session was told by local baillies in January 1575 about the problem of 'common drinking and dancing in houses from eight or nine hours at night', (notice "from"), and in St Andrews in Spring 1591, two women were ordered to do penance 'for singing of bawdy songs, playing at marbles, dancing, and running through the town after supper, and under silence of night on the Sabbath day'. The situation had not changed sixty years later, and so Margaret and her companions may simply have been doing what large numbers of their compatriots had done and continued to do in the face of Kirk disapproval – slip out of the town so as not to draw attention to themselves by the noise they were making, and sing and dance with the man who, according to Margaret, had had sex with at least two of their number and, as we shall see, had sex with a third as well.[50]

Margaret Taylor, another of those questioned by the presbytery in connection with the same set of incidents, had also met the Devil. It was about three years previously, she said, during winter and in the daytime. She was walking with Margaret Duchall to 'the heuch', a crag or a ravine with steep overhanging sides or a mineshaft, when the Devil appeared in the likeness of a young man in black clothes. He bade her renounce her baptism and she agreed to do so; whereupon he promised she should never want for anything, and told her to call upon him in time of need, using the name 'John'. He marked her on her pudenda – unusual in Scotland where the mark tended to appear on the neck, the shoulder, or the arm – and then had sexual intercourse with her. No mention is made of Margaret Duchall. Perhaps we are meant to understand that she went on by herself while Margaret Taylor stayed to talk to the young man. This was the first of several meetings. One happened at twelve at night and involved five other women. They all danced, with James Kirk providing the music on a whistle, and the Devil had sex with Margaret (Taylor) again. At other meetings Satan appeared in his former likeness as a young man dressed in black, as a rough dog, and as a small man. He also appeared to Margaret Taylor after her arrest, while she was interned in a private house – common practice if there was no other more suitable accommodation available at the time. Margaret says he appeared 'like a besom', which could mean like a broomstick or a woman, and promised she would not be executed.

It seems clear from this account that Margaret Duchall, having begun some kind of relationship with 'John', introduced him, either of her own volition or at his request, to a friend or acquaintance, acting, in effect, as "John's" bawd. The record is much abbreviated at this point, with the result that Margaret Taylor's capitulation seems to be immediate; but if Margaret Duchall was indeed performing the role of go-between, the two women would have had much preliminary conversation beforehand, and so the need for tentative steps may not have been necessary. Nevertheless, Margaret Taylor's assignation turned unpleasant. Once Margaret renounced her baptism and agreed to become his servant, "John" proceeded to intimacies by pinching her pudenda. Margaret told the ministers that that was painful, and we may speculate that it caused her to start saying 'no' to his advances, and perhaps trying to get away, because we are then told that 'the Devil struggled with her and did cast her down on her back, and had ado with her as a man has to do with a woman'. In other words, he raped her. Here Margaret added a detail, perhaps in reply to a minister's question, perhaps of her own accord. 'In that time of their copulation, she thought his body was cold'. "Body" here is a euphemism for 'penis'. It was a standard bit of diabolic lore that the Devil's penis was icy cold, and we may ask whether the addition of this detail is not similar to Anna Eberlin's telling her examiners that the boarder/Devil who raped her had a fiery glow, stinking breath, and goat's feet. If this man was the Devil, he must have had certain diabolic traits, and so both Margaret and Anna, *post eventum*, supplied what seemed appropriate.

Why would Margaret Duchall provide "John" with another sexual partner? She may have done so as a favour to a female friend, but it is perhaps more likely that "John" was beginning to tire of her and wanted a younger woman. Margaret Duchall told the presbytery she had been in the Devil's service for twenty years. The fact that she was living alone in a rented house in circumstances of depressing poverty means she could not have been a child when she first met "John". We hear nothing of a husband, nor does the record call her a widow. But it would have been most unusual for her to have remained single, so we may wonder whether she actually was a widow in her twenties. Such an age would have made her attractive enough to be picked up by a stranger; but after twenty years of service, she would have reached that stage in life which her historical period started to think of as 'old', partly because in the seventeenth century (as earlier) the menopause began at about the age of forty. But it is equally possible she was nearer fifty, so the likelihood of advancing years may offer one explanation of Margaret's introducing a younger women to her 'master'.

Margaret Taylor's experience of rape did not put her off meeting "John" again, although their subsequent meetings seem to have been in company with others for the sake of dancing. Even so, she had sex with him on at least one further occasion; under what circumstances, however, is not explained in the record. When they all met, said Margaret, "John" called a roll of their names – not their real names, but those he had given them when they became his servants. Margaret, for example, was known as 'Janet'. Servants, of course, were liable to have their names changed to suit the convenience of their employers. It made life easier if one did not have to keep learning new names to go with new faces every time one employee left and another arrived. But the context in which *this* change of names is described is that of baptism. The Devil's servants renounced their baptism and with it their Christian name and, sometimes after being re-baptised in the Devil's name, were then given their diabolic name which might or might not be different from the one they had before. The 'master-servant' terminology in use here and in a number of other witchcraft contexts, however, suggests that the secular association of that relationship was as strong as the possible theological and liturgical one.

Calling the roll is a peculiar detail, though not unique. In the famous convention of witches in the church of North Berwick in October 1589, the participants gathered round, some standing, some sitting. Next, the Devil, wearing a black gown and a black hat, stood up in the pulpit and, much like a schoolteacher, called his register of those present, each person answering, 'Here, Master', and there was a hubbub with people displaying signs of anger when the Devil called Robert Grierson by his real name instead of 'Robert the Comptroller alias Rob the Rowar', as he should have done. Are we dealing with some kind of semi-formal association? Asking such a question in relation to witchcraft is fraught with danger.

People are liable to shout 'Margaret Murray' at the drop of a hat and talk of the naivety of trusting recorded confessions, and it is perfectly true that one must not push one's question too far down any speculative route. Nevertheless, two points remain. First, as I said before, one cannot dismiss everything which does not accord with the modern 'rationalist' outlook as fantasy or fiction; and secondly, there is some evidence that magical practitioners might indeed form groups, partly for association, partly to work group magic, as in the case of Heinrich Agrippa who seems to have belonged to more than one such group during his lifetime. If, then, we do not trust Margaret Taylor's evidence on this point, there is little more to be said other than to wonder what she meant by it. If, on the other hand, we do trust it, the remark requires some kind of comment. We may care to remember that when some witches met, we are told they were masked, or that they met at night to conceal their identities. Small, informal groups meeting to dance and have sex sound a little like swingers' parties. Their activities would have been illegal in the seventeenth century and heavily censured by their more upright or conforming neighbours. Perhaps the change of name and subsequent roll call were to make sure, if possible, that only consenting members of the group were present, or to remind the group's members of the need for secrecy. It is interesting, in this connection, that Margaret told the presbytery that 'she saw other women in companies going by them at that time'. Is this pure fantasy, or did she catch a glimpse of some other similar group – 'company' implies social gathering – making its way into the countryside in search of privacy for dancing and sex under cover of darkness?

Apart from this roll call meeting when the Devil appeared as a young man, there was another at which he took the shape of a little man accompanied by 'a gentlewoman with a black pouch-like bag, whom she knew not, and was next the Devil'. Women are sometimes said to have occupied this privileged position; Pierre de Lancre, for example, records that 'many have told us that during the Sabbat, during or after the dance, the Devil takes the most beautiful woman for his carnal pleasures. But most often he honours the queen of the Sabbat in this way, as well as the woman he favours by having her sit close to him'.[51] Margaret's designating "John's" favoured one as a 'gentlewoman' is interesting. There must have been something about the way she dressed or spoke which gave Margaret the impression she was not of the same social class as herself or her acquaintance. "John" appears to have had money to spare, and dressed quite often in black, a colour favoured by officialdom and therefore those of a slightly superior rank to many accused of witchcraft. He also wore a black hat, as opposed to a bonnet, another possible small indication of rank. So was the 'gentlewoman' his wife, his current mistress, or simply a member of his own social circle slumming it with the peasants?

One or two details, such as the women turning up to a meeting in the form of cats, "John's" appearance as a dog, and Margaret Taylor's remark that during these meetings, 'their language was not our ordinary language', may have been *post eventum* rationalisations in response to ministers' questions, intended to confirm the diabolical nature of their activities. Her observation that the Devil had to appear to her while she was under arrest and under guard 'like a besom' – a broomstick or a woman – and promised she should not be burned, however, sounds rather like an illusion, a misperception of something which actually does exist, brought on by the stress of her arrest and confinement. She was being held in a private house. The presence of a woman or of a broomstick in her room would therefore not be in the least unexpected. Her interpretation of the 'besom', on the other hand, seems to indicate that she may have been suffering considerably from the circumstances in which she found herself and created a comforting object or individual to see her through her ordeal and keep her spirits up.

A third woman, Katharine Rainie, met the Devil in the form of a man with grey clothes and a blue bonnet. She thought he was not righteous, she told the presbytery. She thought he was the Devil 'and she heard that she signed herself' – an interesting comment which tells us that Katharine was so disconcerted either by the meeting itself or by the realisation she was in the presence of the Devil that she made the sign of the cross without realising she had done so, and had to be told about it later. Was she a Catholic, or had the sign lingered on as a semi-magical protective gesture? Once again, Katharine seems to have been introduced to this man as Margaret Taylor had been, by a woman she knew (Bessie Paton) who turned out to be a member of this same group of witches. Bessie asked Katharine if she would become the man's paid servant. Katharine answered she cared not, an expression of nonchalance meaning she had no particular objection. She and the man thereupon shook hands, and it was at this point that Katharine felt nervous. The man's hand was cold – perhaps not surprisingly, since this meeting took place in February, but coldness was also characteristic of the Devil's body, which is likely to have been the way the ministers interpreted this detail – so Katharine pulled her hand away and made the sign of the cross. In the event, however, she must have overcome her timidity, for she is named as one of the dancers at meetings with the Devil, and Margaret Taylor gave further evidence that Katharine was with her and the Devil in Andrew Thomson's house the night Janet Groat was buried.

What do these three pieces of evidence have in common? It is not suggested in the presbytery records that either Margaret Taylor or Katharine Rainie had done any magical working, although Margaret Duchall had – or at least claimed to have done so. The common thread is that all those women were being examined as witches because all three had had commerce in private and in public with the Devil, and one can see that either the women themselves or the examining ministers made some attempt to equate their dancing and singing with a Sabbat by suggesting that the man seemingly involved with all three was no human but the Devil. A curious narrative told by Pierre de Lancre, however, illustrates some of the difficulties attached to this kind of identification:

> Marie de Chorropique confessed that Augerot d'Armore told her that he would go to find her that night at home; that he would sneak in and she would leave; that he would lead her to a place where she would lose nothing. He did this, and led her, while she was awake, to a property belonging to the Etchenique family. And at the entrance to this property he told her that he had led her there to make her a witch and that she had to renounce God and promise that in the future she would live according to the Devil's will. And as soon as this renunciation was made, d'Armore knew her carnally. And after he led her further into this property, they found a large man whose face was covered, around whom there were countless people whom she names. Upon seeing so many people, she said the name of Jesus with astonishment. Everyone disappeared, even this d'Armore, and she was left all alone. And about three hours before dawn, d'Armore came to find her. Taking her by the hand and making her get up, he scolded her for having said the name of Jesus. And he said that if she ever did that again he would beat her badly. And the second time he went to find her, they went to the Sabbat near the new windmill of the noble house of Haitze, where they found a great lord dressed in black.[52]

Here a man seduces a woman with a promise of future benefit, puts her through a renunciation of her faith, which she is willing to do, and then has sex with her (so far so familiar). Next she is introduced to a big masked man and a large number of people whom she obviously recognises, since she is able to put names to them. Neither her seducer nor the big man is overtly identified with the Devil, and up to this point in the narrative there is no direct evidence of anything preternatural about either the participants or their actions. But when Marie says the name of Jesus, everyone disappears – a preternatural moment. Then naturalism returns – Marie is told off for using the holy name, and taken to another meeting (this time openly called a Sabbat), near the local landowner's house; and there she sees a man of high social rank, dressed in black. With the word 'Sabbat' so clearly in the sentence, we are clearly meant to infer that this man is the Devil, and yet at no point in this or the subsequent passage of the record is he actually identified as such. So what we have is the narrative of a sexual seduction and a meeting of

1. Simon Magus falling from the sky.

2. Bertha Pappenheim, 'Anna O'.

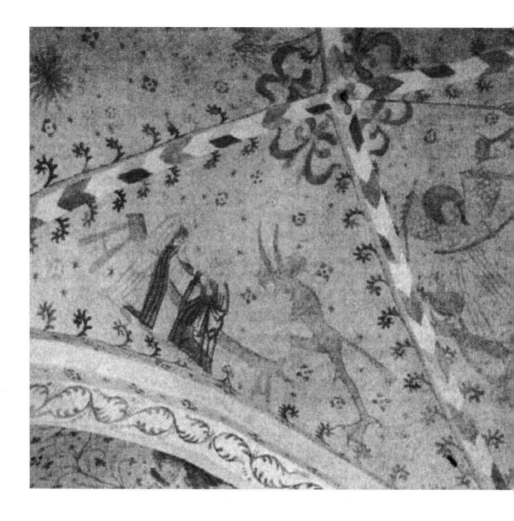

Above: 3. The Devil recording women's gossip.

Left: 4. Sister Lucia de Jesus dos Santos with Pope John Paul II.

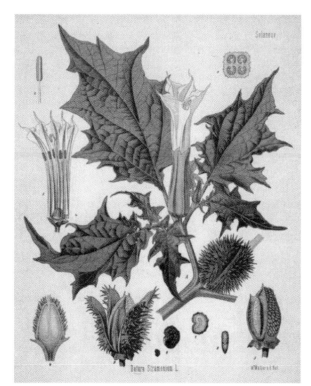

Right: 5. *Datura stramonium.*

Below: 6. The temptation of Job.

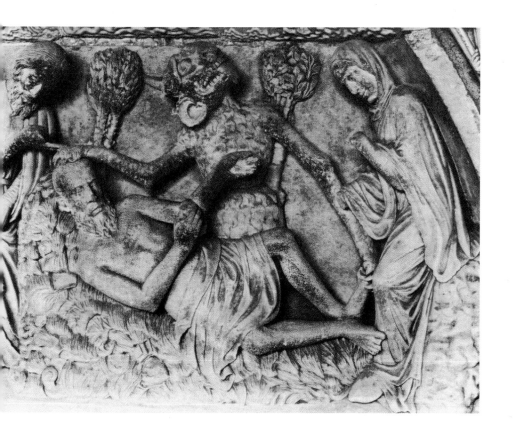

7. The temptations of St Antony.

8. Demons attacking a saint.

Above left: 9. The enemies of the Church attacking the Faith.

Above right: 10. The demon of conceit.

11. A demon costume such as was used in mystery plays in the thirteenth century.

12. The Devil meeting a
Knight.

13. The Devil advising a Monk.

Above: 14. A witch summoning
the Devil.

Right: 15. Satan receiving a child
during Sabbat.

16. The osculum infame.

17. Feasting at a Sabbat.

18. Dancing at a Sabbat.

Above left: 19. Belial standing at the mouth of Hell.

Above right: 20. The seal of Satan from the fifteenth century.

Clericus à tetro possessus Dæmone, frustrà.
Diuorum, uisens. templa, poposcit opem.
Debita nam fuit hæc Benedicto gloria, cuius

27

Ad styga trux hastis uocibus actus abit
Carnibus ordinibusq̃, sacris prohibitus. ad ista
Vt redyt, mortem damniaq̃, prima tulit.

C·19.

21. St Benedict exorcising demons.

22. Nineteenth-century humorous view of the Devil.

Above left: 23. The Devil as Proteus.

Above right: 24. The Devil appearing at a crossroads.

25. Charcot's drawing of an hysteric in Salpetriere Hospital.

26. Charcot's drawing of an hysteric.

27. Charcot's drawing of an hysteric.

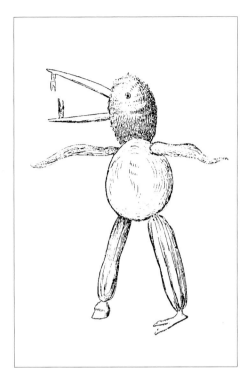

Above left: 28. Cartoon of the Devil disturbing France.

Above right: 29. The ghrol, a desert demon.

30. Lucifer eating Judas Iscariot.

31. The dream of Pilate's wife.

32. Belial dancing before King Solomon.

33. Satan tempting Eve.

34. The fall of the angels. Satan in Hell.

35. The mouth of Hell.

36. Satan presiding over the damned.

people in safe places during the night, with one preternatural element and a few inferential pointers. To an interesting extent, therefore, we can see underlying the statements of all these women a set of actions which is firmly rooted in non-magical, non-preternatural behaviour, and which does not call for suspension of belief on our part. What does require careful comment is the preternatural element, which sometimes takes the form of an intrusion into the flow of the anecdote, and sometimes provides the circumambience of events.

It requires careful comment largely because we do not easily take for granted the interaction between natural, preternatural, and supernatural worlds and partly because we think it reasonable to take into account other possible explanations which belong to the natural realm, just, in fact, as many Mediaeval and Early Modern commentators did. Thus, Johann Wier, a physician, said that some people confessed to being witches because they were melancholic and their unbalanced humour distorted their imagination; Reginald Scot, a Calvinist-inclined landowner, agreed and added that many were old and Catholic, 'doting, mad, and devilish', who bullied their neighbours into believing they had curious powers; Alonso de Salazar, a canon lawyer, criticised the large number of false denunciations he had received during his period of investigating the northern Basque country of Spain, and said he had not been offered a shred of proof of any witchcraft in the area; and Friedrich Spee, a Jesuit priest, was convinced that much of what witches confessed was the result of their being tortured.[53] What these and others were criticising or denouncing, however, was the practice of hostile magic as a result of a pact with Satan. They were not denying the existence and widespread activity of Satan himself. As Wier, for example, clearly states, 'Virtually all the activities hitherto attributed to the [witch] ... proceed not from the [witch] but from Satan himself'. Nevertheless, the points they make are salient, and so we should see how they fit into the picture and affect our view of the available evidence.

Let us begin with the well-known problem of the records, which provide much of that evidence. Sometimes the stories they tell appear as illustrative anecdotes in longer works intended to make theological, moral, or confessional points; sometimes they are included in sermons or journals; often they form the basic material of pre-trial or post-trial papers, and here in particular a largely unknown amount of editing has taken place because, apart from Inquisition records (which are often reasonably full, much fuller than any others), the process of abbreviating much more detailed accounts inevitably loses all kinds of information known to the original audiences but now lost to us. Marion Gibson has directed our attention to many of the essential points to consider in relation to our assessment of this material. She puts them in the form of questions:

Who wrote the account? (tone, access to documents, legal knowledge)
Are the tone and the diagnostic levels of access to events and knowledge constant? Is there more than one author?
Was he/were they at the trial? (description of courtroom scenes, procedure)
Where do specific pieces of information come from? (names, committing magistrate's name, dates, plea, evidence, anecdotes, verdict, sentence)
Are the sources oral or written? (tone, date)
Did the author(s) have access to pre-trial documents? Why and who from?
Did the author(s) understand the minute detail of the legal process, or make obvious mistakes?
Does each author report what he does understand of the legal process accurately? If not, why not?
What is the author's potential propagandist viewpoint?

Already these questions put us at a disadvantage, since all too often we cannot answer them, or cannot flesh out the barest of our answers with any kind of detail. But there is more, because when we are considering examinations before any formal trial took place, we need to bear in mind that questions asked of the accused may well not have been open, but phrased in such a way as to dictate, or at least suggest, the responses of the accused. Thus, questions asked of a witch in Baden-Baden in 1588 included phrases I have italicised:

If the Devil got her signature, was it written in blood, (and if so, in what type of blood), or ink?
   When did he appear to her? Did he want marriage or *merely* dalliance?
   What name did he give himself? How was he dressed? *What did his feet look like?*
   Did she see or *recognise* anything devilish in him?

Now, recognising what was devilish in a person or entity who might turn out to be the Devil was not entirely a matter of guesswork or personal intuition; for ever since the reformulation of witchcraft as a heresy during the fourteenth century, and the recurrent conviction that Satan was loose in the material world, and creating and gathering human agents in a grand conspiracy to achieve individual and general damnation, a growing body of evidence told those in authority not only that such a conspiracy was real but also that its members could be recognised by their conformity to expected types. Those types had been uncovered in the past - sometimes the far distant past - and each examination and each trial served to illustrate the continuing truth of the evidence that put these types on public display. 'Evidence' here means statements emanating from an authoritative source. As far as learned treatises were concerned these sources ranged from Greek and Roman historians and poets to contemporary essays and monographs, their evidence enlivened and reinforced by anecdotes drawn from recent trials and publications. Proving one's argument regularly involved appeals to this long and growing body of authorities. So, for example, when the Jesuit Martín Del Rio wanted to demonstrate that the souls of the dead appeared to the living as a result of demonic activity, he offered proof based upon an enormous range of authors – Scripture, pagan writers, hagiographies, Christian historians, devotional works, letters, collections of *exempla*, dating from very early times to his own, (the end of the sixteenth century) – and noted that 'what they have said should be accepted without qualification and without being regarded as metaphor'. Learned evidence of traffic with the Devil thus tended to be self-referential, and if they were not careful both ecclesiastical and secular courts would labour under an almost irresistible wish to see the answers to their questions conform to the pattern they were told by irrefutable authorities was the correct one.[54]

But making the testimony fit was not always easy. Since meeting the Devil and entering into a pact with him was so often a private experience, proving judicially that it had taken place tended to rely on a confession by the accused, and obtaining a confession when it was assumed the accused was surrounded by diabolic defences presented grave difficulties. Torture was the most obvious way to break down these defences, but everyone knew that confessions made under extremities of pain were not necessarily reliable: hence the usual requirement that questions put during torture must be re-asked outwith the torture chamber. Needless to say, this often produced retractions, in which case the accused might be put back to the torture until her or his testimony remained consistent and conformable to official expectations. So much is well known and a staple of commentaries on witchcraft. Two points, however, tend to be overlooked. They can be seen, to take an example almost at random, in Virginia Krause's remarks on witches' confessions. 'Through confession, accused witches were in effect constrained to reproduce demonological theory, each reiteration serving to confirm both the reality of the Sabbat and the necessity of the witch hunt. How and under what conditions were defendants in witch trials led to confess to implausible crimes that never took place?' The assumptions lying behind this question are (a) that torture never produces the truth, and (b) that the confession of the accused amounts to a work of fiction. Neither of these assumptions is entirely justified.

Let us begin with torture. Leaving aside for the moment the fact that a very large number of confessions was obtained without any torture at all, the truth or otherwise of the replies to questions asked during torture depends on the questions which are asked, and here we need to recall the basis of apparent non-preternatural behaviour informing the narratives from Stirling. Let us suppose a number of open questions thereanent:

> Did you ever have illicit sex with a stranger?
> Was the experience pleasant or unpleasant?
> Did he offer you money?
> Did he make you any promises?
> Did he offer to take you into his service?
> Did you ever meet with others at night?
> If so, where did you meet them?
> Was the stranger present?
> Was there anyone else there? If so, who?
> What did you do?

The answers to these questions can be found in the confessions of Margaret Duchall, Margaret Taylor, and Katharine Rainie without the need to resort to the preternatural, and in complete conformity with behaviour we know was common at the time. Roger Ekirch, for example, has shown that sleep patterns in earlier times were different from ours, and that people tended to break their repose for perhaps one or two hours during the 'middle' of the night before going back to sleep again. They employed this wakeful interval in a number of ways within and outwith the house, often paying visits to one another, or going about other business. So absence from the house during this night period would not, in itself, have been regarded necessarily as odd or suspicious. Questions such as these, then, do not require torture to be answered accurately and truthfully.

Even if we were to continue with open questions involving the preternatural, the answers could well be truthful, too, in as much as they need not take note of the examiners' preconceptions. 'Have you ever performed a magical act, or used magical words in connection with some act?' could easily be answered, 'Yes', since it was entirely part of the normal behaviour of society at the time for individuals to use charms or simple spells to achieve some domestic or personal end. Reginald Scot, for example, in his *Discoverie of Witchcraft* (1584), recorded one intended to preserve cattle from witchcraft:

> At Easter you must take certain drops that lie uppermost of the holy Paschal candle, and make a little wax thereof; and upon some Sunday morning early, light it and hold it so as it may drop upon and between the horns and ears of the beast, saying "In nomine Patris et Filii" etc., and burn the beast a little

between the horns and on the ears with the same wax; and that which is left thereof, stick it crosswise about the stable or stall, or upon the threshold, or over the door, where the cattle use to go in and out; and for all that year your cattle shall never be bewitched.

Isobel Mure, too, had a special charm she used to ward off night fevers and other kinds of evil:

She took fire and ii young women with her, and went to a running water, and light a wisp of straw and set it on the water and said thus, "Benedicite. See ye what I see? I see the fire burn and water run, and the grass grow and sea flow, and night fevers, and all uncouth evils that evil flee, and all other, God will"; and after these words, says XV Paternoster, XV Ave Maria, and three creeds.[55]

None of this requires torture but if torture was used and simple replies were elicited to these questions, the torture would actually have produced the truth, even though in these circumstances it would not have been necessary to use it to get the truth told. Torture, then, does not necessarily produce fantasy. It depends on the questions asked. But now let us introduce preternatural elements into the interrogation.

'Who was this stranger who offered you money, made promises, and invited you to enter his service?' The answer from the two Margarets and Katharine would have been 'The Devil'. Asked, 'What did he look like?' they would have answered, 'He looked like a man with brown clothes and a little black hat'; 'he looked like a young man in black clothes'; 'he looked like a man with grey clothes and a blue bonnet'. Asked, 'What made you think he was the Devil?' they could have answered, but without the direct statements they had been able to offer hitherto. One recognised the Devil by outward signs, by what he said, by what he did, and by what he made others say and do. 'Identity', as Valentin Groebner has pointed out, actually means 'sameness', and this applies a degree of stability not only in people's actual appearance, but also in the appearance they were expected to have. 'In the Middle Ages, people had only the appearance that others perceived in them, regardless of whether this matched their volition'; and not only in the Middle Ages, for it was in the sixteenth century that Arnaud du Tilh managed to persuade a whole village and a grieving wife that he was Martin Guerre, the grieving wife's supposedly dead husband returned to life, and lived among and with them as such for a considerable time. Signs were what counted when it came to identifying people. Clothes, for example, formed one. Fugitives were described by their wardrobes: Hans of Maggena wore 'two red trousers, slit black tunic, a black coat, a black-and-white hat, and had black hair'; Peter of Cirnafs wore 'a red tunic, white trousers, a red hat, and yellow hair'. Change these outward marks and they would pass unrecognised, as in the case of the Duke of Milan who, in the dire straits of a siege in 1500, passed unnoticed during an intense scrutiny of his Swiss mercenaries simply by hiding his long hair under a cap and donning Swiss clothes; or the even more notable case of the Duke of Burgundy, killed at the Battle of Nancy in 1477, who lay naked on the field, stripped by units of the victorious army, and could not be recognised, even by those who had known him well during his lifetime, until he had been washed and dressed in garments befitting his station. Even ghosts needed to identify themselves so as to obviate demonic illusions and human practical jokers.[56] Marks on the body assisted recognition, of course – hence Satan's imprinting his mark on his new human agents, and the importance of such a mark to investigators trying to determine whether X or Y was a witch – and so the Devil's black clothing and cold flesh on the one hand, and his cloven feet on the other, were the most important signs whereby he could be identified.

Here we may note a difference between his appearance at a Sabbat and his appearance to an individual. The Sabbat provided an unmistakable context in which there was no need for the Devil to conceal any of his identifying signs, and therefore he could be recognised immediately for who he was. A personal meeting, however, rarely furnished such a context and so an answer to the question, 'What made you think he was the Devil?' would start to depend partly on personal experience, (suspiciously immoral requests or suggestions, especially in relation to Faith and baptism), and partly in reaction to religious and social expectation, (people were told over and over again, the Devil looks like this, this Devil tempts you to do such and such). When Margaret Bell from Corstorphine met the Devil at night in June 1649, agreed to become his servant, renounced her baptism, and was 're-baptised' *Maggety*, (an affectionate diminutive of 'Margaret'), and then had sex with him, she was doing nothing more preternatural than any of the Stirling women, her apparent phrase 'baptised over again' sounding much like the way her minister or the recording secretary would tend to view and express her being given a new name. Katharine Gibb from the same parish, however, saw the Devil first as a little green man, then as a man clothed in black, and in her case the re-baptism is made more explicit. 'He baptised her with water which he brought in something like a cockle shell, and called her *Catherine*'. Margaret had confessed to the minister and elders on 3 June; Katharine confessed on 22 July. Did Margaret's confession spark an expectation in the Kirk session that renunciation of Christian baptism must imply diabolic re-baptism as part of the naming procedure? There seems to be a pattern to this, for on 19 August Bessie Scott went through a similar process, assisted by Margaret Bell who 'brought water furth of her house in a tong [*half a pair of tongs*], and the Devil sprinkled the water upon [Bessie's] face and called her *Maid*'.

These cumulative details occurring within a relatively short space of time and arising from a small inter-related group of people suggest that interpretation and reinterpretation of a simple claimed event, (the renaming of the Devil's new servant), drew upon the common religious experience of both Kirk session and penitent, with both parties coming to a tacitly agreed version of what 'should' have happened under the circumstances. At least, this is one way of explaining what happened. Another is that the three women in question volunteered the details they gave of their own accord and without any prompting. Since we do not know the exact circumstances of their examinations, we cannot say for certain which is the more likely explanation. But we should bear both in mind, especially when we are told that the Devil appeared in animal form – as a dog to Christian Thomson in September 1644 and to Marion Hunter in January 1650, and as a fettered animal to Margaret Taylor in May 1658. Shape changing was a characteristic of the Devil, but that in itself of course, is not sufficient to determine whether a dog is a dog or Satan in disguise. Circumstances dictate interpretation. For Marion Hunter these seem to be that the dog vanished while she looked at it – just as, in the case of two men who told the synod of Moray in October 1648 that 'they had seen, about sixteen years ago, a little boy to appear unto them upon the way, and that suddenly it vanished and they never did see the same before nor after'. Christian Thomason's mother said Christian, 'had the Devil in a shammy [a piece of soft leather] and being asked how she could prove the same, answered that she could prove easily the thing that she both heard and saw ... And being asked whether the Devil was like a man or a beast, answered rather like a beast, and thereafter that he was like a dog'. Clearly, she was being steered towards this answer, even though the Devil appeared much more frequently as a man. But the preternatural detail of his being magically confined in a piece of leather meant that he ought not to appear in as mundane a likeness as that of a human being, but take some more curious, though not unexpected, shape.[57]

Recognising the Devil, then, came to these Scottish women through the way he looked and the circumstances under which he was seen, what he said, (the demand to renounce God and Christian baptism), and what he did, (giving his mark and a new name). Such recognition of the preternatural elements in what would otherwise have been a natural (or non-preternatural) set of experiences came without torture, although not without the stress attendant upon being accused of witchcraft, being examined by Kirk officials, and, Margaret Taylor's case, confinement in a private house. But if we presume that torture is added to these experiences, the details frequently become much more vivid and extraordinary. During witch-trials in Bamberg, for example, we are told that:

> The witches nearly all say that the Devil first appears to them in the likeness of a lover, worthy of all confidence, but afterwards reveals himself. Sometimes it is misfortune which summons him, when he takes the shape of a rich merchant and promises help, if she will assign her soul to the Devil. When he reveals himself, it is usually in the form of a he-goat, or a green devil, with owl's head, horned, black or fiery visage, goat's feet, long tail and hands with talons. Later the demons show themselves as dragons. When the Devil appears in all his majesty, he requires his victim to renounce God and give himself up to him, body and soul, threatening refusal with twisting his neck and carrying him to Hell.

It sounds nonsensical, and yet even here we must be careful not to take things for granted. Torture may produce lies, distortions, and unlikely or impossible versions of underlying reality, but, as we have seen, beneath the surface of many of these confessions about seeing the Devil a remarkably large number of non-preternatural statements are struggling to get themselves heard, and even in narratives which appear to be exaggerated or fictitious it may be possible to discern a basis of truthful experience.

Let us return to those confessions, which claim attendance at a Sabbat. Their general outline, not to mention individual details, seems to be fantastical and is often attributed to the effects of prolonged and repeated torture. But other possible physiological and psychological conditions in the confessing individual must be taken into account. Was he or she, for example, dreaming? It was a possibility earlier periods considered. In 1586 Pierre le Loyer suggested that *incubi* and *succubi*, demons given to having sex with humans, entered the beds of sleeping individuals and gave them erotic dreams in which the sleepers imagined they flew through the air and had sex with the Devil. Over a century earlier, Jordannes of Bergamo, a Dominican, gave a medical explanation and opined that evil spirits would work upon a witch's humours, stirring them up so that they ascended into the brain and there created all kinds of images which caused the witch to believe that he or she had the power to work all kinds of magic, be transported from place to place, and attend a Sabbat where she or he would worship the Devil; and a few years later, another Dominican, Johannes Nider, recorded that one of his brethren talked to a village woman who boasted that she was able to fly through the air with the goddess Diana and other women, and agreed to demonstrate this in front of the monk and other witnesses. 'She put on a bench the basin in which she usually made dough, sat in it, smeared herself with ointment, pronounced words of harmful magic, laid back her head, and fell asleep. Immediately, with the help of a demon, she had such convincing dreams about Lady Venus and other superstitious things that she began to cry out with a low voice in a song of joy. But when she clapped her hands, she moved the basin in which she was sitting too much and it suddenly fell down from the tall bench and gave the elderly woman's head a hefty blow as she lay on the floor'. The fall woke the sleeping woman who was clearly convinced she had been engaged in sexual intercourse and other unnamed activities, and was chagrined to find she had actually never left her bench.

Now, dreaming alone would probably be a sufficient explanation for at least some of these experiences, but as we are told that Nider's witch applied an ointment to herself, we are led to consider the question and possible role of hallucinogens of one type or another in bringing to birth and formulating the more vivid details of reported journeys to a Sabbat, experiences thereat, and perhaps also a number of the personal encounters with Satan. Again, people of earlier periods were well aware of the effect such drugs could have. Andrés de Laguna, a Spanish pharmacologist, botanist, and Papal physician, described one such incident from his personal experience in 1545. A husband and wife had come to squat in a small hermitage not far from Nancy, and had quickly gained a reputation as malevolent workers of magic. They were soon arrested and questioned under torture by the Duke of Lorraine, and claimed to have killed the Duke's father by magic at the instigation of the Devil who told them how the murder should be done. After their arrest, a search was made of their quarters with notable results:

Among the materials found in the hermitage of the wizard and witch was a pot full of a certain green ointment like poplar ointment, whose smell was so heavy and pungent that it proved to be composed of extremely cold and soporific herbs such as hemlock, nightshade, henbane, and mandrake. Through the constable, who was a friend of mine, I obtained a good supply of the ointment and later in the city of Metz I had the wife of the public executioner anointed with it from head to foot. She through jealousy of her husband had completely lost the ability to sleep and had become half-insane in consequence. This seemed to me to be an excellent opportunity to undertake a test of the witch's ointment. And so it turned out, for no sooner did I anoint her than she opened her eyes wide like a rabbit, and soon they looked like those of a cooked hare. She then fell into such a profound sleep that I thought I should never be able to wake her. However, by means of tight ligatures and rubbing her extremities and applications of

castor oil as well as euphorbia and frequent inhalations, and finally with
cuppings, I was so successful that after a lapse of thirty-six hours, I restored
her to her senses and sanity. Her first words were, "Why did you wake me
at such a bad moment when I was surrounded by all the delights in the
world?" Then turning her eyes towards her husband (he was beside her, she
stinking like a corpse), and smiling at him, she said, "Skinflint! I want you to
know I've put horns on you, and with a younger and lustier lover than you!"
She said many other strange things, and wore herself out beseeching us to
allow her to return to her pleasant dreams. Little by little we distracted her
from her illusions, but forever after she stuck to many of her crazy notions.
From all this we may infer that all those wretched witches do and say is
caused by potions and ointments which so corrupt their memory and their
imagination that they create their own woes, for they firmly believe, when
awake, all they had dreamed when asleep.

De Laguna is clearly in agreement with several experimenters of the period,
that witches' imaginations were stimulated by narcotics or hallucinogens in the
drinks and ointments they used, but he does not for a moment deny the existence
of the Devil who had worked upon them through natural means and causes. He
says, for example, that the coldness they felt during sexual intercourse with the
Devil might actually result from 'a humour as cold as ice which enters into their
intestines like hail stones', but it was the Devil who, 'because of his wisdom and
shrewdness, teaches [the drinks and ointments] to the foolish witches in order to
make them dream and imagine an infinite number of stupidities'. So the dreams
may have been false, but their origin was real enough, and so too were the pain
and anxiety which accompanied them and followed in their wake.[58]
Nevertheless, other Early Modern writers dismissed the notion that witches'
salves could cause any such effects, on the grounds that their contents – mainly
the fat of murdered children – would not produce the claimed experiences; that
witches often anointed their broomsticks rather than themselves; or that if there
was any effect, it came from the magical incantation recited during the smearing
process, or from the actions of a demon, and not from the ointment itself. But the
drugs theory continued to be popular among later historians and commentators.
In 1882, Ludwig Mejer advanced the notion that witches drank a brew of thorn
apple, *Datura stramonium*, (fig. 5) which gave them visions so intense they seemed
to be real, and modern users of the drug report that they do not realise they
are hallucinating and interact with objects and people no one else can see. Mejer
suggested that the plant was brought into Europe by gypsies from the east in
about 1420, but this idea was flattened the following year by J.B. Holzinger who

pointed out that the earliest mention of *Datura stramonium* says it was first brought to Vienna in 1583. It also appears that *Datura* needs to be ingested or smoked for its effects to take place, whereas witches were said to use an ointment; so it might be thought that even if we allow the presence of hallucinogens such as atropine, scopolamine, and hyoscamine in its ingredients, absorption through the skin would not readily produce the results reported in witchcraft confessions. But Edward Bever begs to differ. There is plenty of evidence, he says, not only that individuals in the Early Modern Period ate hallucinogenic substances in their bread, but also that salves with similar properties were both known and used. Nightshade, henbane, mandrake, and thorn apple all belong to the family *Solanaceae*, and solanaceous hallucinogens, however ingested or absorbed, produce hallucinations and dreams that seem completely and utterly real. These hallucinations and dreams are filled with people or entities which appear to have a separate existence from the dreamer and may therefore seem to interact with him or her while the drug is having its effect; and that effect may last for several days, the individual continuing his or her experience to the bewilderment of any sober person in the vicinity. In consequence of his investigations into this subject, then, Bever comes to three conclusions: (i) some people deliberately did indeed use psychoactive substances to produce altered states of consciousness; (ii) a number of people would get together every so often in order to participate in some such activity; and (iii) these groups often taught each other magic.

So while no one can claim that these experiences account for all narratives about the Sabbat, derived from confessions free or otherwise – Bever himself does not, and neither do I – they do provide evidence that behind some of the confessions may lie genuine 'trips' and genuine interactions with hallucinatory beings; and therefore when we examine any narrative telling of a meeting with the Devil, flying through the air, feasting and dancing and being sexually promiscuous, we (as did their original examiners) may be listening to a person telling us the absolute truth as she or he experienced it, with leading questions, psychological pressure, cultural and religious expectation, and possible torture perhaps contaminating the evidence, but not inventing it outright.[59]

On the other hand, neither dreaming nor drugs nor hallucinations can be said to cover the wide range of disparate experiences, which may have lain behind either the Sabbat or individual meetings with Satan. For there were also those who had contacts with the dead or with fairies, and made special journeys to the Other World by means of trances or similar out-of-body journeys. When Katharine Gibb in Corstorphine met the Devil while she was watching sheep in the park of Kinneill, for example, ' the Devil appeared to her in the likeness of a little green man and asked her what age she was of, and if she would be his servant'. This sounds like a fairy encounter, fairies being associated with the colour green and small stature, and the boredom of watching the sheep may have made her drift off into a sleeping or half-sleeping state. Entry into trance-like states may be deliberate or involuntary. Shamans embrace the former, and we know of several individuals who took messages back and forth between the worlds on behalf of their communities. Thus, the seventeenth-century historian, Bartholomaeus Anhorn, quoting the earlier Olaus Magnus, observed, 'This is where the satanic raptures of the Laplanders belong, along with the midnight peoples who are devoted to the Devil's service', as described by Olaus Magnus, when he writes:

> If a stranger wants to know how things are back at home, they can tell him within twenty-four hours even if it is 300 miles away or more, and this they do in the following manner. After the magician has performed certain ceremonies and has addressed his hellish gods with certain words, he falls to the ground, like a corpse from which the soul has gone; and it seems that there is neither movement nor life in him.

Further south, Chonrad Stoecklin, a herdsman from Oberstdorf in the territory of Augsburg, told investigators that, after a warning to reform his life, given by the spirit of a dead friend who had appeared to him in February 1578, he had been carried away in a trance – not bodily but in spirit – had seen Heaven and Purgatory, and returned with a message for his wife and children to pray with great devotion and attend Mass eagerly; and a professional diviner, Hans Tscholi from Switzerland, testified to a court that 'in his family there always had to be someone who was ecstatic from time to time, and who had to travel among the dead, and now he was the one who had to undergo this'. These experiences have something in common with such groups as the specialised healers of Romania, who travel to the Other World to learn their craft, and, of course, with saintly mystics everywhere who fall into trances and travel or experience in spirit. Such journeys, needless to say, run the risk of falling foul of official opinion and if they appear in confessions are most likely to be interpreted in a way that makes them conformable to the prevailing orthodoxy. But, once again, confession of spirit-travel may well be made in good faith, and accepted as such by the person's interrogators. Indeed, when it comes to going to the Sabbat and taking part therein, a number of key-points quickly turned into orthodoxy and were therefore expected – flight through the air, meeting Satan, re-baptism, feasting, orgy, magical instruction – and if they did not appear in the confession were treated as serious and deliberate omissions so that the confessing individual might be pressured maltreated, tortured, (I emphasise *might*), until she or he provided the requisite details and made the confession full.

The *leit motiv* of these discussions of meeting and interacting with the Devil is the reality which underlies so many of the details, a reality which may be distorted or wrenched from one context and applied to another, or reinterpreted to satisfy a number of preconceptions, but a reality nevertheless. It means we should be prepared to accept that there is much less outright fiction in accounts of witches' and magicians' behaviour than has often been allowed or realised. In addition to this, we need to be aware of the reality of the central figure, Satan himself, in the perception of earlier periods. His presence in daily life was palpable. Luther reported in conversation:

Almost every night when I wake up the Devil is there and wants to dispute with me ... I instantly chase him away with a fart ... The Devil looks for me when I am at home in bed, and one or two devils constantly lie in wait for me. They are clever devils. If they can't get anywhere in my heart, they grab my head and torment me there.

He was not speaking metaphorically. Both the Devil and his demons were capable of entering the human body and taking up residence there, as we shall see when we discuss demonic possession, and it is in this physical sense, too, that we should understand Richard Norwood's description of Satan's assaults upon him:

Sometimes he seemed to lean upon my back or arms or shoulder, sometimes hanging on my cloak or gown. Sometimes it seemed in my feeling as if he had stricked [struck] me in sundry places, sometimes as it were handling my heart and working withal a wonderful hardness therein ... Also in bed sometimes pressing, sometimes creeping to and fro, sometimes ready to take away my breath, sometimes lifting up the bed, sometimes the pillow, sometimes pulling the clothes or striking the bed or on the pillow.

Our thinking of these and other encounters with Satan is therefore not adequate to the occasion unless we realise that in many instances what is happening in the individual who experiences them is much more than daydreaming or hallucinating in their commonly understood senses.

'Seeing' Satan, for example, was a complex business. The 'seeing' itself will have been different in certain respects from the 'seeing' to which we are accustomed, for in the modern West especially devices to correct defective or failing vision are almost universally available, and in consequence we have little prolonged experience of the blurring, swimming, distorting nature of uncorrected sight. If outlines are indistinct, if floaters in the eye intrude upon that fuzziness, if individuals or objects at a distance, or in the edge of peripheral vision, cannot be recognised except at close quarters, then 'seeing' and 'recognising' will not have the same sharp meaning they have for us. Add to this that clinical studies have shown that imagining a figure and projecting it into one's visual field involves 'a profound alteration of the functioning of the nervous system', and that 'the physicality of this sort of experience can go beyond even 3-D projection into the visual field to an actual experience of physical contact' – actual enough to produce real bruises and welts on the body. So if we re-read Cecilia Ferrazzi's account of her ordeal at the hands of the Devil in this light, we can begin to appreciate that her narrative will have been truthful, perhaps entirely truthful. For as far as Cecilia and all the others we have been discussing were concerned, meeting the Devil did not feel like a hallucinatory experience, no matter how we may care to suggest that experience could have originated. On the contrary, nothing could have felt more real, more intense, more substantial; so the problem for Cecilia's listeners was not really to question whether the meeting she described had happened at all – for all concerned it clearly had – but whether her experience at the hands of the Devil sprang from causes requiring medical help, (an effort to rebalance the humours in her body and redress the superfluity of black bile, for example), or whether she needed immediate and drastic spiritual intervention; and this is where our discussion must follow theirs.[60]

CHAPTER 7

Demonic Possession: Theatre or Reality?

In 1654, Elias Wellhöfer, a Catholic engraver who spent nearly forty years of his working life in Augsburg, published a set of fifteen scenes illustrating the story of a woman possessed by the Devil. They begin by showing her walking in the countryside with a fashionably dressed gentleman. Nothing seems untoward until one looks at the man's hat. A long feather rises from each side, to present the unmistakable appearance of horns - an indication to the reader, as perhaps it should have been to the woman herself, that the gentleman's appearance was deceptive and that she was in fact conversing with the Devil. The result of this converse is shown in the following eight pictures. The woman is in bed, distracted, while priests and monks attempt to calm her screaming by touching her with holy objects. Then she is taken to church to be exorcised and betrays yet more hysteria, her body distorted, her hair flying wildly, her mouth constantly open in a scream, while Mass is celebrated and she is shown the consecrated Host. Finally, in picture 10, she is depicted writhing on the floor of a house, a priest's stole about her neck, while a priest and a monk make one more attempt to drive the demon out of her. In picture 11, however, she seems to be perfectly calm. Fully dressed, her hair back in place under a cap, she explains to two priests that she has been accustomed to flying with witches. We know this because she holds out a long stick with a curved end for the priests to examine, while through the open window we see four women flying beneath the clouds on just such a stick. But her confession appears to have unhinged her again, for in the next picture we see her seated in her night dress, hair flying everywhere, while a girl holds down her hands; an old woman wrenches her tongue, and two demons stand looking on- one with the face of a bird, the other humanoid with a bull-face, horns and long curved ears, insect wings, shaggy animal legs, and cow's feet. The open window shows the four flying witches, but two are tumbling off the stick, an indication perhaps that in spite of the demons' presence, the woman's maleficent power is on the wane. In the next picture she is no quieter, but a priest and a layman are in attendance, and the scene through the window, clearly depicting terra firma and many trees, has two sketchy figures whose purpose cannot be discerned from the drawing. Pictures 13-15 illustrate the woman's unhappy fate. She is seated before three officials at a table and seems to be giving an account of her meeting with Satan, for through the window we see a horned demon, (or perhaps the gentleman with the horn-like plumes in his hat), and the woman herself, bending towards him, one arm held out in a gesture – but a gesture of what? Submission? Worship? It is difficult to tell. The last pictures show her being branded on the breast on her way to execution, and finally a composite illustration of the execution itself.[61]

It is an odd concoction, comprising scenes of diabolic possession and confession to witchcraft, and it is interesting that Wellhöfer used some of them again in 1666 and 1669 to illustrate an account of a trial for blasphemy and another of witchcraft, since the three offences were often interconnected at the time. But the series makes it plain that to converse with the Devil, albeit as a private and not as a communal experience during the Sabbat, could lead to his appropriating the individual, quite literally taking possession of her or him and using her as his instrument to convey messages directly from the demonic plane. Possession, however, should be distinguished from obsession. When St Antony of Egypt, like so many other desert saints, was tormented by demons who tried to distract him from prayer or meditation, he was being obsessed, that is 'besieged' by them. They never sought to enter his body and take up residence there, but remained always exterior to him and intermittent, so that the saint enjoyed periods of freedom from their attentions before they started to attack again. Possession on the other hand, involves an external force or entity, which takes control of someone's body and launches attacks from within, the only relief afforded the unfortunate host being when the occupying force or entity lies dormant. This occupying force or entity may not always be demonic, of course, although it may be interpreted as such in certain cultural contexts and under certain historical circumstances. One can be possessed by the dead, by fairies, and by God Himself, and the reasons for one's being possessed may be equally varied. Possession may be genuine or faked, voluntarily induced or involuntarily endured, and of whatever kind it may be, is likely to be disconcerting or frightening to those who witness it. Hence the call for ritual expulsion of the force or entity – the exorcism which seeks to restore the expected balance between the physical and preternatural worlds and discourage any untoward repetition of spirit invasion.

Being possessed by a divinity is often difficult to separate from being possessed by some other, less desirable or even dangerous entity. The most obvious examples of the former in the Jewish and Christian traditions are the descent of the spirit upon the prophets – 'The spirit of God came upon him, and he prophesied among them', (I *Kings* [*Samuel*] 10.10; 'the spirit entered into me when [the Lord] spake unto me, and set me upon my feet ... The spirit took me up ... The spirit lifted me up and took me away', (*Ezekiel* 2.2; 3.12, 14); 'The spirit of the Lord is upon me', (*Isaiah* 61.1) – and its entry into St Paul and other early Christians, 'As I began to speak, the Holy Spirit fell upon them, as on us at the beginning', (*Acts* 11.15); 'Paul was pressed in the spirit, and testified to the Jews that Jesus was Christ', (*Acts* 18.5). Often, as in the case of the Jewish prophets and St Paul, possession results in the transmission of a message, and so possession may be difficult to distinguish from mediumship, and perhaps the most spectacular example of this comes from Tibet where, right up until the mid twentieth century, a monk fulfilling the role of State Oracle would dislodge his own spirit from his body and so create a vacancy within it, which a god could enter and possess for the time being. Heinrich Harrer described one such session, which he saw for himself at the Nechung monastery:

Hollow, eerie music greeted us at the gate of the temple. Inside the spectacle was ghastly. From every wall looked down hideous, grimacing faces, and the air was filled with stifling fumes of incense. The young monk had just been led from his private quarters to the gloomy temple. He wore a round metal mirror on his breast. Attendants robed him in gay silks and led him to his throne. Then everyone drew back from round him. No sound could be heard except the hollow music. He began to concentrate. I watched him closely, never taking my eyes from his face – not the slightest movement of his features escaped me. He looked as if the life were fading out of him. Now he was perfectly motionless, his face a staring mask. Then suddenly, as if he had been struck by lightning, his body curved upward like a bow. The onlookers gasped. The god was in possession. The medium began to tremble; his whole body shook and beads of sweat stood out on his forehead. Servants went to him and placed a huge, fantastic headdress on his head. This was so heavy that it took two men to carry it. The slender body of the monk sank deeper into the cushions of the throne under the weight of his monstrous mitre. It is no wonder, I thought, that these mediums die young. The spiritual and physical strain of these séances must be killing.

The trembling became more violent. The medium's heavily laden head wavered from side to side, and his eyes started from their sockets. His face was swollen and covered with patches of hectic red. Hissing sounds pierced through his closed teeth. Suddenly he sprang up. Servants rushed to help him, but he slipped by them and to the moaning of the oboes began to rotate in a strange exotic dance. Save for the music, his groans and teeth-gnashings were the only sounds to be heard in the temple. Now he started beating on his gleaming breastplate with a great thumb-ring, making a clatter which drowned the dull rolling of the drums. Then he gyrated on one foot, erect under the weight of the giant headdress which just now two men could hardly carry. The attendants filled his hands with barleycorns which he threw into the awe-struck crowd of onlookers. All bent low before him, and I feared lest I be noted as an intruder. The medium became calmer. Servants held him fast and a Cabinet Minister stepped before him and threw a scarf over his head. Then he began to ask questions carefully prepared by the Cabinet about the appointment of a governor, the discovery of a new Incarnation, Matters involving war and peace. The Oracle was asked to decide on all these things. Often the question had to be repeated several times before the medium began to mumble. I tried to pick out intelligible words but made nothing of the sounds. While the Minister stood humbly there trying to understand the answers, an old monk took them down with flying pen.

Techniques for achieving such a state can be taught and learned. Joseph Karo (1488-1575), for example, had an angelic mentor who gave him detailed instructions about his conduct as part of a rigorous preparation for the descent of the possessing spirit which Karo identified as the Shekinah, the female aspect of divinity, important in the Kabbalah; Isaac Luria (1534-72) would prostrate himself on the grave of one of the Mishnaic sages and concentrate upon conversing with the dead sage's spirit, a technique he passed on to his principal student, Hayyim Vital; and a century later, Nathan of Gaza (1643-80) used techniques drawn from Abulafian instruction manuals which had been well known in the sixteenth century. An account of one of his trances, which happened in 1665, tells us that in the middle of the night, Nathan suddenly began to recite one of the tractates of the Torah, then asked the young scholars who were with him to sing hymns, at which point a wonderfully fragrant smell pervaded the house. Next, Nathan started to jump and dance and remove his clothing, the preface to his suddenly falling down and lying as if dead. Indeed, the attendant scholars thought he was dead and laid a cloth over his face as they would have done over that of a real corpse. But after a while they heard Nathan speak very quietly – not in his own voice, but in that of what they took to belong to some divine entity, a spark of God, which had caused the pleasant odour. Similar prophets and mystics abounded in Europe, their trances and prophecies given extensive publicity after the invention of the printing press which churned out increasing numbers of pamphlets describing them, often in a sensational fashion, during the sixteenth and seventeenth centuries. Indeed, like elements of the popular press today they tended to concentrate on the more bizarre or histrionic aspects of possession, and bred an unfortunate assumption in their readers that the more extreme the screaming and writhing, the more the possessed person's saintly virtue was demonstrated and proved. It is a point to which we shall return in due course.

One aspect of possession, closely connected with possession by the dead, is a feature of central and southeastern Europe in particular – possession by fairies. These, of course, are not the dainty butterfly figures of nineteenth-century imagination, but humanoid entities of human size, connected with dancing, fertility, and illness, able to bless and able to inflict pain. They often carry off sleepers to a world or state of existence where time means nothing, 'carrying off' being an expression for entering into possession although sometimes, as in Serbian belief, this 'entering' is exactly what they do, for when the soul leaves the body during sleep, a fairy may enter therein and dance the sleeper to death. Elsewhere the belief is somewhat different. When a fairy enters the body, the face becomes disfigured and the hands and feet are 'taken away', that is, rendered useless. Illness itself, of course, may be regarded as a form of demonic possession, and curing charms are often expressed in exorcistic form:

Behold Thou, o Christ,
This breast, and it so swollen.
Tell that to Mary;
It was she who bore the Son.
Rash between swellings,
Leave this bed.
Take yourself to another bed.
Send the milk from the breast.
Transmit the rash to the stone,
And through the stone to the ground.

The dead, too, may take over the bodies of the living, it may be perforce, or it may be via what Evan Zeusse called 'invited spirit mediumship', whereby they speak or act through them. Most famous from its nineteenth-century history of Spiritualism, this type of mediumship has a much earlier history. Indeed, it goes back to Biblical times and King Saul's consultation of the dead prophet Samuel whose spirit was raised by the so-called witch of Endor, an episode whose exact meaning was fiercely debated during the sixteenth century by theologians and demonologists alike.[62]

There existed, therefore, a wealth of ways in which human beings lay open to attack from and possession by spirits of one kind or another, so much so, in fact, that possession could be regarded simply as the most theatrical way in which an individual entity from the spirit world was likely to manifest itself in the world of matter, since it did not appear in its own form or as a separate entity disguised as someone or something else, but hid within the body of a human whom it compelled to behave in ways both frightening and sensational, thereby creating in onlookers a sense of disjunction from normality, greater than that which might flow from a disguise or even a separate manifestation. Recorded accounts of these incidents are extremely common. The following is one that took place in a domestic setting and lacks most of the spectacular trappings attendant on more public displays of possession. For that reason it is worth considering in some detail.

In June 1598, Françoise Secretain was accused of sending five demons into Loyse Maillat, the young daughter of a couple whom Françoise had asked for a night's lodging. The husband was not at home and the wife, Humberte, refused, but Françoise persisted and eventually Humberte gave in and left Françoise in the house with their eight year old daughter Loyse and two younger girls while she went to attend to the cattle. 'Françoise', says Henri Boguet who recorded the narrative in his *Discours des Sorciers*, 'went up to Loyse and two of her younger sisters as they were warming themselves by the fire, gave Loyse a crust of bread resembling dung and made her eat it, strictly forbidding her to speak of it, or she would kill and eat her, (those were her words); and on the next day the girl was found to be possessed'. The symptoms were typical, but mild in comparison with some:

> [She] was struck helpless in all her limbs so that she had to go on all fours; she also kept twisting her mouth about in a very strange manner. She continued thus afflicted for a number of days, until on the 19th of July her father and mother judging from her appearance that she was possessed, took her to the Church of Our Saviour to be exorcised. There were then found five devils, whose names were Wolf, Cat. Dog, Jolly and Griffon; and when the priest asked the girl who had cast the spell on her, she answered that it was Françoise Secretain, whom she pointed out from among all those who were present at her exorcism. But as for that day, the devils did not go out of her. But when the girl had been taken back to her parents' house, she begged them to pray to God for her, assuring them that if they fell to their prayers she would quickly be delivered. Accordingly they did so at the approach of night, and as soon as her father and mother had done praying, the girl told them that two of the devils were dead, and that if they persevered with their devotions they would kill the remaining ones also. Her father and mother

were anxious for their daughter's health and did not cease praying all night. The next morning at dawn the girl was worse than usual and kept foaming at the mouth; but at last she was thrown to the ground and the devils came out of her mouth in the shape of balls as big as the fist and red as fire, except the Cat, which was black. The two which the girl thought were dead came out last and with less violence than the three others; for they had given up the struggle from the first, and for this reason the girl had thought they were dead. When all these devils had come out, they danced three or four times round the fire and then vanished; and from that time the girl began to recover her health.

Here we can discern five episodes: (i) Loyse eats dark bread forced on her by Françoise; (ii) her legs give way and her mouth keeps twisting; (iii) she is taken to church where the possessing demons are identified; (iv) a rational interlude in which Loyse asks for prayer and says that two of her demons are dead; (v) a fit, foaming at the mouth, and the exit of all five demons. It is tempting to see the whole episode as stemming from Lyse's ingestion of the bread and to suggest that this precipitated a hallucinogenic experience. The bread of the poor – and we are told that Françoise was poor – certainly might contain some unusual or unexpected ingredients. As Piero Camporesi has pointed out:

> The scarcity of precious grains [such as wheat] resulted in bread-making which paid little attention to the quality of the mixtures, into which entered grasses with stupefying seeds such as darnel ... When bread was made in this desperate way with the most impure and heterogeneous mixtures, every pernicious adventure was possible.

So it might be possible to speculate that Françoise's piece of bread could have been tainted with ergot, and that Loyse's reaction to eating it was therefore a form of convulsive ergotism, which tends to produce delirium, hallucinations, and convulsions. Speculation, however, is what such an explanation would remain, for Loyse's initial symptoms are not really those of ergotism, (although her later symptoms could be), and the period of rationality between the two outbreaks needs to be accounted for, as does the difference in her behaviour during the two periods of possession.

First let us note that we know nothing about Loyse Maillat beyond what Boguet records. We do not know if she was naturally sickly, weak, healthy, strong-willed, naughty, given to tantrums, religious, or self-centred, and therefore if her crawling and mouth-twisting was genuine or merely a theatrical performance; nor have we any notion of the state of her relationship with her parents. On the other hand, there was a lapse of forty-four days between the onset of her symptoms and her parents' decision to take her to church, far too long a period for an eight year old to sustain theatrics, if indeed the symptoms lasted more or less unabated during that time. Notice that Loyse herself never suggested she was possessed – again, perhaps her age was against her having such a conception. It was her parents who came to this conclusion. Why? Did she merely crawl and twist her mouth, or did she display other behavioural signs, which provided clearer indications of demonic interference? We are not told. Neither are we told whether the parents consulted a doctor or an apothecary in the first instance before turning their thoughts to a preternatural explanation. Boguet includes this narrative as part of his drive to show that witches could indeed send demons into the body of another person, his affirmative contribution to a debate on the subject in which others denied the possibility. It was thus in his polemical interest to concentrate on the demonic side of the incident, and to omit anything which might interfere with the clear exposition of the point he wanted to make. On the other hand, he may have recorded accurately everything he knew or wanted to know. It is a good example of the amount of attendant detail to which we have no access and whose lack should therefore make us cautious in jumping to easy conclusions.

Loyse's trials began after she had eaten bread given to her by Françoise Secretain. This was actually a commonplace among causes of possession. William Sommers, for example, said he had been pestered by an old woman while he was going to and from the town of Walton, and at last, when they met once more beside a deep coal-pit, gave her three pence in response to her insistent begging:

> After this she put her hand to a bag she had about her, and taking thence a piece of bread with butter spread on it, bade him eat it. He refusing, she threatened him ... to throw him into the pit and break his neck if he would not eat it. Whereupon (greatly against his will, and for fear), he did eat it, and in the eating it seemed as sweet as any honey.

But this was the beginning and source of his possession. Likewise, an unfortunate woman who, according to a news pamphlet published in 1607, became demon-possessed after eating an enchanted orange, and similar entries into the body can be illustrated by the comic sub-plot of a Spanish play, *La Duquesa de la Rosa*, written in the early 1560s by an actor from Seville, Alonso de la Vega. The major-domo of the Duchess sends some jellied eels as a gift to his brother, but chooses a simpleton, Thomé Sanctos, to deliver them. Worried that Thomé may be tempted to eat some of them, the major-domo tells him they contain a demon and that if

Thomé eats any of the eels he will die. Naturally, Thomé cannot resist temptation, and he and a page that he has met on the way eat some and immediately believe they are possessed by demons and about to die. Both, however, survive their ordeal, only to be beaten for their greed at the end of the episode.

Claude and Humberte Maillat, then, perhaps guided by the fact that their daughter ate bread given to her by a stranger and soon after began to display peculiar but also particular symptoms, decided their daughter was possessed and took her to their local church to be exorcised. The process of exorcism is complex. First the priest must have been authorised by the Church to conduct exorcisms. Secondly, he must consider other possible explanations for the patient's behaviour before deciding that this is indeed a case of genuine possession, for there were frauds, and sometimes very skilful frauds. Marthe Brossier, for example, was a draper's daughter who in 1598 claimed to be possessed as a result of witchcraft, and quickly turned into a national celebrity because of her highly theatrical performances and, (a key point), her anti-Protestant utterances while supposedly in her trance-like states. Many people, however, were sceptical and had no hesitation in saying so, and saying so in print. The *Rituale Romanum*, therefore, properly and cautiously advises, '[The priest] should not readily believe that someone is possessed, but should take note of those signs whereby a possessed person is distinguished from those suffering from melancholia or some other illness', and gives three examples of the most common of such signs: speaking or giving evidence of understanding languages he or she does not know; having knowledge of what is happening in distant places, or of things he or she cannot be expected to know about; displaying strength beyond his or her age or natural condition. Loyse, one may remark, showed no such symptoms, according to Boguet's account, and if she had done, it is most unlikely that Boguet, who was keen to claim that she was genuinely possessed as a result of witchcraft, would have omitted to mention or describe them. So the priest must either have taken into account signs about which we do not know, or have yielded to the persistence of Loyse's parents who had convinced themselves that their daughter was possessed.

If the priest were doing his job properly, however, he would have been circumspect. Moshe Sluhovsky notes the careful steps designed for the exorcist by Cardinal Giulio Santorini, some of whose preparatory work to produce an official rite of exorcism for the Church was incorporated into the authorised Roman Rite in 1614:

Santorini describes four causes for possession: despair, sin, salvation of souls and witchcraft ... He warns against mistaking melancholy and mental retardation for possession and makes a special mention of women's natural inclination to be deceived. It is important to interrogate the possessed person's state of mind and health history, and to question relatives whether the victim suffers from melancholy, depression, wild imagination, or other mental troubles ... However, the possibility that alleged demoniacs suffer from natural afflictions neither excludes diabolic aetiology, nor does it mean that melancholics should not be exorcised. Often they are victims of the demon, and in such cases the exorcist ought to adjust his techniques to the personality of the demoniac and to refrain from agitating her too much. Following consultation with physicians, an exorcist should also consider administering natural medicine.

In other words, the priest will neither assume that the affliction whose symptoms he is witnessing are preternatural in origin, nor that they are natural, but will be prepared to take steps to employ whatever type of remedy he judges appropriate to the individual case. So if we suppose that Loyse's parish priest observed these various strictures, he will have taken into account that she may simply have been ill or downright naughty, and come to the conclusion she really was possessed. But possessed by what? A good spirit, a ghost, some unknown entity? Or had she been occupied by an evil spirit? Telling the difference between the various possible possessing entities was not always easy, so this is where experience and precedent came in. An older priest may have dealt with such problems before; a younger priest may have read the latest literature on the subject. There will have been much for him to ponder, but having made up his mind anent the type of spirit with which he was being called to deal, the priest will then have embarked on the long, hazardous, exhausting job of trying to determine the personal identity of the spirit or spirits occupying the little girl. Such identification is crucial to the success of the exorcism, because control of the name brings control of the individual who will respond to it and to no other. Once known for who he is, the spirit can then be addressed directly, and the exorcism proper can begin.

First the priest will want to know why the spirit has possessed the girl. Was it by accident or design? If the latter, by whose design – his own or the Devil's? If by design, who sent him into the child's body, the Devil or a human agent such as a witch? If by a witch, who is she? Secondly, while endeavouring to extract this information, the priest will be assessing the state of the possessing spirit. Is he frightened? If so, does this make him aggressive verbally or physically (through the girl's body)? Is the spirit speaking with the girl's voice or his own? If he is not frightened, is he in control of the situation? Is he dominant? If either of those, what will be the best way to wrest control from him without causing damage to the girl? Regardless of the nature of the demonic spirit, however – and this, according to the record, is clearly the type of entity which had entered Loyse – the spirit was in the wrong place and needed to be dislodged. A demon's ultimate proper place was Hell, although it may have inhabited the sub-lunar air for the time being, a region we have noted before as one teeming with such creatures, and so the priest will have endeavoured to send it back – an expulsion and fate the spirit would clearly try to resist. So it needed to be reminded of its true condition, rejection by God and consignment to a place of perpetual subjection and alienation from Him, and of its lack of power n the face of divine authority wielded in this instance by the Church through her representative, the priest. Hence, Gospel readings from *Luke* 10.17-20 which proclaim, 'Lord, even the devils are subject unto us through thy name', and *Luke* 11.14-22 which tells of Jesus casting out an evil spirit, and the fragility of the rule of Satan in the world.

Then, after prayer, according to the *Rituale Romanum*, the priest places his stole round the possessed person's neck and his right hand on his or her head, and, after further prayer, begins the first of three exorcisms:

I exorcise you, most unclean spirit, every assault of the Adversary, every illusion, every Legion, in the name of our Lord Jesus Christ, [and conjure you] to uproot yourself and put yourself to flight from this being created by God. He who enjoined that you be [expelled] from the highest heavens and immersed in the depths of the earth commands you. He who has commanded the sea, the winds, and storms commands you. Listen, therefore, and be afraid, Satan, enemy of the Faith, enemy of the human race, bringer of death, robber of life, diverter of justice, root of evils, kindling which sets vices on fire, seducer of people, betrayer of nations, inciter of envy, source of greed, cause of dissension, rouser of sorrows. Why do you stay in place and put up resistance when you know that Christ the Lord is destroying the means of achieving your object? Be afraid of Him who was sacrificed in [the person of] Isaac, sold in [the person of] Joseph, slaughtered in [the person of] the lamb, crucified [in the person of] a human being, and then was triumphant over Hell'. (The priest now traces crosses on the forehead of the possessed individual). 'Withdraw, therefore, in the name of the Father + and of the Son + and of the Holy Spirit +. Give place to the Holy Spirit by this sign of the holy cross + of Jesus Christ, our Lord, who with the Father and the same Holy Spirit lives and reigns for ever and ever, Amen.

The exorcism bristles with authority and injunctions to be afraid, but perhaps most noticeably it addresses the spirit as 'Satan', and delivers a string of identifying phrases which underline the assumption that, whatever name the possessing demon may supply to the exorcising priest, it is no more than an agent of its master, the Devil, and can therefore be treated as his mouthpiece and his limb.

The second exorcism reinforces the first, but at greater length, and with many more words of command using the verb *impero*, essentially a military term, implying instant and unquestioning obedience. The third exorcism, with a mixture of *Matthew* 8.29 and 25.41, reminds the possessing demon of his proper place. 'He stings you with divine lashes. In His sight you with your legions trembled, cried out, and said, "What is it to us and to you, Jesus, Son of God most high? Have you come here to torture us before the proper time?" He subjects you to everlasting flames, He who, at the end of time, will say to the impious, "Depart from me, you who have been cursed, into the everlasting fire which has been prepared for the Devil and his angels"'. With the demon thus reminded, the priest recites the Athanasian Creed – a statement of faith – seven psalms whose burden is that the individual is under attack from hostile forces and needs God's help, and a final prayer that the evil spirit in control of the possessed may lose that power, flee and not come back, and that it may be replaced by the goodness and peace of Jesus Christ.[63]

We can see several of these stages in the sequence of engravings by Elias Wellhöfer, which we discussed earlier, and although they were drawn over fifty years after Loyse Maillat's possession, the procedure followed by her parish priest will not have been all that different. He was successful in three of his endeavours. He ascertained that Loyse was being occupied by demons – five of them – he discovered their names, and he found out the reason for her possession: she had been occupied at the behest of Françoise Secretain whom she identified as the source of her possession by pointing her out in the congregation. The names of the demons appear to resemble those of familiars uncovered by the English witch-finder, Matthew Hopkins. The frontispiece to his *Discoverie of Witches* (1647) shows two witches naming their demons who are portrayed as a cat, a hare, a dog, a mouse, and a cow, and labels them as Holt, Jarmara (possibly *Jar* = 'discord' + *marrer* = 'spoiler'), Sack-and-Sugar, News, Vinegar-Tom, Ilemauzar (i.e. *Ail* = 'trouble' + 'mouser'), Pyewackett (*Pie*, perhaps a reference to its colouring), Peek-in-the-Crown, and Griezzell Greedigutt. There is clearly a folk element in this naming as, indeed, there may be in the names of Loyse's spirits; but it is worth asking who provided the names, the most likely answer being Loyse herself, either in her own person and voice, or in the person and voice of the demons themselves. Wolf, Cat, Dog, Jolly, and Griffon are just the kind of name one might expect a child to produce, knowingly or unconsciously, and they stand in sharp contrast to the names of, for example, the seven demons who took possession of the Ursuline nun, Jeanne des Anges, in the convent of Loudun in 1632: Astaroth,

Zabulon, Cham, Nephtalon, Achas, Alix, Uriel. These are Biblical, Apocryphal, and magical names such as may be found in grimoires containing the ceremonies of ritual magic, a set of learned techniques far removed from the popular magic Loyse and her parents may have seen or known about.

Still, childish or 'folk' in origin, the type of name made no real difference. The occupying demons had yielded up names by which they could be addressed, exhorted, and threatened, and had thus surrendered to the exorcising priest a useful and important mean whereby he could begin to impose order on the chaos the demons had created within their little victim. Unfortunately, however, the mean was not sufficient and the demons did not depart. But they do seem to have been subdued for a while, because upon being taken home Loyse was calm enough and rational enough to ask her parents to pray for her. Prayer, she suggested, after they had done so, had now killed two of her demons. What made her think so? (We have to proceed as though Loyse was telling the truth, as she perceived it. If we dismiss her observations, or indeed her whole narrative, as lies, our inquiry simply turns into wondering how she was able to dupe so many adults for so long, and why they were unable to see they were being fooled. This is not an impossible version of events, of course, and there are several examples of deliberate fraud by children. But we must also allow for the possibility that no fraud was intended and no lies told - no deliberate lies, at any rate - and in this case, our questions must obviously take a different turn.)

So, what made Loyse think that two of her demons were dead? Here we must remind ourselves of the close relationship between spirits and human physiology. Spirits, as opposed to souls, were actually material in nature, although very much refined, and occupied different organs of the body, such as the heart, liver, and brain, according to their specific type and function. Now, demons are similar to spirits in as much as they are a created part of Nature, and although they have no bodies as humans have, they still behave in a way analogous to the spirits which are present and operate within the human body from their principal bases therein. Demons, being impure substances, occupy the bowels. Nancy Caciola quotes Gerald Cambrensis by way of illustration. 'When the Eucharist was given to a certain woman in whom there was a demon, the demon was asked where it was, and if it was with Christ. It answered, "No, the Lord is in her soul and I live in her intestines"'. Caesarius of Heisterbach was even more specific. 'When it is said that a devil is inside a person, we must not understand this to mean the soul, but the body; for the Devil can live inside the body's open spaces and in the bowels where the shit is contained'. If, then, we posit a situation in which Loyse felt pain or disturbance or cramps in the region of her bowels or stomach, and then noticed that these had subsided once she got back home and her parents had finished praying, knowing, (because the adults round her had told her so), that these discomforts were caused by five demons, she could well have assumed that easement of her pains had resulted from the death of some of her tormentors: hence her announcement, and her request to her parents to keep on praying. If their prayers had already killed two demons, more prayers would surely kill the rest.

Claude and Humberte started their prayers 'at the approach of night'. This implies they waited for a while. Why should they have done so? Why not begin praying at once? If there was a delay, the reason probably lies in the fact that night was regarded as the dangerous time, the hours during which evil might be abroad and the powers of darkness at their most potent. As the Bible said by way of comfort, 'Thou shalt not be afraid for the terror by night ... Nor for the pestilence that walketh in darkness', (*Psalm* 91.5-6). Prayer by night would therefore be that much sharper and more potent against an enemy whose special time this was. Unfortunately, despite a night of prayer, Loyse's period of remission did not last and at least one of the symptoms of possession had returned.

Now, contemporary medicine taught that if the body was purged, the balance of humours would be restored and health would thus return. Purging included substances to induce vomiting, and it would therefore be natural to conclude that possessing demons would eventually leave the body via those orifices which led to the stomach or the bowels: the mouth and the anus. Hence, at the crisis of her suffering, Loyse fell to the ground and vomited up her demons. Four came out of her in the shape of fairly large red balls, one being coloured black. Possessed individuals were frequently seen to vomit a great range of objects during the course of their torments - pins, feathers, small creatures, stones - as, for example, in the case of Christian Shaw from Renfrewshire, who in 1697 claimed to have been possessed by demons as a result of witchcraft:

> Being on her way to her grandmother's house at Northbar, she did thrust
> or spit out of her mouth parcels of hair, some curled, some plaited, some
> knotted, of different colours, and in large quantities; and thus she continued
> to do in several swooning fits every quarter of an hour, both in her passage
> to Glasgow, which was by boat on Thursday, November 12th, and when
> she was in Glasgow. For the space of three days ensuing she put frequently
> hair out of her mouth, and in as great quantities as the first day, her former
> swerffing or swooning fits recurring as often throughout the days as before.
> And thereafter from Monday to Thursday following she put out of her
> mouth coal cinders about the bigness of chestnuts, some whereof were
> so hot they could scarcely be handled, one of which, Dr Brisbane being
> by her when she took it out of her mouth, felt to be hotter than the heat

of anyone's body could make it. Then for the space of two days in these swooning fits, as formerly, there was put, or taken out of her mouth, straw in great quantities, though but one straw at once folded up together, which, when put out, returned to its length, was found to be both long and broad, and it was remarkable than in one of them there was a small pin found. There after were put out of her mouth, bones of various sorts and sizes, as bones of fowls, and small bones of the heads of kine, and then some small sticks of candle fir, (a sort of fir in the country, that burns like a candle), one of which was about three or four inches long: which, when any upon sight of either bones or sticks took hold of to pull out, they found them either held by her teeth set together upon them, or forcibly drawn back into her throat; particularly Archibald Bannatyne of Kellie, younger, observing a bone in her mouth like a duck shank or leg bone, and essaying to pull it out, he declared he found something drawing it back into her throat, so that it took a great deal of force to get it pulled out. It is to be noticed that she never knew how these things were brought into her mouth, and when they were got out of it, she immediately recovered of her fit for that time.

After this, she put out of her mouth some quantity of unclean hay intermixed with dung, as if it had been taken out of a dunghill, which was so stinking that the damsel could not endure the nauseating taste and vile relish those things produced in her mouth, which did necessitate her still to rinse her mouth with water, after the putting of that sort of matter out of it. Then for more than a day's space, she put out of her mouth a number of wild fowls' feathers; after that a gravel-stone which, in the judgement of beholders, had been passed by some persons in a gravel fit, with some small white stones, and a whole nut gall, (wherewith they use to dye and to make ink), together with lumps of candle grease and egg shells; during which time she continued as formerly in her recurring swooning fits, with some intervals wherein she was in perfect health: of all which there were many famous [respectable] witnesses who, in that city, (besides those who were continually with her) came frequently to visit her.[64]

Now, while some of these cases were undoubtedly fraudulent, and proven to be so at the time, others were not, or were not so proven, and this last seems to have been true of Loyse's allotriophagy. But did anyone else see the demons either as balls or as themselves while they danced about the hearth? Boguet's text keeps the statement impersonal, so we do not know. In Loyse's heightened state, however, (presuming, as we have chosen to do, that she was not creating or involved in a fraud), it would have been perfectly in keeping with her dissociated state of consciousness genuinely to have seen such things, and her report of them, transmitted to her parents who would have been in an emotionally receptive condition, could have allowed them to agree that if this is what she was seeing, it must have been so. After all, it was they who declared Loyse was possessed in the first place and they who took her to church to be exorcised. They therefore had little if any need of being convinced that demons had inhabited their daughter and were now expelled by her retching and vomiting.

Demonic possession such as that suffered by Loyse, however, was not confined to the laity. The business of exorcism itself was highly dangerous, and in 1615 a meeting in Antwerp noted that a number of exorcists had been taken over by the demons they were trying to expel, while in 1616 the Archbishop's court in Mechelen heard a Capuchin monk admit that he had thrown in his lot with Satan and deliberately sent evil spirits into other people. But monks themselves did not become possessed – at least, not according to the records. For example, in spite of the fact that two Capuchin novices from a Sicilian monastery in 1671 exhibited many of the usual symptoms of possession – immense strength, shrieking and screaming, and aversion to holy objects – the account of their experience says merely that they were 'obsessed', that is, besieged by demons who did not actually enter their bodies. This is partly because the nature of the incident seems to have been peculiar – the demons offer long disquisitions on the need for everyone to repent, and describe the torments of Hell and Purgatory, so their 'task' is to preach rather than force their human agents into theatrical performances – but also because male bodies were believed to be less open than those of women and therefore less likely to be invaded, 'less open' here meaning controlled and impenetrable. Female bodies by contrast 'by virtue of their reproductive capacities [were] seen as more open, more grotesque, less autonomous ... flowing with substances which threatened to get out of hand'. In consequence, 'women's bodies in particular were inferior, and therefore more prone to become unbalanced; inferior because moister, colder, wetter than the masculine'.

This view, developed by contemporary medical theory, means not only that one expects to find more instances of demonic possession in convents rather than in monasteries, but that manifestations of typical or expected symptoms among nuns will be described as 'possession' rather than 'obsession'; and such indeed is the case. Moshe Sluhovsky has pointed to a remarkably large number of mass possessions breaking out in convents all over western Europe between the mid fifteenth and late seventeenth century, only one or two of which have been the subjects of intensive study. At Louviers in 1647, to take only one example, Sister Madeleine Bavent, aged eighteen, suddenly claimed that two men, one a priest, had taken her to a Sabbat where she had married the Devil and had sex with him on an altar. Her confession set in train further investigations which rapidly uncovered similar confessions from some of the other nuns, who also exhibited signs of being possessed: screaming obscenities and blasphemies, contortions of the body, speaking strange or unknown languages, a horror of confession and communion, and suffering mysterious wounds which came and then vanished of their own accord. All in all, eighteen of the fifty-two nuns in the convent displayed some or all of these symptoms, and the exorcisms intended to free them became a public spectacle, tentacles of hysteria reaching out from the nuns themselves to affect many in the watching crowds.

The reasons for these outbreaks in convents have been much debated, with writers concentrating on the most famous episodes from the early seventeenth century. They have suggested that possessions in these contexts played an important part in the contemporary search for witches, since the nuns' identification of named witches as the sources of their affliction could be taken more or less at face value, emanating as it did not from the nuns themselves, but from the voices of the demons within them. It has also been opined that some of these outbreaks were recorded by people whose intention was to use them in polemical fashion to advance, say, the Catholic cause against the Protestant, or orthodox Catholic piety against illuminism, the notion that individuals can receive enlightenment of a spiritual kind from some interior source – clearly an idea fraught with danger since the nature of that source could be divine or angelic, but also demonic or illusory. But one of the most popular explanations has centred upon the idea that cloistered women, particularly if they were young and healthy, must have been sexually frustrated, and that these incidents of possession acted as outlets for that frustration – witness (they say) the obscenities frequently characteristic of the possessed nuns' outbursts. This notion, however, smells of one of the twentieth century's obsessions, a post-Freudian pudendum gazing which makes quite unwarranted, and indeed unsustainable, assumptions about the nature of conventual life and, as Moshe Sluhovsky has said:

A pre-Freudian world in which sex was not as central to self-identity as it is for us, and where sexual and erotic symbolisations were natural means of expression for nuns, who were constantly warned of sexual temptation, who equated tensions with danger, and therefore with the erotic, and who were all familiar to a certain degree with the mystical-erotic language of late Mediaeval spirituality.

In other words, they were tense because they felt themselves possessed, and gave voice to that tension and anxiety in lewd and blasphemous language because that was the natural way for them to acknowledge the essentially blasphemous, but religious, nature of their possession.

It is also important to be aware that until it became clear that the source of the nuns' possession was demonic, nobody could be quite certain whether or not they had been taken over by a good or an evil spirit, and in consequence the first step in what might prove to be their rehabilitation was to discern which kind of spirit had taken them over. The dangers attendant upon this invasion of one entity by another quite different in kind are not to be exaggerated, and the experience for the nuns themselves must have been both frightening and exhilarating. What we should not do is diminish such an experience by dismissing it as intentionally fraudulent, hysterical, or pathological – and no one is denying that any or all of these are possible in some individual cases – but empathise with those undergoing it and involved with it, since those who sincerely believed and felt they had been entered by something powerful and alien which used and misused them in ways they knew to be sinful, would have been terrified not only by the experience itself, but also by those lucid intervals during which they would have been acutely aware that the possessing demon would take over again in full force and subject them to physical and spiritual torment.

These cases, then, especially those which fall outwith the favoured 1600s deserve more attention and closer scrutiny than they have generally received so far, for they are likely to reveal much about the nature of male and female spirituality, which has escaped notice hitherto. The case of Loyse Maillat, too, helps to show that, as with accounts of personal and communal experiences of the Devil, it is possible that there is much more to the narrative than meets the eye at first, and that modern assumptions about imaginative children, hysterical girls at their first menstruation, sexually anxious adults, and downright frauds are not sufficient to 'explain' every recorded incident of demonic (or indeed other) possession. That said, of course, it would be foolish not to point to those cases that certainly were fraudulent. I have already mentioned Marthe Brossier, a twenty-six year old who convinced her family she was possessed by a demon, and in 1598-9 went on a tour of France, performing wonders of clairvoyance on the way, before arriving in Orléans where a number of priests were fooled before the dean and canons of the cathedral decided to call in doctors from the university and authorise them to administer trick tests, all of which she failed. Wherever she went she was exorcised, thereby providing the general public with free theatre, herself a leading role, and physicians a chance to cross swords with theologians in a protracted argument about whether Marthe was genuinely possessed or merely ill. At the same time in England, William Sommers, aged nineteen or twenty, alleged that he had been persuaded by an exorcist, John Darrell, to feign demonic possession and to stick to this story by the Devil himself who appeared to him in the likeness of a mouse while Sommers was in prison. Sommers displayed many of the behaviours associated with possession: unnatural distortions of the body, extraordinary strength, trance-like states, and the utterance of strange or unknown words. In both cases, the possessed individual had her or his supporters and defenders, and it might be possible even now to make out a case in favour of at least some of their claims. Twenty year old Anne Gunter from Oxfordshire, however, was fraudulent through and through, although it is clear from the testimonies given before Star Chamber in 1605 that she had been induced and bullied into it by her father. Again, her symptoms were very much those which people expected to see, including vomiting up pins, which she also expelled from her nose through sneezing. Fraudulent, too, was a French woman in 1599, 'whose face turned black, whose tongue protruded the length of four or five fingers, whose eyes rolled back and mouth gaped, while she leaped, cried, and twisted in different directions'.[65]

Frauds apart, however – and both the sixteenth and seventeenth centuries were well aware of their possibility and uncovered them without hesitation unless, perhaps, it was politically or confessionally expedient for them not to do so – the growing number of cases of possession served to underline the common perception and assertion that Satan had been let loose and was busy preparing the destruction of humankind. These cases went hand in hand with an immense upsurge in cases of witchcraft all over Europe during the 1590s and early decades of the 1600s especially, proving to anyone who had eyes to see and ears to hear that the Church, (whichever Church they acknowledged), was right in her warnings to repent of personal sin, reject or abjure heresy, and turn to God before the final catastrophe. Loyse Maillat's case, then, is one among thousands, but it is notable perhaps for its relative lack of drama. Much, much more could be and was expected of possessed individuals, and a list of some of these behaviours was drawn up in the case of five children and two adults from Lancashire, all belonging to the same household, who began to show symptoms of possession in February 1595:

It is worthy to be marked that, though these possessed had every one some things peculiar to themselves which none of the rest did show, and that so rare and strange that all the people were forced to confess it was the work of an evil spirit within them, so had they also many things in common with one another, and were in their fits for the most part handled alike.

1. They had all and every one of them very strange visions and fearful apparitions, whereupon they would say, "Look where Satan is. Look where Beelzebub is. Look where Lucifer is. Look where a great black dog

is, with a firebrand in his mouth. See how Satan runs at me with a spear in his hand to stick me to the heart, but God will defend me".

2. They had every one of them two spirits at the least, one to torment them inwardly, with all the torments of Hell, as it were, for the present, and either one or more to stand before their faces, most ugly and terrible to behold, to drive them into all fear and astonishment.

3. They heard very hideous and fearful voices of the spirits sundry times, and did make marvellous answers back again to them very directly and strangely.

4. They were in their fits ordinarily so held in that captivity and bondage that, for an hour, two, or three, and longer time, they would neither see nor hear nor taste nor feel anything but the devils, they employing them wholly for themselves, vexing and tormenting them so extremely, that for the present they could feel no other pain or torture that could be from the body.

5. They, all of them, were taken suddenly with a very fearful shrieking and a marvellously strange howling and shouting, making a noise as it were to call on and to waken one another, so that the spirits, being raised up, might go to their work and proceed to torment their subjects according to their custom. When one began, they all followed after in order, observing time and tune, as if it had been the ringing of seven bells. And such was the strangeness of these voices, that the uttering and framing of them exceeded all cunning invention or the skill of any counterfeit imitation. And the effect was also so fearful, that it was both terrible and troublesome to the whole country [nearby district], and wrought a wonderful astonishment in all that heard it.

6. Further, they all of them had their bodies swollen to a wonderfully huge bigness and almost incredible, if there had not been many eyewitnesses to it.

7. They had also a marvellously sore heaving and lifting, as if their hearts would burst, so that with violent straining of themselves, some of them vomited much blood many times.

8. They had their faces disfigured, and turned towards their backs, a fearful thrusting out of their tongues with a most ugly distorting of their mouths, being drawn up, as it were, to their ears.

9. They were all of them very fierce, offering violence both to themselves and others, wherein also they showed very great and extraordinary strength.

10. They blasphemed God and the Bible, they reviled the preachers, railed on such as feared God, scorned all holy prayers and wholesome

exhortations, which being offered and applied to them, they became ever much worse.

11. For the most part, they delighted in filthy and unsavoury speeches, very agreeable to the nature of the unclean spirit which then dwelled within them, in so much that, in the very sermon, time when such unseemly behaviour was spoken against, the evil spirit wrought most maliciously and spitefully against the grace of God. And it forced one of them, though she was a maid, to utter openly in the hearing of the people such filthy uncleanness as is not to be named.

12. Most of them were blind, deaf, and dumb for divers days together.

13. They were out of their right minds without the use of the senses. They were especially void of feelings, as much sense in a stock as in one of them. Or, in a way, it was as possible to bring a dead man back to life as to later or change them in their trances or fits, in anything that they either said or did.

14. They were kept fasting a long time. And divers of them, for the space of three days and three nights, did neither eat, nor drink anything, Satan intending thereby to procure their pining away.

15. In their fits, they had divers parts and members of their bodies so stiff and stretched out as were inflexible, or very hard to be bent.

16. They showed very great and extraordinary knowledge, as may appear by the strange things said and done by them ...

17. They all in the end of every fit always said thus, "Jesus, bless me". Yea, though they had forty or a hundred fits in one day, as it is certain some of them had, yet they never missed saying thus. But as sure as they had a fit, whether it were long or short, so sure it was that it would be ended with this prayer, "Jesus, bless me". This was ever a sure sign that they were restored to the use of their senses for that time, which never failed.

18. After their fits, they were always as well as might be. And they felt very little or no hurt at all, although they had been every so sorely tormented immediately before.

Now this harmony and consent in signs and actions, both for the matter and manner of strange handling of all these in their several fits, does make it evident that they were all really and corporeally possessed.

However one may care to interpret these modes of behaviour, whether individually or collectively, their spectacular theatricality is tailored for an audience, and that being so, their potential as propaganda cannot be overlooked. Nor was it. Marthe Brossier was used for just such a purpose, and so was Nicole Obry from

Vervins, aged about sixteen, who was exorcised more or less every day for more than two months in 1565-6 in front of large crowds. Beelzebub, her occupying demon, made several interesting demands: first, that the exorcists move from Vervins to the much larger city of Laon; secondly, that he must be exorcised in the cathedral, not in a private chapel; thirdly, that a stage be built within the cathedral so that people could have a better view of the proceedings; and fourthly, that a demon of his high rank could not be expelled by anyone of lesser position than a bishop. All these demands were met, and in February 1566 the final performance started. Nicole was taken to the cathedral, the Bishop said Mass, and then began a conversation with Beelzebub. One of the demon's replies reveals the import of the performance. 'I entered here by the commandment of God because of the sins of the people, to show that I am a devil here to convert or harden my Huguenots'. *My* Huguenots. Here for the onlookers there was irrefutable proof that Protestants were in thrall to and inspired by the Devil, for Beelzebub himself acknowledged as much. The point was underlined when the Bishop threatened the demon with a consecrated Host:

> 'You must show who is your master', said the Bishop, 'who will make you leave'.
> 'Who? Your Jean le Blanc?' replied Beelzebub in a sarcastic reference to the Host.
> 'Who taught you to call it by this name?' asked the Bishop.
> 'It was I who taught my Huguenots to call it that', replied the demon.

His mockery did him no good, however, for the Bishop raised the Host and commanded Beelzebub to leave, whereupon Nicole's face became horribly distorted, her body rose six feet into the air, and she cried out in a dreadful voice.

Eventually the demon receded, withdrawing at last into her left arm from which, on 8 February, he finally departed. Not only had the whole incident disseminated propaganda against Huguenots in general, and the local Huguenots in particular, one of whom had also attempted to exorcise Nicole and had been rebuffed by Beelzebub who observed that one devil could scarcely expel another, but the power of the consecrated Host, and therefore the doctrine of transubstantiation, rejected by Protestants, had been thoroughly demonstrated. Not that Protestants quietly accepted their losers' role. In England, for example, George More put the case for Protestants' engaging in a battle of exorcisms:

> If the Church of England have this power to cast out devils, then the Church of Rome is a false Church. For there can be but one true Church,

the principal mark of which, as they say, is to work miracles, and of them this is the greatest, namely to cast out devils. And hereupon, conferring at another time with two [sceptics], they brought out this bold protestation, that if we could prove any such power to be in our Church and show them infallible instance or example to justify the practice thereof, then they would join themselves to our Church assemblies, and freely embrace our religion.

But while some Protestants were willing to fight Catholics on the same demonic ground, others were equally clear that they neither would nor should do so. 'Wheresoever the Scriptures so speak of the possession of devils', wrote John Deacon and John Walker in 1601:

They speak it only by metaphor ... And this I say further, that you cannot possibly allege throughout the whole Scriptures any one text wherein either angels or spirits or devils are otherwise spoken of than only by metaphor: the which places being interpreted literally would pester the Church with many absurd and inconvenient opinions.

For all this, however, very many Protestants accepted that Satan could both obsess and actually possess, and used all their own endeavours as well as those of Protestants exorcists to combat the Devil and drive him from people's bodies, not only to rid them of a dire and unwanted enemy, but also to demonstrate to others the godliness of their faith and so provide occasions of moral inspiration at least as effective as any polemic or sermon.[66]

Exorcisms, of course, were only one example of demonic theatre. Another was the theatre itself which continued to take full advantage of the opportunities presented by various dramatic plots, as well as the deep-seated belief in the active presence of Satan and his demons in the Mediaeval and Early Modern worlds, to stage presentations of that activity, although while the Devil had been a figure of religious drama in the past, during the sixteenth century he or his spirits became increasingly part of a secular, often confessionally polemical theatre. As Anthony Munday noted in 1609 in his blasts against playhouses, England was under attack from various reprehensible sources, namely, the Devil, Catholics, and actors. 'I would gladly separate them', he wrote, 'for ... the Devil, and Papists, and players do mock at religion, and abuse the Holy Scriptures'; while in 1624 William Prynne made much the same connection, and linked them all with dancing and with witches at a Sabbat:

Dancing is the pomp of the Devil, and he that danceth, maintaineth his [the Devil's] pomp and singeth his Mass ... The woman that singeth in the dance is the prioress of the Devil, and those that answer are clerks, and beholders are parishioners, and the music are the bells, and the fiddlers, the ministers of the Devil.

A touch exaggerated, perhaps, but the mood among many of England's Puritans when it came to the subject of Satan's influence in society tended to be dramatic, as can be seen from Stephen Gosson's contention that Satan was flooding England with imported Italian books in order to poison the English with a desire for sinful foreign delights. Fortunately however, he observed, Satan appeared to have forgotten that the English were largely illiterate.

Still, amusing as these rhetorical flourishes may be to our modern ears, they should not mislead us into thinking that the Devil in the theatre (or elsewhere) cannot be taken altogether seriously. On the contrary, Puritan fulminations are evidence that the sixteenth and seventeenth centuries took him very seriously indeed, and Nathan Johnstone has summed up the points succinctly:

> The Protestant emphasis on the Devil's power to intrude into the consciousness should not be interpreted, as Jeffrey Burton Russell would see it, as evidence of a greater concern with the purely human potential for evil, forced to rely on the Devil for its expression until the enlightenment provided a new language more capable of encompassing conflicting psychological experiences. For internal temptation in Early Modern culture was not used as a metaphor but as the description of a real event. We should be wary of imposing psychological explanations on a culture that would not have recognised them. Whilst the inhabitants of Early Modern England were as capable of diagnosing delusion as diabolism, their inclination was to accept the possibility (if not always the certainty) that the experience of internal conflict or dislocation or the sense that the commonwealth was being subverted by a hidden agency, was the experience of the Devil.

This is an important point to note, because the discourse of Early Modern theatre, (and not merely English theatre), tended to concentrate on the fraudulent or the deceptive aspects of possession and exorcism, partly because this reflected a genuine contemporary theological debate on the relationship between spirit entities and the human body, partly because it offered opportunities to make anti-Catholic or, indeed, anti-Puritan points, but also partly because a fraudulent possession and a fraudulent exorcism provided more fun for the audience. In Juan de Timoneda's *Los Menemnos*, one of the dramatis personae has his hands tied as part of a ritual of exorcism, before managing to obtain a sword and cut himself free; in Shakespeare's *Twelfth Night* (1601) when Malvolio pays the penalty for his presumption that his mistress is in love with him, the characters pretend he is possessed, lock him up in a dark cellar, and say they are sending a specimen of his urine to 'the wise woman' to see if it is black – a sign of demonic possession; and in *El pleyto que tuvo el Diablo* (c.1639), a stage-priest conducts an exorcism offering a close parody of the character and wording of that used by the Church:

> I unworthy minister and priest of God, by the authority that I have from the Church, command, force and compel the infernal spirits that after this our commandment be notified, intimated, and read to you, you declare, manifest, and discover all that which be asked by us of you. The first thing, that you confess how you are in that body, and how many there are of you, and why you entered it. And from that point we cite, command, and compel, and force Lucifer, prince of the demons, and Leviathan, Beelzebub, Asmodeus, Behemoth, and Astaroth, and Belial, and all the other captains and infernal ministers: that this our notification being heard, within three moments, and the last one for peremptory, the triune canonical entrenchments being set forth, that you torment the demons who are in the said Catalina molesting her, and that you force them with the most intense penalties of a hundred thousand years, which you should execute in each moment they refrain from completing our commandment. And if by obstinacy you do not obey, I excommunicate you, and I anathematise you, and I command that you do not torment more the said Catalina. And that you say the cause for which you molest her: and three moments after the notification, you will incur the said penalties.

In Protestant England, as one might expect, such scenes provided ideal material for both anti-Catholic invective and anti-Catholic hilarity. Barnabe Barnes's *The Devil's Charter* (1606/7) depicts Pope Alexander VI using exorcism as a means of summoning rather than banishing spirits; and George Ruggle's *Ignoramus* (1615) contains an extensive scene of pseudo-exorcism (Act 4, scene 11) in which Ignoramus, having been designated a demoniac, is tied to a chair but then subjects his 'exorcists' to a bombardment of names and phrases, (the general tenor of his message being, 'I'll have the law on you!') which the 'exorcists' then pretend to recognise as the names of his possessing demons:

> *Cola*: You who stand waiting with palm branches and blessed herbs, bind him tightly to the chair.
> *Ignoramus*: Why are you attaching[67] me with ropes and cords?

Cupes: Shut up!

Ignoramus (calling upon his servant): O Dulman, Dulman! You said today that you would fight like a devil for me. Where are you now, Dulman?

Cola: I exorcise you, Dulman. Flee, cursed Dulman, flee.

Ignoramus: He's already fled today, but if Dulman comes now ...

Cola: He's invoking Dulman. Dulman is certainly [his] name.

Ignoramus: Plague on you! [My] name is Ignoramus.[68]

Cupes: Go away, Ignoramus.

Ignoramus: Go away yourselves, scoundrels that you are, along with your 'riotous behaviour' and 'unlawful assemblage'.

Cupes: Forsake [him], utterly depraved spirit Ignoramus! I conjure you, Ignoramus. Refuser of justice, seducer of humankind, sower of discord, transgressor of the truth, dissipater of peace, I exorcise you.

Since James VI and I, before whom this play was performed more than once, had personally investigated cases of claimed possession after his accession to the English throne, the inclusion of such a scene and its extended joke can be interpreted partly, at least, as a piece of carefully directed anti-Catholic propaganda as well as a flattering reference to the King's own perspicacity in unmasking frauds of this type.[69]

The expression of political or confessional views through scenes of possession and exorcism, however, or indeed the laughter roused by their use as vehicles for humour or farce, should not mislead us into thinking that they necessarily represented a move towards scepticism about the reality of Satan or of demons among any of the social classes. Nor should the attribution of certain experiences such as flight to the Sabbat or absorption of hallucinogenic agents through the use of certain ointments be mistaken for dismissal of the notion that there were preternatural agencies behind them. As we have seen, Andrés de Laguna subscribed to physiological and humoural theory describing the outcomes of their use, but acknowledged their source in Satan's extensive knowledge of the natural world, and the malevolent purpose, which drove his making this available to less knowledgeable humans. Stuart Clark has protested against the tendency among some modern historians to try to erase this extra-natural component of Mediaeval and Early Modern beliefs, as though it were too embarrassing or too inconvenient a mode of thought for their readers to entertain. But we must come to terms with both the supernatural and the preternatural in history and, as Hilaire Kallendorf says, 'learn from [our predecessors] to be more open to seeing supernaturally influenced or genuinely religious figurations of the early modern self'.[70]

So to answer the question whether demonic possession was theatre or reality, we must allow that it could be both, and both simultaneously, provided we do not turn 'theatrical' into a synonym for 'fraudulent'. Living with the belief that an alien entity can enter one's body, take up residence there, and use one's body in whatever way it wishes, regardless of the pain and fear it causes, is immensely frightening, and none of those who seriously claimed to have endured the experience, or any of those who witnessed their endurance and sought to cope with its symptoms and dislodge its cause, were in any doubt that if they were engaged in some kind of game or some type of drama, it was a game or drama with serious consequences which stretched far beyond this world and into the next.

CHAPTER 8

Satan's Vengeful Return

When audiences attended the theatre or listened to the lengthy sermons of the day, what kind of mental image sprang to their minds when mention was made of Satan, and did the actor-demon they saw on stage correspond at all to that personal mental image? In Marlowe's *Dr Faustus*, the demon Mephistophilis, conjured by Faust, appears first in ugly shape and is commanded by Faust to go away and come back as 'an old Franciscan friar' because 'that holy shape becomes a devil best'. The initial ugliness, however, happens for the sake of the engineered anti-Catholic joke, and also accommodates the actor who is to spend quite a lot of time on stage with the protagonist, and may have found it easier to wear a friar's habit than the more elaborate costume required for a frightening demon. Moreover, the initial shock delivered to an audience by a demon-mask and so forth cannot be sustained throughout a whole play, and the more homely, more human costume of a friar serves to render the anti-Catholic message of the play much more vivid and memorable, and perhaps reminds the audience of the unfrightening way Satan regularly appeared to individuals in real life. This reassuring Satan, to judge by the confessions of those who claimed to have had personal dealing with him, seems to have lain at the forefront of people's minds, the other, repulsive image lurking further back, to be remembered and seen when circumstances or context demanded. Thus on the one hand we have the Devil of Milton's Puritan epic, which claimed to 'justify the ways of God to men', and to throw light upon the vexed theological debate anent God's omniscience and humankind's free will. Having successfully tempted Eve and thereby seduced Adam, Satan returns to Hell to boast his double triumph, only to find that he and all his angels are transformed into snakes and other poisonous monsters:

A while he stood, expecting
Their universal shout and high applause
To fill his ear; when, contrary, he hears,
On all sides from innumerable tongues
A dismal universal hiss, the sound
Of public scorn; he wondered, but not long
Had leisure, wondering at himself now more;
His visage drawn he felt to sharp and spare,
His arms clung to his ribs, his legs entwining
Each other, till supplanted down he fell,
A monstrous serpent on his belly prone,
Reluctant, but in vain; a greater power
Now ruled him, punished in the shape he sinned,
According to his doom; he would have spoke,
But hiss for hiss returned with forked tongue
To forked tongue; for now were all transformed
Alike, to serpents all, as accessories
To his bold riot; dreadful was the din
Of hissing through the hall, thick-swarming now
With complicated monsters, head and tail –
Scorpion, and asp, and amphisbaena dire,
Cerastes horned, hydrus, and ellops drear,
And dipsas (not so thick swarmed once the soil
Bedropped with blood of Gorgon, or the isle
Ophiusa); but still the greatest he the midst,
Now dragon grown, larger than whom the sun
Engendered in the Pythian vale on slime,
Huge python; and his power no less he seemed
Above the rest still to retain; they all
Him followed, issuing forth to the open field,
Where all yet left of that revolted rout,
Heaven-fallen, in station stood or just array,
Sublime with expectation when to see
In triumph issuing forth their glorious chief;
They saw, but other sight instead – a crowd
Of ugly serpents; horror on them fell,
And horrid sympathy; for what they saw
They felt themselves now changing; down their arms,
Down fell both spear and shield; down they as fast,

And the dire hiss renewed, and the dire form
Catched by contagion, like in punishment
As in their crime.
(*Paradise Lost* 10.504-45).

This is the traditional picture of Mediaeval demonology, quite at odds, one may note, with the overblown Romantic reinterpretation foisted upon Milton by the pernicious sentimentalism so characteristic of the nineteenth and early twentieth centuries. Contrast this with young Mercy Furtado's experience on Great Island in New Hampshire, who described the Devil she saw as having the figure of a short black man. 'He was not of a Negro, but of a tawny or Indian colour. He wore a high-crowned hat, with straight hair' – just the kind of look and clothing common among the local Wabanaki people. Circumstances and context, the two great moulders of the imaginative process. So while Milton's Satan may have been a traditional image in the grand style, it is unlikely to have been the first to enter the theatre audience's imagination, or indeed that of a church congregation. Still, a glimpse into the mind of a private individual reveals the variety of diabolic images stored therein. Johann Haizmann, a twenty-five-year-old painter from Bavaria, was possessed by the Devil on two August days in 1677, having made (according to his confession) a pact with Satan nine years earlier. He was exorcised by monks from the Abbey of Mariazell, and celebrated his release by painting a triptych and a series of eight portraits showing the Devil as he had seen him during the past few years. Erik Midelfort describes how those changed over time:

The paintings Haizmann completed shortly after his first liberation confirm the suggestion that at first the Devil appeared as an ordinary part of the world, but that slowly the Devil assumed a grotesque, monstrous, draconian appearance. In the triptych, for example, Haizmann painted his first encounter (the left panel) as a meeting in a peaceful countryside with an elderly gentleman in a red cloak with a long walking stick and a black dog. Haizmann showed himself, wearing a green smock or dress, signing an agreement in black ink. In the right panel Haizmann depicted his yielding up the pact in blood. The countryside is now wilder, and the Devil appears as a bearded red monster with horns, four breasts, and claw-feet. The final, central panel presents the return of the bloody pact at the altar of the Blessed Virgin. The Devil now appears as a red flying dragon with green wings and tail and the whole centre of the panel is exploding in red and white flames.

It has been suggested, more than once, that Haizmann was schizophrenic, but this does not really affect the point I am making here, which is that within Haizmann's developing images of the Devil we find not only those traditional and highly conventional pictures he may seen again and again in the stained glass and painted walls of Bavarian churches, but also that unthreatening, human-like appearance which people so often reported when they described their first personal contact with Satan; and it is this reassuring, comfortable image which occurs to Haizmann first.

Images from beyond the bounds of Europe, however, were not so genial, and while the earlier Middle Ages had been content to interpret the deities of other nations according to information derived from Classical explorers and anthropologists such as Ktesias and Herodotos, once the non-European world began to open up to the astonished gaze of sailors, merchants, missionaries, and makers of empires, the more the delineations and expectations of demonology came into their own as a last flowering of the diabolic imagination before enchantment in Europe drained away from the literate classes, leaving either a cold 'scientific' eye or a blowsy, 'Romantic' vision in its place. An illuminated fourteenth-century manuscript, *Le livre des merveilles*, contains pictures purporting to illustrate the travels of Marco Polo and Odoric of Pordenone, among others, and shows such scenes as Sir John Mandeville praying in a desert valley while horned, winged demons torment lost souls who have fallen into a deep cleft in the ground, while another picture transfers the demons' horns to the heads of Indian deities who receive the prayers of worshippers in a building remarkably like the interior of a Christian chapel. But however much or however little direct knowledge of Indian gods and goddesses may have underlain this version of their religion, the impression that Indians actually worshipped the Devil was given a fillip by the publication of Ludovico di Varthema's *Itinerario* in 1510. This Bolognese explorer had travelled in south India between 1503 and 1508, and now described what he had found in a temple in Calicut, an important trading city in Kerala:

The King of Calicut keeps this Deumo [Devil] in his chapel in his palace, in this wise; this chapel is two paces wide in each of the four sides, and three paces high, with doors covered with devils carved in relief. In the midst of this chapel there is a devil made of metal, placed in a seat also made of metal. The said devil has a crown made like that of the Papal kingdom, with three crowns; it has also four horns and four teeth with a very large mouth, nose, and most terrible eyes. The hands are made like those of a flesh-hook and the feet like those of a cock; so that he is a fearful object to behold. All the pictures round the said chapel are those of devils, and on each side of it there is a Sathanas seated in a seat, which seat is placed in a flame of fire, wherein are a great number of souls, of the length of half a finger and a finger of the hand. And the said Sathanas holds a soul in his mouth with the right hand, and with the other seizes a soul by the waist.

Varthema's book proved popular and ran into several editions. Five years after its first publication, an illustrated edition was brought out in Augsburg, its pictures helping to fix the demonic version of India's deities even more firmly in the heads of its European readers, and encouraged later travellers and writers to be free with the words 'devilish' and 'Devil'. Hence Edward Terry, chaplain to Sir Thomas Roe who travelled in India between 1614 and 1619, wrote of the Hindus, 'I know Satan (the father of division) to be the seducer of them all', while Abraham Rogerius, a Dutch missionary who spent ten years (1630-40) on the Coromandel coast, wrote in his *Open Door to the Secrets of Paganism* (1651) that Indians worshipped a supreme god, lesser gods, and the Devil, and that the images with many arms, which he saw everywhere around him, were demonic and embodiments of the Devil. Variants upon Varthema's Deumo persisted. In 1550, for example, Sebastian Münster from Basel published his *Cosmographia Universalis* with a picture of Deumo looking remarkably like European versions of the Devil, and as late as 1667 Athanasius Kircher was still happy to reproduce Varthema's description which he reinterpreted as India's version of Typhon, the hideous monster of Greek mythology, chthonic embodiment of volcanic forces, later identified with the Egyptian god Set.[71]

But if early travellers and missionaries in India found much to reinterpret in confirmation of one of their visual paradigms of Satan, those who went to central and south America encountered other difficulties. Jesuit missionaries, for example, while sympathetic in many ways to the native cultures they met, were convinced that wherever they went they were seeing evidence of Satan's rule over the indigenous peoples, in spite of the fact that, let us say in northern Mexico, the inhabitants had no conception of a personal expression of evil who sought the downfall of humankind. The deities of the Indians, wrote Friar Barnardino de Sahagún, '[are] not gods, but lying and deceitful devils', and even after the native peoples had been converted, one's vigilance could not be relaxed, for 'I am also certain that the Devil neither sleeps nor has forgotten the worship that these Indian natives offered him in the past, and that he is awaiting a suitable conjuncture to return to his lost lordship'. Illustrations of these deities in missionaries' reports and histories underline the point by showing the type of demonic figure - half human, half bestial, winged and frequently horned - which their European readers could recognise and identify at once. Thus, in Diego Muñoz Carmago's *Descripción de la ciudad y provincial de Tlaxcala*, Franciscans have set up a cross and demons are falling from the sky, their eyes and mouths wide open in panic; the gods Tlaloc and Huitzilopochtli are shown staring out of the cellae of their temple in goat-like and demon form in Sahagún's *Historia General*; and the *Codex Maglabecchi* depicts a grotesque and bestial demon encouraging Indians to worship him and practise cannibalism.

After conversion, natives sometimes confirmed the missionaries' point of view. As Pérez de Ribas recorded in 1645:

> This nation was so entombed in darkness that a woman who had been enlightened by the teaching of the Gospel declared and so stated to one of the priests who preached the Gospel: "Father, look across the river. Do you see all those hills, mountains, peaks, and heights there? Well, we revered all of them and there we practised and celebrated our superstitions". The old woman certified that the Devil appeared to them in the form of dogs, toads, coyotes, and snakes – forms that correspond to what he is. Indian principals and fiscales declared as a fact widely accepted among them that at night the sorceresses used to attend certain dances and gatherings with demons and that they returned through the air.

But even after conversion, when the new Christians' perceptions began to change, they did not necessarily do so in ways the Jesuits could altogether approve. When the 'Indians' fell ill, for example, they were told that God had sent the disease as a spur to make them listen to the missionaries who were offering them a way to break free from the dominion of the Devil and, by being baptised, ensure their possible salvation. Their own religion told them they were falling ill because they had offended local spirits, whereas the Jesuit explanation let them see that they were not to blame at all; they were simply, without realising it, victims of a cosmic struggle between God and Satan, and their illness, if it was anyone's fault, was the fault of Satan. It was a view, which could be seen, in frequent battles between missionaries and native shaman-priests. These last were clearly Satan's agents, exercising great authority by reason of their claims to cure illness and appease the anger of the gods and spirits. If, however, the missionary could demonstrate a greater magic, he would demonstrate that his version of the relationship between God and Satan was correct, and thus persuade his native audience to abandon the latter and become worshippers of the former. This is how Father Gabriel Druillettes achieved immense status among the Kennebec Abenaki in the 1640s:

When a particularly virulent epidemic struck, Druillettes gave close personal attention to the sick, and confounded and discredited his rivals when some of those he baptised survived. Consciously aiming to outdo his native shamans, he reversed their traditional social role to his own advantage. Understanding that shamans required payment for their attentions and did not nurse the sick, he eschewed gifts and lavished care, thus undermining the shamans' prestige. Because the Kennebecs believed that beneficent power rested in manifest social concern, his behaviour proved he was more humane than the medicine men. It was the Jesuit's psychotherapeutic skills, as much as his medical ones, which earned him respect. Druillettes's role as a curer, and his resistance to disease and the threats of the shamans, made him a formidable charismatic figure, to whom even the shamans themselves succumbed. One sent for Druillettes when he fell ill and allowed himself to be baptised, and had his drum and charms destroyed, after which he recovered. This act conferred tremendous authority on the Jesuit since the drum was the heart of ritual power, the Abenaki word for shaman means 'sound of drumming', and the word for 'drum' refers to the act of beseeching supernatural powers for help ... Druillettes compared favourably with shamans because he acted as the man of power that the Kennebecs expected him to be, and because he addressed the tribe's sense of crisis and offered solutions that accorded with the Abenaki's opinions of good and evil.

Further south, in Brazil, a similar situation obtained. Friar Vincente do Salvador noted in his *História do Brasil* (1627) that the Devil had lost his control over Europe and had now directed his efforts towards the Americas where the inhabitants of Brazil in particular gave many evidences of being in thrall to Satan, a state of affairs which was still being remarked in the late eighteenth century. Indeed, so ubiquitous did the Devil seem to be that setbacks in missionary efforts, for example, could be and were attributed to his intervention. Thus, Father Jerônimo Rodrigues noted of an incident during a journey towards Laguna, when he and his fellow Jesuits embarked on a small canoe, 'As the Devil so greatly felt our coming into the land which for so many years he had possessed, he ordered, (God our Lord so permitting), that the weight be greatly increased ... and thus the canoe overturned and everything sank to the bottom ... whence with great labour everything was removed, wet and damaged'. Nor was the Devil merely an invisible, malevolent force. He could be seen in many guises. José Martins saw him as a hairy half-caste, fat above the waist, thin below; Manuel João saw him in the shape of a large beetle, Antonia Maria as a small black pig, Luzia da Silva Soares as a stinking he-goat; while José Francisco Pereira, on trial in 1730-31 for working magic, told the court that Satan had appeared to him at various times under the form of a white man, a black man with duck's or hare's feet, a woman with backward-pointing feet, a black he-goat, a donkey, a lizard, a toad, a tortoise, a spotted cat, and a hen with her chicks. What these descriptions show is the original native awareness of being surrounded by a spirit world which manifested itself in Nature, and the post-Christian demonization of that world, which allowed almost constant sensitivity towards spirits to be translated into an almost constant sensitivity towards demons and their controlling master.[72]

Pacts with the Devil, again a notion brought in by European missionaries, also informed and continue to inform aspects of Dominican and Haitian magic; and in Africa, both Christianity and Islam had and continue to have an immense impact on the concept of personalised evil, as can be seen, for example, among the Ewe of Ghana where, as late as the nineteenth century, missionaries regarded their converts and potential converts as living in thrall to Satan. Thus, a German Pietist minister opined that the 'heathen' were 'not merely unknowing, weak and frail people [who] felt their poverty and misery and longed for salvation'. The situation was more complicated than that because 'among them the Devil has had his unlimited kingdom for such a long time that they have become his slaves and have sunk into bestial and demonic conditions. One has to break chains to free them, one has to overcome Satan's bulwarks to save them from the government of darkness and transfer them into the realm of God's dear son'. In consequence, missionaries played up the concept of Satan and Christianity's role in setting people at liberty from him, and thus encouraged a vivid, recurrent, and long-lasting awareness of him which continues into the present, especially among those peoples in Ghana, Liberia, and many other African countries where Pentecostalism and its variants have proved to be particularly successful in their missionary efforts.[73]

Further north, the same kind of diabolism of local religions took place. In his True Relation, George Percy described his experiences in Jamestown, Virginia between 1609 and 1612, and noted that the Algonquins whom the colonists defeated:

Fell into their exorcisms, conjurations, and charms ... making many diabolical gestures with many necromantic spells and incantations ... But neither the Devil whom they adore, nor all their sorceries did anything avail them. For our men cut down their corn, burned their houses and, besides those which they had slain, brought some of them prisoners to our fort.

It was not, however, only the indigenous peoples who had dealings with or experience of the Devil. Satan frequently manifested himself to some of the inhabitants of the Thirteen Colonies, too, in the guise of natural creatures. In 1662, Ann Cole from Hartford, Connecticut, started to show signs of being possessed, and disturbed church services with her fits and peculiarities, as did two other women with her. One of these was arrested on suspicion of being a witch. She did not deny the charge, and confessed a familiarity and pact with the Devil whom she first saw, she said, in the shape of a deer or fawn gambolling around her. In January 1684, a Harvard College tutor noted in his diary that the Devil appeared to him, making a noise like a bird; eight years later, William Branch, aged thirty-three, testified that one night while he was in his bed, 'there was a light all over the chamber like fire, and there came a thing upon me like a little boy, with a face as red as fire'; and a teenage boy from Bradford, Connecticut, (known as a thief and a liar), said that the Devil appeared to him in the shape of a fox and threw him into a pig-sty. The same year, Nathaniel Wyatt's maid had a fit while she was working in the yard, and claimed to be possessed by the Devil whom she had seen in the form of a black cat in the hen house. Under subsequent questioning, she said she also saw him as a white dog, then as three women whom she refused, though pressed, to call witches. The Cole and maid cases are interesting, since both purported to be cases of demonic possession, in as much as the first woman may have been genuine, whereas the second was almost certainly a fraud – as, indeed, some people openly said at the time. Other New Englanders testified that the Devil might appear as a white calf, a black dog with eyes in his back, or in the shape of a black man, this last being his most common guise in the Salem testimonies where he is said to be 'like a black man' sometimes wearing a hat, further detailed as a high crowned hat.

Local contexts and local circumstances, of course, helped shape the details of these appearances. The settlers were surrounded by indigenous peoples whom they regularly referred to as 'black', and therefore it is not surprising to find Increase Mather overtly linking them with demons, 'whose Powawes used all their sorceries to molest the first planters here'. But the local Indians were not the only ones who were deemed to be a kind of diabolic threat to the colonists. Demons, he said, were like 'vast regiments of cruel and bloody French dragoons, with an Intendant over them, overrunning a pillaged neighbourhood', with which two similes he not only summed up many of the local tensions which helped to produce the notorious outbreak of witch trials in Salem, but also encapsulated the feeling of being under siege and fighting a battle for God against the encroaching forces of the Devil, a feeling which characterised the particular religious confession of the region. As John Demos expressed it, 'witches – Satan – God's overarching "providence" – the warfare of opposing spiritual kingdoms – New England as an especially important battlefield: key strands, all, in a highly stretched and broadly shared web of associations'.[74]

Travellers and missionaries, then, took with them certain preconceptions of how evil worked in the world and what its manifestations should look like. In India, Central and South America, reinterpretation of indigenous deities in conformity with European expectations was made easier because the natives personified their deities in statues whose distinctive features readily enabled Europeans to see them as demons or forms of Satan. In North America where these visual representations were not found, the spirit world was nevertheless immediate and sensible to its worshippers, and both colonists and missionaries thus made a slightly different connection with their own culture, turning to the phenomenon of witchcraft and its demonic familiars, who so often appeared in the forms of animals, to explain to themselves what they felt was happening around them. In Europe, the Devil was a potent force for evil, who may have operated for the most part invisibly, but whose effects could be seen in natural disasters and personal damnations. When he did appear, he took a multitude of forms, but preferred the human since that was initially less frightening and therefore laid his intended victims more open to his allure and seductive persuasions. Hence in the North American colonies he was more likely to betray his presence through witchcraft and possession than via the visual images so blatantly put on show in other American and in Indian temples.

Increasing familiarity with statues, however, took the edge off such reinterpretation, and once the eighteenth century had set in, the impulse to see Indian religions in demonic terms had weakened considerably. There were similar regressions in Europe. Confessional wars and rivalries had sharpened participants' sense of evil to a remarkable pitch of acuity, and their ability to see and feel demonic presences had perhaps never been more remarkable. In many religious confessions God Himself had become frightening, a looming patriarchal figure full of prohibitions, a strait-jacket for the soul, and His enemy Satan had grown large in proportion. But once the vicious wars of the first half of the seventeenth century had begun to cease, and their aftermaths had lost their immediacy of pain and suffering, and once the intensive waves of witch-prosecutions during the same period began to die down, certain intellectual debates involving the nature of God, evil, and the material universe stated to make themselves felt in a wider public than that of the proponents and their interested circles. Descartes proposed that God created the universe but then withdrew from His own creation and left it to function by itself. If one accepted this, what place was there for the Devil? Was he also part of the created universe, left there to wreak havoc upon humankind, unchecked; or had he been relegated to a hellish world of his own, from which he could not emerge, as Balthasar Bekker suggested in his *De Betroverde Weereld* (1691); or had he entered the human mind at some stage, a figment to explain disaster or ill-fortune or human wickedness, as Daniel Defoe seems to imply in the second part of his *Political History of the Devil* (1726)? Those devoting their lives and attention to the sciences increasingly left God out of their equations if they could and gradually a rift opened up between what the learned and their admirers chose to believe, and the beliefs and mores of the bulk of the uneducated society which, on the whole, continued to behave and believe in much the same way it had always done – a fragmentation of society, which threatened to leave its diverse parts speaking different intellectual languages and therefore in danger of not understanding one another. It was a rift symbolised, perhaps, by the withdrawal of the aristocracy and their learned satellites from living in society to living in their own enclave – the Court at Versailles instead of their country chateaux, the New Town in Edinburgh instead of the Old City tenement-lands – and by the separation of town from country dweller, most evident in England during its industrial revolution.

For the educated, Satan became a figure in a wider battle, that between defenders of the proposition that non-material worlds and entities existed and interacted with the material world and its inhabitants, and those who regarded the reality of non-material worlds and entities as unimportant or irrelevant in their increasing emphasis on research into the material universe. There was also a note of snobbery in the writings of the latter. 'Superstition' turned into another word for 'irrationality', and was applied to beliefs and practices current among peasants and the unlettered in general: witness, for example, the title of a book by Pierre le Brun, *Critical History of the Superstitious Practices which have seduced the People and embarrassed the Learned, with the Method and Principles for distinguishing Natural Effects from those which are not* (1702). Anti-Catholic and anti-clerical propaganda, too, masqueraded as history, as the beliefs and practices of an earlier Europe were dubbed 'superstitious' in contrast with the 'rationalism' which was now deemed to have supplanted them among right-thinking people – a skewed and negative legacy which lingers on today.

Not that the proponents of the new 'rationalism' had everything their own way, at least, not without a fight. Religious groups such as the Methodists, Moravians, Behmenists, and Swedenborgians preached a world dominated by both God and Satan, and even the French, among whom the decline of traditional views on this cosmic division can be said to have started, continued to be fascinated by witchcraft during much of the eighteenth century, publishing no fewer than 122 titles on the subject by clerics, magistrates and doctors – just the professions who had taken an active interest in witchcraft, demonology and the operations of preternatural entities during the previous two centuries. Thus, in 1717 an anonymous writer published a defence of the older modes of perception: *Dogmatic and Moral Discourse on the Temptations of the Demon: where it is shown by Scripture and the Fathers of the Church what is his Force, the Extent of the Power of the Spirits of the Shadows, the Excess of their Fury, and their different Artifices against Men, and the sure Means of Protecting oneself against them*; while in 1725, a physician produced a reinterpretation of the notion of the Devil as an interventionist in the workings of the physical world, proposing instead that he was a shadowy tempter who concentrated on putting ideas and images into people's minds and thereby tricking them into behaving ill: *Letters to several of his Friends on the Subject of Magic, Acts of Harmful Magic, and Sorcerers: where he gives explanations of the most surprising Effects usually attributed to Demons, and shows that their guiding Spirits often play no part in them*. But if the Devil had not disappeared entirely from everyone's discourse, he was retreating into the human psyche and beginning to take up residence there, envisaged no longer as a spirit raging through the world, but as a producer and manipulator of immoral impulses.

The enthusiasm for providing 'natural' explanations for events, which had hitherto been seen under the light of preternatural or even supernatural happenings can be illustrated by Jean-Baptise de la Chapelle's monumental work, *Le ventriloquiste, ou l'engastrimythe*, published in 1772. He begins with the long-debated Biblical case of the witch of Endor and the ghost of Samuel whose voice, says La Chapelle, was undoubtedly produced by ventriloquism. This art of 'stomach-speaking' owes nothing to demons and everything to technique, a technique which can be learned by anyone – as he illustrates with two anecdotes, one about a Viennese baron, the other about a grocer called Saint-Gille, both contemporaries of La Chapelle. Saint-Gille invited La Chapelle to his home in February 1770, and there the two men began their conversation about the art:

M. Saint-Gille asked me to a little room on the ground floor, (what those in the trade call a back-shop), and each of us occupied a corner of a little fireplace which warmed us, with a table beside us. We were alone. My eyes did not leave his face, which I saw almost continuously from the front.

For about half an hour he had been relating to me some extremely comic scenes arising from his talents as a ventriloquist, when, in a moment of silence on his part and of distraction on my own, I heard myself called, very distinctly, with the words "M. l'Abbé de la Chapelle", but from so far off, and in such a strange voice that all my entrails were disturbed. As I was warned, I said to him, "I believe that you have just spoken to me ventriloquially". He responded only with a smile; but, as I was indicating the direction of the voice which seemed to me to come from the roof of a house opposite, I heard, through the floor of the room above the one where we were, quite distinctly, and with the same character and tone as that which had just caused me such surprise, "It is not from that direction"; and then the voice seemed to come from a corner of the room in which we were conducting our experiment and observation, as though it had emanated from the very midst of the earth.

Not, in fact hostile to religion – on the contrary, La Chapelle wanted to defend it by purging it of the tendency to assign demonic causes to what he saw as natural phenomena – his book nevertheless provided a popular fillip to the cause of those for whom cries of priestly fraud and trickery were becoming a clichéd response to anything in religion which smacked of the preter- or supernatural; and this theme of priestly fraud and popular superstition was carried forward in studies of the ancient world and of contemporary peoples beyond the magic circle (so to speak) of Europe and North America, which mingled overt anti-Catholicism and studied racism in a brew unmistakably tasting of the nineteenth century.[75]

The urge to demote the non-'natural' elements of religion, however, was not confined to learned works. It washed through the fiction of the period, too, and we can see a good example of it in Matthew Lewis's novel of 1796, *The Monk*, a story of passion, rape, murder, incest, and the dark superstitions of Madrid during the days of the Inquisition, which ends in a bargain with Satan and the spectacular death of the eponymous hero at the hands of Satan himself. Tempted by a witch to save himself from further torture and the death sentence of the Inquisition, Ambrosio, the renegade monk, opens a magic book and summons Lucifer who appears:

> In all that ugliness, which since his fall from Heaven had been his portion. His blasted limbs still bore marks of the Almighty's thunder: a swarthy darkness spread itself over his gigantic form: his hands and feet were armed with long talons: fury glared in his eyes, which might have struck the bravest hearty with terror: over his huge shoulders waved two enormous sable wings and his hair was supplied by living snakes which twined themselves round his brow with frightful hissings.

The Devil and the monk strike a bargain. In return for his soul, Satan promises to remove him far from the Inquisition's grasp, a pact that Ambrosio makes in the extremity of his terror. Needless to say, however, the Devil deceives him. Once the monk makes over his soul to him, the Devil carries him out of prison but, instead of granting him further liberty, soars high into the air with Ambrosio in his talons, then lets him go and fall to a dreadful death. The melodrama is effective, the moral message apparently clear, and the depiction of Satan based firmly on Mediaeval iconographic tradition. But the fact that the book is a novel and that its action is set in a time and place the reader is invited and expected to despise means that the figure of Satan is not intended to be taken seriously. He has been reduced to a Pollok theatre cut-out in an overblown plot – a far cry from the ubiquitous, frightening demon who terrorised real lives in the previous century, and is little more than part of the machinery of an anti-Catholic rant designed to please a public well-disposed to respond favourably to such crudities.[76]

Not that the older notion and beliefs had disappeared. On the contrary, in Hungary in 1745 an accused witch was asked specifically about her participation in a Sabbat:

Primo: Were you in alliance with the Devil? When did this come about, where, and in what manner? Who provoked you to make this alliance?
Secundo: When alliance with the Devil was sealed, did you deny God? In what manner? And did you worship the Devil? What form did this take? And furthermore,
Tertio: What did you do there? Were you entertained there? And did you take part in such entertainments on several occasions and where? Was this when you had communion with the Devil?

As Owen Davies has shown anent England, 'the idea of the Devil stalking the country promoting mischief continued to be held by not a few Anglican clergymen and was certainly widespread in popular culture and the literature that was produced for it'. Thus, a ballad tells the story of a spoiled rich child who, after one act of disobedience too many, was confined to her room by her parents:

The Devil to her did appear straight,
In human shape and manner like a man;
And then he seem'd to take her by the hand.
He said, "Fair creature, who do you lament?
What is it fills your heart with discontent?"
She said, "My parents cruel are to me,
And keep me here to starve in misery".
He said then, "If you will be rul'd by me,
Revenged of them thou shall quickly be."

The promised revenge was death by poison. Coroners' courts retained a clause relating to motive for committing a crime, 'being moved and seduced by instigation of the Devil', until well into the nineteenth century; and late eighteenth-century examples of young persons being asked whether they understood what an oath is, reveal that they were acutely conscious of the Devil's being a real and active entity who was keen to promote sin (and therefore crime). Accused persons in both the eighteenth and the nineteenth century were prepared to offer the Devil's instigation or temptation as a perfectly serious explanation for their actions, as in the case of William Tustin who in 1817 was found to have three stolen geese in his oven, and pleaded that the Devil had bewitched him to do it: or of a woman tried for infanticide in 1838 who told the court that Satan had commanded her to kill her child. In 1775, too, several remarkable cases of demonic possession gripped the attention of Bristol, all of which were recorded by one William Dyer in his diaries, and also by Dyer's friend, Henry Durbin, whose narrative was published after his death in 1800. The details of these cases are striking, but entirely familiar to anyone who is acquainted with earlier descriptions of possessed behaviour:

> The doctor thought her incurable and would take no fees. She used to bark four or five times, and then crow somewhat like a young cock, turning her head from the right shoulder to the left, backwards and forwards twenty times, and yet her neck not swell. I have seen her tongue pulled, as it were, out of her mouth very long, then doubled down her throat; then after having rolled on the ground in great agony, she would go about the house as usual, or sit and sew, barking and crowing all the time. She has continued very well ever since it stopped.

The eighteenth-century German states, too, had sufficient cases of demonic possession to keep exorcists very busy, as we can see from the career of Johann Joseph Gassner (1727-79), a Catholic priest originally from Vorarlburg in Austria, who in a series of diaries during the 1760s and 1770s kept records of those whom he had cured of their possession. Starting with a cure of his own ill health, which he attributed to the influence of an evil spirit, he went on to apply his method to others, first ordering the possessing demon to give some sign that he was indeed occupying the patient's body, and then, after receiving such a sign, exorcising the spirit according to the usual rites of the Church. An engraving of 1775 shows him seated at a table, his right hand placed on a possessed man's head, his left raised in a gesture of command or blessing, and a black dragon-like demon hurtling in the midst of a long airy stream out of the patient's mouth. A monk sits nearby benevolently looking at the patient, while a large crowd of men and women watch the proceedings with a mixture of pleasure and astonishment. But if Father Gassner's career illustrates a widespread willingness to believe that illness might be caused by demonic or diabolic malevolence, it was merely acting within a structure of belief in the active presence of the Devil in everyday life, which continued into the nineteenth century. The priest of Konfeld in the diocese of Trier, for example, felt it both useful and necessary to keep a collection of charms intended to protect their reciter against demonic assault:

> Bethzairle and all evil spirits, spirits human and airy, watery, seeds of fire and earth and all ghosts, I [name] forbid you my bed and the beds of my children. I forbid you in the name of God my house, stables, barns, the flesh and blood of myself, my wife, and my children, our bodies and souls. I [name] forbid you all holes, even nail holes, in my house, stables, barns, everywhere around my house until you ... [illegible] all the little hills and empty all the little brooks, count all the little leaves on the trees and all the stars in the heavens, until the dear day comes unto us when the Blessed Virgin Mary bears her second son. + + + These I forbid you in the name of the most holy Trinity, God the Father + the Son + and the Holy Spirit + Amen.

Such beliefs continued more or less unabated throughout the nineteenth century. In 1890, Getrud Püllen from Giesenkirchen, aged thirty-three, had visions of both the Blessed Virgin and the Devil, and when seeing the latter behaved as though she were possessed, blaspheming and vomiting coins, needles, steel pen nibs, and bloody bile. It was a phenomenon not confined to the German states, for in the later years of the same century, in the French parish of Boulleret, people vomited blood and claimed to have been wounded by the Devil who appeared in the guise of a man dressed in black. Pacts with the Devil also continued to be made. Between 1680 and 1789 at least twenty-nine such cases appear in the records of Sweden's highest legal institution, all of which strongly suggest that among the common people at least belief in the Devil's powers was as strong as ever. So too in Spain. In 1742 Angela Jiménez, a widow, was brought before the Inquisition, charged with being under suspicion of making use of superstitious practices and entering into a pact with the Devil. In 1751 a Franciscan friar, Brother Judas Morales, actually signed a pact, which was produced in court; and at the beginning of the nineteenth century, a gipsy called Ana Barbero was accused of practising amatory magic and of making a diabolic pact. In mid nineteenth-century France, an old man told the Comte de Résie, who was recording such things for his book on the occult sciences, that if one wanted to make a pact with the Devil, one should go to a cross-roads where there was a wayside cross, sacrifice a black hen, and invoke Satan who would then appear, sometimes visibly, sometimes not. This practice seems to have been widespread and relatively common, at least once with near fatal results, for when the widow of a shepherd who was supposed to have been killed by Satan read out an invocation she found among her late husband's effects, the Devil suddenly appeared and attempted to force her to sign a pact with him. She resisted heroically for three days, but her screams and wailing frightened her neighbours who did not venture near her until her ordeal was over.[77]

All this, of course, was taking place against a background of official disapproval, some of it learned, some of it secular, some ecclesiastical. Debunking belief in the Devil, possession, witchcraft, and indeed much that had to do with any form of spiritual existence was, in Roy Porter's phrase, a 'crusade of the radical enlightenment', along with a specific target which Voltaire and his fellow-travellers and supporters had in their sights – Roman Catholicism. The eighteenth century debated the subject and produced various compromises between Protestant Christianity and 'scientific' atheism; the nineteenth century banished God to the sterile formulations of lip-service, and the Devil to the close prison of the individual psyche where, from the mid century onwards, the new priesthood of the couch, psychiatrists and their clinical assistants, could visit him, analyse him, challenge his existence, and, having 'cured' his human host of any notion that he was anything more than a figment of degenerationist pathography, move on to the next patient, like penny visitors peering at the mad in their Bethlehem cells. The most influential centre for the development of theories pertinent to this subject was the Salpêtrière in Paris under the leadership of Jean-Martin Charcot (1829-93) who was convinced that hysteria, originating as he saw it in the patient's weak neurological system, played a major role in demonic possession. His study on the portrayal of demoniacs in European art was written to illustrate this very point, as we can see from his remarks on Adam van Noort's picture of St Clare delivering a Pisan woman from five demons:

> The possessed woman is in the agitated phase. Half upside-down, she is supported by two men. On one side, her right foot rests on the ground and on the other, her head rests on the chest of one of those assisting her. The sick woman seems to be striving to lift her torso in an arc, an attitude which, as we have seen, is common among hysterics. The right hand of one of her supporters presses against the side of her stomach and resists this movement. Her head is stretched out, her mouth open, her eyes distorted upwards. Lastly, we shall draw attention to the gesture of her left hand, which opens her dress, completely uncovering her breast. This is a characteristic feature of attacks of hysteria.

Charcot's work was continued by one of his pupils, Pierre Janet (1859-1947) who coined the terms 'disassociation' and 'subconscious', publishing the fruits of his research in 1892 under the title, *The Mental State of Hysterics*, while another pupil, Sigmund Freud, went on to develop a particular form of psychotherapy, having been much influenced not only by Charcot, but also by an Austrian psychiatrist, Josef Breuer (1842-1925), who had developed *his* psychological theory of hysteria after treating a twenty-one-year-old hysteric, Bertha Pappenheim, to whom he referred in his study of the case as 'Anna O'. Bertha exhibited her symptoms over a period of three and a half months, from mid December 1880 to the beginning of April 1881. These consisted of paralysis of her right side, visual problems, temporary deafness, incomprehensible speech, hallucinations, and irregular behaviour, some of which, at least, can be correlated with those of people suffering from possession. Freud, of course, went his own way and invented a battery of technical terms to describe aspects of the hidden personality which he claimed to be analysing – unconscious, id, ego, superego, death wish, and so forth – so that by the time the twentieth century began, demonic possession had been wrested from the charge of the Church and delivered into the hands of the *bien pensants* who were only too keen to dub it 'hysteria' and use it as the thin end of a wedge to try to crack open and break the rock on which the Church was built.

Meanwhile, art and literature took advantage of the growing scepticism, or claim to scepticism, among the lettered classes to turn the Devil into a character in the Gothic horrors which became fashionable during the eighteenth and nineteenth centuries, or, with that moral frivolity masquerading as high-minded earnestness which is so typical of certain coteries of the same period, to adopt him as a kind of anti-hero. French novels such as *Le diable boiteux* (1707), *L'histoire et imaginations extravagantes de Monsieur Oufle* (1710), *Le diable amoureux* (1772), or *Vathek* (1782) lampooned both magic and the Devil, while the Scots poet, Robert Burns, treated Satan as a comic figure, fit for a tale or two to frighten children:

Address to the Deil
O thou, whatever title suit thee!
Auld Hornie, Satan, Nick, or Clootie,   [*left-handed*]
Wha' in yon cavern grim an' sooty
Clos'd under hatches,
Spairges about the brunstane cootie,   [*splashes, brimstone, tub*]
To scaud poor wretches!

Hear me, auld Hangie, for a wee,   [*hangman*]
An' let poor, damned bodies bee;
I'm sure sma' pleasure it can give,
Ev'n to a deil,

To skelp an' scaud poor dogs like me,
An' hear us squeal! ...
I've heard my rev'rend Graunie say,
In lanely glens ye like to stray;
Or where auld, ruin'd castles, gray,
Nod to the moon,
Ye fright the nightly wand'rer's way,
Wi' eldritch croon.   [*hollow-sounding screech*]

When twilight did my Graunie summon,
To say her pray'rs, douse, honest woman,   [*respectable*]
Aft 'yont the dyke she's heard you bumman   [*droning*]
Wi' eerie drone;
Or, rustling, thro' the boortries coman,   [*elder trees*]
Wi' heavy groan ...
An' now, auld Cloots, I ken ye're thinkan,
A certain Bardie's rantin, drinkin,
Some luckless hour well send him linkan   [*walking fast*]
To your black pit;
But faith! he'll turn a corner jinkan,   [*dodging*]
An' cheat you yet.

On the other hand, Charles Baudelaire (1821-67) played with the idea of the Devil, toying with images of willing possession, or blasphemously parodying the litanies of the Church, just as possessed individuals were reported to do:

Without ceasing, at my side, the Demon moves restlessly;
He swims round me like an air which cannot be touched;
I swallow him and the sense which turns my lung
And fills it with an eternal, guilty desire.

Sometimes, knowing my great love of art,
He takes the shape of the most seductive of women
And, under the specious excuse of a sneak,
Accustoms my lip to vile love-potions.

This is how he leads me, far from the eye of God,
Gasping for breath and broken with fatigue, to the middle
Of the plains of Boredom, [which are] deep and deserted,

And throws into my eyes [which are] filled with confusion Soiled clothes,
open wounds, And the bloody machinery of Destruction.
(*Fleurs du Mal*: Destruction = no.109).

O thou, the wisest and most beautiful of angels,
God betrayed by fate and deprived of praises,
O Satan, take pity on my long wretchedness.
O Prince of exile, who has been done wrong,
And who, vanquished, always stands up stronger,
O Satan, take pity on my long wretchedness ...

Glory and praise to you, Satan, in the heights
Of Heaven where you reigned, and in the depths
Of Hell where, vanquished, you dream in silence!
Grant that one day my soul, under the Tree of Knowledge,
Rest next to you, at the moment when, on your brow
Like a new Temple, its branches spread out.
(*Fleurs du Mal*: *Les litanies de Satan* = no.120)[78]

To be sure, Baudelaire's intentions are complex, his poetic relations with Satan
reflecting a personal tension between his Catholic upbringing, the rampant
scientism of the day which encouraged an easy lapse into atheism, and a sense
(not confined to himself) that evil was not merely a set of internal impulses, but
an external reality which was busy alienating humanity from itself and driving it to
some felt but unseen catastrophe. It is a complexity and an intimation of despair,
which also comes out well in his short prose poem, 'The Generous Gambler' which
first appeared on 7 February 1864. The narrator is prowling the streets of Paris
when the Devil suddenly appears and winks at him to follow. The narrator does so
and finds himself in a subterranean dwelling luxuriously appointed. There he sees
men and women with whom he feels an immediate rapport, recognising in them a
fellow-horror of boredom, 'and the everlasting desire to feel that one is alive'. The
Devil and prowler drink and smoke, the prowler feeling relaxed enough to offer the
Devil a toast, 'To your immortal health, old Goat!' Together they talk, dismissing
modern philosophies as worth little consideration, and then the Devil complains
about the bad reputation he has in every part of the world, saying that he lives in
fear of the day when 'a preacher, more subtle than the rest of his brethren, says
out loud in the pulpit, "My dear brethren, never forget, when you hear people
trumpeting the progress of the enlightenment, that the Devil's finest trick is to
persuade you he does not exist!"' – in fact, a boast disguised as pseudo-timidity.

Baudelaire's Devil is quite right, of course, but he is right in a context which, in the words of J.A. Hiddleston, 'is predominantly pessimistic, and the world [Baudelaire] invokes is one in which order and reason have been replaced by anarchy in both the moral and the physical spheres'. It is, actually, a context applicable well beyond the narrow world of Baudelaire's prose poems, to the nineteenth century in Europe as a whole, in fact, and to western Europe in particular, a Europe to which the saying wrongly attributed to G.K. Chesterton is apropos: 'When men stop believing in God, they don't believe in nothing, they believe in anything'. Loss of belief in, or increase of doubt anent God could thus have two contradictory effects upon belief in the Devil: rejection or commitment.

Rejection was simple. If neither Burns' mockery nor Baudelaire's apparently blasphemous dalliance was to an author's taste, he could either gloss over Satan's existence as too embarrassing to mention, or embrace him with a view to joshing him away. The former was the path taken by the eighteenth-century English hymn-writer, Isaac Watts, who in his *The World To Come, or Discourses on the Joys or Sorrows of Departed Souls at Death, and the Glory or Terror of the Resurrection* (1718) devotes two of the book's fifteen discourses to the punishments suffered by the damned in Hell, but manages to avoid any mention of Satan at all, even though he (Watts) acknowledges the existence and activity of demons. Twee leg-pulling, however, was the choice of John Beard (1800-76) who published an *Autobiography of Satan* in 1872, although one can see that his intention was not to be twee so much as commonsensical. Beard was a Unitarian minister and somewhat radical theologian with an extensive reputation, so much so, indeed, that foreign correspondents were able to reach him if they addressed their envelopes simply 'John R. Beard DD, Manchester, England'. His aim in writing the book was polemical, 'aimed at nothing less than to deal a blow at Traditionalism, Sacerdotalism, and Satanism, which reciprocally evoke and support each other, and which, in a brood of superstitions, have inflicted on our race many of the direst evils under which it has suffered'. In other words, it was largely another anti-Catholic tract.

Satan begins by saying that he is not 'a personal concentration of transcendental vice, wickedness, and woe', but 'a personification of the dark side of humanity and the universe' and with this planted in the reader's mind, he proceeds to assert, ('argue' would be somewhat misleading a term), that belief in a personal Devil has been created and sustained throughout the ages by a combination of fear and ecclesiastical chicanery. We are then taken through the Bible where, says Beard, both 'Satan' and 'possession' can be, and should be, interpreted as metaphors often springing from linguistic misunderstandings or misinterpretations. A similar review of Church history follows, with Rome receiving the lion's share of condemnation: 'The priests, by working with and on the weak and bad side of human nature, having made me what I am, naturally employed me for their purposes'. Finally, Satan skips through the controversies of the eighteenth and early nineteenth centuries, the attempts to defend his existence and the denials of it, always, however, directing his readers' attention to Beard's central point – 'I am a product of man's imagination excited and controlled by external nature' – until he bids his readers farewell with the repeated refrain, 'Great Pan is dead!' and the observation that 'you have become adult, and henceforwards will do far better without me than you did under my inspiration'.[79]

Mockery, flirting, dismissal: these by and large turn out to be the principal mechanisms which the eighteenth and nineteenth centuries used to cope with their determination that the Devil should not exist, their hope that he did not, and their latent fear that perhaps, after all, he might. Particularly successful at reducing him to a cosy figure of legend were British folklorists, the collectors (and sometimes, one suspects, the inventors) of country traditions and ear-catching whispers of supposedly long-standing local beliefs. Hence 'legends' about the Devil's digging a dyke in the north face of the Sussex Downs, because he was annoyed by the piety of the villagers north of the Downs, and wanted to let in the sea to drown them; or the Devil's dying of a cold caught on Stourton Moor in Devon, and being buried under the village cross; or the Devil's leaving his footprints in stone near the Lancashire village of Pendleton as he strode across the moors to destroy Clitheroe Castle. Similar stories can be found elsewhere, of course. Iceland tells us that Christ, St Peter, and the Devil were once walking beside the sea. Christ spat on the water and created the halibut; St Peter spat and created a lumpsucker, not as noble a fish as the halibut; but when the Devil tried the same, he made the jelly-fish, a quite useless creature. In the eastern Alps, he appears to travellers on Twelfth Night at crossroads, in the shape of a hunchbacked dwarf, and asks them seven questions, and if they answer correctly without saying 'yes' or 'no', he gives them a treasure.

Still, one cannot dismiss every story or tradition as dubious because of its suspect origin or unconvincing detail. The magical tradition, for example, is strong and very long-lasting, and many a surviving tale or belief 'discovered' and recorded by anthropologists or folklorists actually never disappeared, its use or importance or validity remaining strong throughout the passing of centuries, and thus never actually standing in need of being 'discovered'. Its apparent disappearance is the result of the lettered classes' ending their dialogue with everyone else and cantering after scientific gods, leaving a living tradition to be nurtured and continued in their absence until the learned or curious stumble across it and publish it as part of a set of oddities. The nineteenth-century folklorist was, in fact, a collector in the manner of contemporary entomologists: track down an unusual story in the wilds of nowhere, capture it in a net of words, and pin it to a page for the amusement of passing readers and the instruction of enthusiasts in this branch of study.

Beyond Victoria's home shores, however, traditions were more vibrant and therefore less quaint. In Estonia, for example, the Devil maintained a long and constant presence in everyday consciousness. In 1894 Mats Jäger was met on the road, in the middle of the day, by a very tall woman dressed in white, who would not let him pass. Mats reacted stereotypically with the adjuration, 'If you are a Christian, step out of my way and let me pass. If you are Satan, begone!' whereupon the woman withdrew and vanished. This, then, turned out to be an encounter with a ghost, but people were just as liable to meet the Devil himself in a pub or on a pitch-black road. When they did, they saw him as unnaturally short; big, ugly, and old; extremely fat; remarkably thin; black – but always, under these circumstances, as a man. He could, however, appear as a woman or take the form of a coachman, a soldier, and so forth. When he was not seen in anthropomorphic form, he might appear as an animal such as the usual dog, cat, horse, or goat, or any one of nearly fifty non-human shapes:

> One crone said that this is a true story that happened in Korgepalo. A man went to the barn. The door of the barn was open and something like a goat walked there across the floor: tap, tap, tap! and walked over the feet of the man. The man shouted, "What?" Then he started to read the Lord's Prayer. But the animal licked the man with its tongue. This was the Devil himself. The man often read the Bible; he was there in the barn reading the Bible. Then the Devil came from the top of the oven, took the Bible and threw it into the fire.

In short, Estonian tradition says that anyone can meet the Devil, and the Devil has a place in everyone's life, a living legacy which can be seen elsewhere in Europe, though often hidden from outsiders who, it is felt, might not understand or be sympathetic to its survival.[80]

So, taking Europe as a whole, we have a continuation, inherited from the eighteenth century, of active belief in and encounters with Satan or his demons, masked by official denial and embarrassment in many quarters. But exorcism even now continues to be a necessary and powerful tool in countering aspects of human experience that used to be called 'possession'. On 15 August 1972, Pope Paul VI suppressed the minor orders of porter, lector, exorcist, and acolyte, but suppression does not mean abolition and exorcists have continued to function as they always did, but as priests specially trained for and committed to this dangerous work. Father Gabriele Amorth (1925-), for example, acted until recently as the exorcist for the diocese of Rome and, like all priestly exorcists, advocates caution as well as boldness in approaching cases of possession. During his period in office, he says, nearly 50,000 cases were brought to his attention, and yet only 84 of these individuals turned out to be authentically possessed. 'It is essential not to confuse demonic possession with ordinary illness', he told Gyles Brandreth during an interview in 2001. 'The symptoms of possession often include violent headaches and stomach cramps, but you must always go to the doctor before you go to the priest'.

An Anglican exorcist, Donald Ormond, took much the same attitude in another interview:

> In the Church of England, and in churches based on the Church of Rome, you require the permission of a bishop before an exorcism can be performed ... [and] I should explain that apart from permission from my bishop, I do nothing without the full knowledge of members of the medical profession, and if possible in the presence of a doctor.

The two men were also clear, (as indeed one might expect), that the Devil is no figment of the imagination, but a reality, and a very dangerous one. 'I do think a tremendous harm was done when the Church ceased to teach about the Devil', Dr Ormond observed, 'because therein lies his strength. If nobody believes in his existence he has the power to do anything'. Likewise, in answer to Brandreth's question about the ritual of exorcism, Fr Amorth spoke in a matter-of-fact way, as though the existence of demons and Satan were something to be taken for granted:

> Demons are wary of talking and must be forced to speak. When demons are voluntarily chatty, it's a trick to distract the exorcist. We must never ask useless questions out of curiosity. We must interrogate with care. We always begin by asking for the demon's name.
> And does he answer? I ask.
> Father Amorth nods.
> Yes, through the patient, but in a strange, unnatural voice. If it is the Devil himself, he says, "I am Satan" or "Lucifer" or "Beelzebub".

The increasing need for exorcists can be gauged from Fr. Amorth's own figures – 'Fifteen years ago there were twenty Church-appointed exorcists in Italy. Now there are 300' – and with that need there has also emerged an army of charlatans, 'spell-breakers' of one kind and another who charge large sums and affect little or nothing. Cashing in on a trend is not in the least new, of course. The interesting question is why the Modern Period should have witnessed such a trend. Michael Cuneo suggests that possession and exorcism in the USA may have become particularly noticeable during the mid 1970s as a result of popular entertainment with *The Exorcist* (1973 film) and *Hostage to the Devil* (1976 book) playing major roles in firing popular imagination and moulding the expectations of at least some exorcists themselves:

> Although he might not care to admit it, the priest-exorcist is also operating in the shadow of the popular media. Those sacrificial Jesuits immortalised by William Peter Blatty, those embattled hero-priests risking life and limb and dignity in Malachi Martin's Hostage to the Devil – these are the mythic figures, the pop cult icons that real-life priest-exorcists are forced to contend with. Their stories, their fictionalised narratives, constitute the inevitable standard against which [some American exorcists], at some level, sooner or later, measure their own performances.

This certainly has a large element of truth in it as far as it refers to North America and Western Europe, but one must not leave out of account certain forms of evangelical Christianity, which lay emphasis upon both the figure, and influence of Satan, and emotional engagement in the expression of one's faith. Bill Ellis has traced the influence of some Pentecostalist movements in the USA which, with their strong condemnation of any form of magic, no matter how trivial, their consequent demonization of folklore, and their innate tendency to value intense personal religious experience over official Church teachings, led their members into strange byways wherein, for example, according to the highly influential theories of Kurt Koch, author of such books as *Between Christ and Satan* (1962), *The Devil's Alphabet* (1970), and *Occult Bondage and Deliverance* (1970): and H.A. Maxwell Whyte, founder of a Charismatic movement in Toronto and author of *The Power of the Blood* (1959), parents' participation in any practices deemed 'magical' was deemed to lead to mental disorders in their children, and was therefore a form of occult child abuse. What practices did these people have in mind? Consulting or raising spirits by means of the Ouija board, even in fun, was one. Some participants claimed they had been inspired to do so by seeing *The Exorcist*, but their experience could easily become unpleasant. Edmond Gruss found that half the students at his Baptist-run college had either used the board themselves or knew someone who had done so, and he relates what happened when four students, after attending church, retired to their room, lit candles, and called up spirits with their board:

[After a while] they became quite bold and said, "May we have Satan in our presence". Nothing happened, but the pointer began to go in circles. All of a sudden the pointer flew out of their hands and went off the table. They put it back on the board and asked if Satan was present. The indicator went to YES. They asked several questions and became more frightened, as the answers were too accurate for comfort. The young man stated that fear gripped them all, as the candles dimmed, and a feeling of evil pervaded the room. One of the fellows threw his pocket New Testament on the Ouija board, only to have it scoot off in a different direction. They all joined in prayer at this point, asking for the evil presence to leave ... This experience ended their use of the Ouija board.

The combination of certain religious confessions' attributing many mental and physical illnesses and disabilities to the operation of evil spirits, and the explosion during the 1970s in particular books promoting these ideas and offering a variety of remedies largely based on psychiatry and exorcism, also happened to coincide with a conscious movement in society aimed at highlighting and combating the sexual abuse of women and small children, a coincidence from whose fertile soil sprang the belief that there existed parents who were binding their children to Satan through demonic ritual, blood sacrifice, and sexual abuse – a belief intensified in the 1980s by the publication of books purporting to be the accounts of children (now adults) who had survived these experiences and were 'remembering' them via dreams, and certain psychotherapies whose techniques and expectations themselves owed much to blind trust in this type of story. All these reports helped to reinforce the conviction, bolstered by overarching myths and assiduously spread by the media, and conferences of committed professional physicians and sociologists, that there existed conspiracies involving groups of individuals (small groups at first, then, it was alleged, whole swathes of the population) who were being Satanically inspired to corrupt and the overthrow existing Christian society. As the *Sunday Pictorial* informed its readers on 28 October 1951:

There are many men and women in Britain today who delight in wickedness and who, subscribing to the cult of Black Magic, take part in unbelievable debauchery ... 1. Black magic is Not practised by a few crazy individuals. IT IS THE CULT OF MANY ORGANISED GROUPS. 2. Most of the men and women involved are not only sane – THEY ARE HIGHLY INTELLIGENT. 3. They include people who are nationally and internationally famous. A revival of witchcraft is sweeping the country, and people must be warned against it.

Testimonies from Christian converts who had once, according to their own assertions, taken part in the worship of Satan fed the media, which in turn fed the public appetite for sensationalism. Doreen Irvine was one such convert who had had sixteen demons expelled from her during a period of seven months. According to her account, *From Witchcraft to Christ* (1973), her troubles had begun one day in the mid 1950s when two girls in the strip-club where she worked approached her, who told her they were Satanists and invited her to join them. She was taken, she said, to a temple where a throned man representing Satan received a lengthy adoration from thirteen black-clad, hooded figures. Impressed by what she had witnessed, Doreen later allowed herself to be initiated into the sect at an elaborate ceremony attended by 8,000 people:

> Two priests disappeared behind the black drapes ... and returned with the sacred white cockerel. Its neck was broken ... and its blood caught in a silver cup. More chants and prayers to Satan followed ... The chief Satanist approached me and made an incision in my left arm, and my blood was caught in the cup that contained the blood from the slain bird ... I dipped my finger in the mixed blood and signed a real parchment, thereby selling my soul to Satan for ever and ever ... The people went crazy, and all kinds of evil scenes followed ... To my surprise I was sworn in as High Priestess.

Whoever wrote this had clearly picked up a few details from popular accounts of a witches' Sabbat, even down to the ridiculously large number of participants. Despite its being patent nonsense, however, the book sold well and similar tales were revived in a variety of tabloid newspapers during the following decade – *The Sunday Sport* (13 March 1988), *The Colchester Evening Gazette* (27 January 1989), *The Sunday Mirror* (21 May 1989 and 25 March 1990) – along with a number of notorious child-abuse cases alleged to be connected with Satanic rites – Nottingham 1986-7, Rochdale, 1989, and Orkney 1991 – stirring the mixture and adding what appeared to be self-authentication to a growing media frenzy. 'By the year 2,000', opined the Bishop of Oxford on BBC 4, 'Satanists will be sacrificing one baby per minute'.[81] Since no Satanists, no Devil-worship, no ritual abuse were ever substantiated after considerable investigation of all these claims, it would be easy to dismiss talk of Satan, demons, possession, and the need for exorcism as mere nonsense the result of fantasy concocted by sick or devious persons, and reported and encouraged by media always alert to what may titillate jaded readers and viewers, and thus sell copies or advertising. In Britain this criticism may have some substance to it; for in a society which has largely decided to turn its back on God, Satan, demons, and possession have become little more than vehicles for a series of delicious *frissons*, interesting because they smack of beliefs long past and discarded, diverting because it is thought they can do no harm. Nothing, perhaps, illustrates more clearly the proposition that, to all intents and purposes, Britain remains stuck in the eighteenth century with a façade of technology added, and that the tabloids and the television offer the equivalent of the earlier printing presses, which sent out Gothic thrills to shiver the spines of the middle and upper classes with pleasurable agitations which could be relied on to disappear once the diversion had been sucked out of them.

It might be argued, too, that elsewhere in the West attitudes may not be altogether different. Victoria Nelson has articulated the situation from an American perspective, notable since the USA is taken to be a set of fundamentally Christian societies.

Today the supernatural grotesque is most readily found in popular entertainments – and in this venue, at the turn of the new century, it is undergoing a profound shift ... Because the religious impulse is profoundly unacceptable to the dominant Western intellectual culture, it has been obliged to sneak in this back door, where our guard is down. Thus our true contemporary secular pantheon of unacknowledged deities resides in mass entertainments, and it is a demonology, ranging from the "serial killers" in various embodied and disembodied forms to vampires and werewolves and a stereotypical Devil ... To give a secular explanation for our fascination with the supernatural grotesque ... It is because our culture's post-Reformation, post-Enlightenment prohibition on the supernatural and exclusion of a transcendent, non-materialist level of reality from the allowable universe has created the ontological equivalent of a perversion caused by repression. Lacking an allowable connection with the transcendent, we have substituted an obsessive, unconscious focus on the negative dimension of the denied experience. In popular Western entertainments through the end of the end of the twentieth century, the supernatural translated mostly as terror and monsters enjoyably consumed. But as Paul Tillich profoundly remarked, "Wherever the demonic appears, there the question of its correlate, the divine, will also be raised".

This appearance of the demonic and the divine coincided not only in waves of popular films, of which *The Exorcist* is merely the most notorious, but also in the creation, apparently intended to be serious and certainly taken seriously by many, of organisations purportedly devoted to the worship of Satan. Of these, the best known is the Church of Satan, founded in San Francisco on Walpurgisnacht, 30 April 1966, by Anton LaVey (1930-97). According to his *Satanic Bible*, (a mishmash of ideas drawn from several sources including Nietzsche, Aleister Crowley, and H.L. Mencken), the Satanist is at liberty to define for him or herself what he means by 'God' and should, if he has correctly understood LaVey's philosophy, in effect worship him or herself as 'God'. Sin is natural to the human condition and should be embraced, not condemned, although certain forms of sin, such as rape or paedophilia, are to be shunned because they transgress the maxim, 'Satanism encourages any form of sexual expression you may desire, as long as it hurts no one else'. There is no after-life and therefore no Heaven or Hell. Self-indulgence in this life on earth, within the prescribed limits, is thus the desirable goal of the Satanist. So the 'Satan' of the Church's title is somewhat misleading, since the movement's rituals are not designed to worship a personification of evil, but to achieve certain specific ends through magical means: to attract someone sexually to you, to increase worldly gain for someone of your choice, or to destroy someone you regard as an enemy. Essentially an atheistic 'church of egocentricity', the Satanic title is partly a gesture of defiance in the direction of conventional Christian confessions, and partly an advertising slogan designed to attract a certain type of individual to the product, a product which might be described as a parody of teenage rebellious play-acting. Indeed, LaVey himself admitted as much, calling his organisation 'showmanship ... nine parts outrage and one part social respectability ... just Ay Rand's philosophy, with ceremony and ritual added'.[82]

If LaVey himself did not take his organisation with particular seriousness, many of his imitators and successors certainly did, perhaps because they were caught up in a maelstrom of euphoria about what seemed to be the limitless possibilities human 'progress' and freedom from traditional constraints which blew up in the 1960s, and threatened (or promised) to sweep everything away and replace it with a terrestrial utopia – a euphoria which was bound by its very nature to be transitory. For the Western twentieth century, while priding itself on its rationality and freedom from the superstitions of the past, was as filled with irrationalities and contra-sensical fears or hopes for the present and future as any century which had preceded it; and within this choking atmosphere, prophecies – religious, sociological, millennarianist, ecological – abounded, seeming to see the immensity of Satan's presence (Capitalism, Communism, Terrorism) overshadow humankind as he and his demon-followers and human agents (Jews, Freemasons, Communists, Terrorists) pursued their great end of bringing about the destruction of the present order. As Eugen Weber expressed it, "Rationalism did not mean rationality; secularism easily adjusted to magic, mysticism, and astrology; and a diet of second-hand, second-rate religion-substitutes created more demand for religious revival and revitalisation'.

The concurrence of the demonic and the divine in such frenetic circumstances should therefore, *pace* the rationalists and the media, not come as any surprise, and we have a good example of this conjunction in the memoirs of Sister Lucia de Jesus dos Santos, one of three shepherd children to whom the Blessed Virgin appeared near the Portuguese town of Fátima between May and October, 1917. Among other visions, the children were granted a sight of Hell, which made a deep impression, as well it might:

> Our Lady showed us a great sea of fire which seemed to be under the earth. Plunged in this fire were demons and souls in human form, like transparent burning embers, all blackened or burnished bronze, floating about in the conflagration, now raised into the air by the flames that issued from within themselves together with great clouds of smoke, now falling back on every side like sparks in a huge fire, without weight or equilibrium, and amid shrieks and groans of pain and despair, which horrified us and made us tremble with fear. The demons could be distinguished by their terrifying and repulsive likeness to frightful and unknown animals, all black and transparent. This vision lasted but an instant. How can we ever be grateful enough to our kind heavenly Mother, who had already prepared us by promising, in the first Apparition, to take us to heaven? Otherwise, I think we would have died of fear and terror.[83]

To those who have reservations in the face of this, Keith Fernandino's observation may be apposite: 'If one concedes the existence of at least one supernatural spirit-being, God, there is no logical basis for denying the possibility that other spirits, albeit of a different order, may also exist'; while for those who still feel an inclination to scoff, Fr Gabriele Amorth may perhaps be allowed a final word: 'Remember, when we jeer at the Devil and tell ourselves that he does not exist, that is when he is happiest'. So maybe if Satan were ever to be interviewed and asked whether he actually exists and, if so, what he thought was his greatest achievement, he could gesture towards the twentieth century and the start of the twenty-first, and reply with the epitaph of Sir Christopher Wren in St Paul's Cathedral, *Si monumentum requiris, circumspice*: 'If you are asking about a record of what I have done, look around you'.

Notes

Chapter 1

1. Ferrazzi, *Autobiography of an Aspiring Saint*, trans. A. Jacobson Schutte, (Chicago & London: University of Chicago Press 1996), 25-6. On hairiness, see Russell, *Lucifer*, 68, 225. One of Satan's many nicknames was 'Old Hairy', *Ibid.*, 66.
2. Roberts,*The Earliest Semitic Pantheon*, 145-64. Bottéro, *Religion in Ancient Mesopotamia*, 45-7, 48-51, 87. Quotation, *Ibid.*, 57.
3. Spell: Frankfurter, *Evil Incarnate*, 15-26. El's tent: Mullen, *The Divine Council*, 133. Wright, *The Early History of Heaven*, 48. Bottéro, *op.cit.* supra, 86, 221.
4. Tiamat: Russell, *The Devil*, 88-9. Hittites: *Ibid.*, 97-8. Ereshkigal etc.: *Ibid*, 90-2. Jacobsen, *The Treasures of Darkness*, 21. Wray & Mobley, *The Birth of Satan*, 81-4. Toorn, Becking, Horst, *Dictionary of Deities and Demons*, cols. 1170-2, 852. Ben Sira: Stern & Mirsky, *Rabbinic Fantasies*, 183-4. A similar Mesopotamian female demon was Lamashtu who also harmed new-born children as well as pregnant women, and brides and grooms on their wedding-night, Toorn, Becking, Horst, *op.cit.*, col.1604.
5. Russell, *op.cit.* supra, 78-82. Forsyth, *The Old Enemy*, 50-2. B. Watterson, *The Gods of Ancient Egypt*, (London: Batsford 1984), 112-22. Griffiths, *The Conflict of Horus and Seth*, 1-11. Note that in Greek papyri, Seth has gradually turned into a major demon, at once a diminution of his status and yet still a figure of importance, albeit in relation to his newer, evil functions rather than his older, more benign persona, *Ibid.*, 128.
6. Wray & Mobley, *op.cit.* supra, 85-7. The translation from *Yasna* 30 of the Zoroastrian sacred hymns, the Gāthās, is adapted from three sources: (i) W.W. Malandra, *An Introduction to Ancient Iranian Religion*, (Minneapolis: University of Minnesota Press 1983), 40; (ii) M. Wilkins Smith, *Studies in the Syntax of the Gathas of Zarathushtra*, (Philadelphia: Linguistic Society of America 1929, 70-1); (iii) H. Humbach, *Die Gathas des Zarathustra*, 2 vols. (Heidelberg: Carl Winter Universitätsverlag 1959), 1.84-5. Dastur, *The Moral and Ethical Teachings of Zarathushtra*, 14, 19. Boyce, *History of Zoroastrianism*, 199, 232.
7. Pagels, *The Origin of Satan*, 39-42, quotation, 44. Kelly, Satan, 14-18, 21-3, 26-8. Forsyth, *The Old Enemy*, 113-15, quotation, 117. See also Marvin Pope's notes on *Job* 1.6-9 in his translation of *Job*, (The Anchor Bible), (New York: Doubleday & Company 1965), 9-12. Wray & Mobley, *The Birth of Satan*, 52-68. It is interesting to compare this Hebrew *śtn* with Egyptian Seth whose name means 'instigator of confusion', 'deserter', and 'drunkard', Te Velde, *Seth, God of Confusion*, 7.
8. Belial: Toorn, Becking, Van der Horst, *Dictionary of Deities and Demons*, cols. 322-7; Forsyth, *op.cit.* supra, 200-1. Mastemah: Toorn, Becking, Van der Horst, *op.cit.*, cols. 1033-5; Kelly, *op.cit.* supra, 35-41; Pagels, *op.cit.* supra, 53. Wray & Mobley, *op.cit.* supra, 102-5. 'Beelzebub', another

of these names, is in fact a deliberate misspelling of *b'l zbl* = 'Baal the Prince', a deity invoked to cure illness, Toorn, Becking, Van der Horst, *op.cit.*, cols. 293-6: and 'Lucifer' has a complex history and was not identified with Satan until the second or third century AD. Russell, *The Devil*, 188-9.

9. NT names for Satan: Russell, *op.cit.* supra, 229, note 6. Cf. *Babylonian Talmud*, 'Satan the evil prompter and the angel of death are all one', *Baba Bathra* 16a. Satan as ruler of the world: Russell, *op.cit.* supra, 234-6; Kelly, *Satan*, 95-7. Wray & Mobley, *The Birth of Satan*, 115-36. Forsyth, *The Old Enemy*, 266-76. Pagels, 'The social history of Satan', 487-8.

Chapter 2

10. Vivian & Athanassakis, *The Life of Antony*, 65-73, 79-85, 87, 89-91. I have by and large followed their translation, but have chosen to differ here and there. For example, they choose to translate Greek *drakōn* as 'dragon' which in English has too many Chinese associations to be helpful. Homer used the word to refer to a serpentine creature of mythological aspects, but also as an ordinary term for 'snake', and, bearing in mind the evil's later mergence with the snake of Eden, I prefer 'serpent' in this context. When St Antony defies Satan who has taken the form of a black child, Satan runs away at the sound of *his* (St Antony's) voice, not 'frightened by his own cries', as Vivian and Athanassakis translate; and when the saint retreats on Mount Pispir, it is unlikely he occupies deserted 'barracks'. *Parembolē* here surely refers to something much smaller, such as an outpost, to be occupied by only a few soldiers at a time. The date of the *Life* is discussed by B.R. Brennan, 'Dating Athanasius's Vita Antonii', *Vigiliae Christianae* 30 (1976), 52-4.

11. St Justin Martyr, *Dialogus cum Tryphone Judaeo* = *Patrologia Graeca* 6.573. Vivian & Athanassakis, *op.cit.*, 119, 137, 143, 169, 191, 171, 145-7. On the dangers of importing modern notions into the past with a view to explaining it, note Philip Rousseau on the fourth-century AD Egyptian ascetic, St Pachomius. 'The imaginative vigour of any ascesis that involves, among other elements, a demonology is likely to awaken the scientific suspicions of a modern student, but the last thing we are thereby entitled to doubt is that consistency, purpose, and indeed perception lay behind it. "Demon language" involves categories and descriptions which may be hard to translate into moral alternatives', *Pachomius: The Making of a Community in Fourth-Century Egypt*, (Berkeley & Los Angeles: University of California Press 1985), 135. There are interesting parallels between the demonic experiences of St Antony and St Pachomius who were more or less contemporaries. The Devil set demons to attack the latter in the form of dogs; a demon appeared to him in the form of a woman; and he experienced tricks which were not actually illusions – a pit suddenly appeared in front of him, a demon shape-changed into a cock which crowed in his face, and several demons pretending to be a group of workmen tried to distract him by making a lot of noise. See the Bohairic *Life of Pachomius* in A. Veilleux (trans.), *Pachomian Koinonia* Vol.1, Kalamazoo, Michigan: Cistercian Publications 1980, 25, 36, 44. See also Flint, 'The demonisation of magic', 310-15. It is perhaps no coincidence that many of the earliest Christian heresies involved disputation over the exact nature of the relationship between God the Father and God the Son, and whether Jesus had been an entirely corporeal figure, or entirely spiritual, or a combination of the two, in which case the debate centred upon the proportion of these two natures in the single divine figure, and their relationship with each other. Indeed, St Athanasius wrote a short book on *The Incarnation of the Word of God*, directed against the heresy of Arianism which had begun in Egypt during the early fourth century AD and maintained that before His incarnation, Jesus had been a spiritual being created by God the Father and was therefore not co-eternal with the Father. On *phantasia*, see the detailed discussion by Gerard Watson in *ANRW* II.36.7, 4766-808.

12. Nugent, 'Black demons in the desert', 209-11, quotation 210. Frost, 'Attitudes towards blacks in the early Christian era', 5. The reason for the Devil's appearing to St Antony as a black

child seems to be mistranslated in Vivian & Athanassakis – 'as though out of his mind'. This is not the meaning of the text. On perception of images, see Heinrich Institoris, *Malleus Maleficarum*, trans. P.G. Maxwell-Stuart, (Manchester: Manchester University Press 2007), 151-2. Wolfson, 'The infernal senses', 114-24. Quotations from St Antony: Vivian & Athanakassis, *The Life of Antony*, 113 (modified), 115. Ethiopians: Nugent, *op.cit.*, 217-18. Cf. *Acts of Andrew* 22 = James, *Apocryphal New Testament*, 345. St Augustine, *De civitate Dei* 22.8.

13. Lucifer: Kelly, *Satan*, 191-208. Cf. *Apocalypse* 9.1, 'I saw a star fall from heaven unto the earth: and to him was given the key of the bottomless pit'. Forsyth, *The Old Enemy*, 134-9. Wray & Mobley, *The Birth of Satan*, 108-12. Manichaeism: Forsyth, *op.cit.*, 390-5. Lieu, *Manichaeism*, 22-132, 245. Pseudo-Dionysios: *The Complete Works*, trans. P. Rorem, (London: SPCK 1987), 90. Forsyth, *op.cit.*, 359-60. Council of Braga: quotation from J. Pelikan, *The Christian Tradition*, Vol. 1, *The Emergence of the Catholic Tradition (100-600)*, Chicago & London: University of Chicago Press 1971, 136.

14. She'ol: *Ezekiel* 31.14; *Proverbs* 9.18; *Job* 11.8; *Amos* 9.2; *Job* 17.16; *Psalm* 115.17; *Job* 10.21, 22; *Psalm* 17.6 (Vulgate) = 18.6 (AV). Gehenna, ('the ravine of the sons of Hinnom'): 2 *Chronicles* 28.3; Talmud, '*Erubin* 19a; Cf. *Book of John the Evangelist* = James, *Apocryphal New Testament*, 192. Charlesworth, *Old Testament Pseudepigrapha* 1.789; Talmud, *Pesahim* 54a; Charlesworth, *op.cit.*, 909, 574-5, 587-9. See also Lehtipu, *The Afterlife Imagery*, 271-5. *Apocalypse of Paul* 31, 32, 35 = James, *op.cit.*, 542-3. Cf. *Apocalypse of the Virgin* = James, *op.cit.*, 563. *Apocalypse of Peter* 22-4, 26-30 = James, *op.cit.*, 509. *Acts of Thomas* 55 = James, *op.cit.*, 390. Watterson, *Coptic Egypt*, 96, 97.

15. Porphyry, *De abstinentia* 2.38, 39, 40. Notice the admixture of corporeality and incorporeality in Rabbi Jeremiah Ben Eleazar's statement that Adam begot ghosts and male and female demons, Talmud, '*Erubin* 18b. Ancient notions of the differences between soul and body were not the same as ours. Their position is best explained by Outi Lehtipu. '[The ancient philosophers held the view that] the soul was made of matter, such as fire, ether, or atoms. This, however, did not mean they thought the soul was corporeal, for "material" did not mean the same as "corporeal" and "immaterial" did not equal "incorporeal". The soul was different from the body and thus incorporeal, yet it occupied space and was material. Even Plato, who makes a sharp distinction between body and soul, does not understand them as representing different realms (such as physical and spiritual or material and immaterial) but as different parts of one spectrum', *op.cit.* supra, 223-4. This view was contradicted by St Thomas Aquinas, but it has its uses in helping us to understand the complexities underlying the constant questions about the relationship between spirit and matter which occupied much time and debate during the Mediaeval and Early Modern centuries. On Ephesians, see Lash, 'Where do devils live?' 163-5, 170-4. *Isaiah* quotation: Charlesworth, *Old Testament Pseudepigrapha* 2.174. Hall, 'The Ascension of Isaiah', 289-306. On the date, see *Ibid.*, 300.

16. Egypt: Trombley, *Hellenic Religion and Christianisation*, 5-6. Frankfurter, 'Syncretism and the holy man', 352. Asia Minor: Trombley, *op.cit.*, 75, 78-9, 81. Syria offers a similar picture, *Ibid.*, 134-43. Frankfurter, *op.cit.*, 382, 383, 384 (his italics). Flint, 'The demonisation of magic', 324-47. Mango, 'Diabolus Byzantinus', 217, 221. For an exorcism from the Milanese liturgy, which threatens Satan directly on the assumption that he is present in or near the candidate for baptism, by reminding him of his various defeats at the hands of God, see Kelly, *Satan*, 212-14.

Chapter 3

17. Reed, *Fallen Angels*, 49-53, 93-4, 113-16, 149-55, 160-89. The names of the principal demons and the secrets they taught to humans are listed in 1 *Enoch* 69.4-15, part of a section of Enoch known as *The Book of Similitudes*. Knust, 'Enslaved to demons', 442-9. VanderKam, '1 Enoch, Enochic motifs, and Enoch in early Christian literature', 62-87. *Clementine Homilies*, chaps. 13-14, 17 in Roberts & Donaldson, *The Ante-Nicene Fathers*, 8.273.

18. Theodoret, *Graecarum affectionum curatio*, sermon 8 = *Patrologia Graeca* 83.1033. Arab polytheism: Trombley, *Hellenic Religion and Christianisation*, 173-84. Henniger, 'Pre-Islamic Bedouin religion', 9-12. MacDonald, Boratav, Nizami, 'Djinn', 546-9. Chabbi, *'Jinn'*, 43-9. Rippin, 'Devil', 524-7. Doughty, *Travels in Arabia Deserta*, 2.100; 1.53-4. As in Christian tradition, the Devil had or acquired more than one name. Apart from Iblīs, he was also known as 'Azāzīl before he fell from Heaven, and sometimes Hārith. See Awn, *Satan's Tragedy and Redemption*, 25. *Life of Adam and Eve* in Charlesworth, *Old Testament Pseudepigrapha* 2.262. Kelly, *Satan*, 182-6. Russell, *Lucifer*, 54-7. Awn, *op.cit.*, 33-44.

19. Satan-Iblīs: Awn, *op.cit.* supra, 46, 48-56, (quotation, 54), 111-12. Chabbi, *'Jinn'*, 45. Dubois, *Nordic Religions*, 49, 84-5, 79. Woolf, 'The Devil in Old English poetry', 1-2. St Augustine: Kellogg, 'Satan, Langland, and the north', 413-14. Fletcher, *Conversion of Europe*, 228-84, (quotation from Pope Gregory, 254). See also J. Strzelczyk, 'The Church and Christianity about the year 1000, (the missionary aspect)' in P. Urbanczyk (ed.), *Europe around the Year 1000*, Warsaw: Wydawnictwo DIG 2001, 56-61. Jones & Pennick, *A History of Pagan Europe*, 171-2. Russell, *Lucifer*, 70-1. Kelly, *Satan*, 223-4. Battista, 'Blámen, djöflar, and other representations of evil', 2-7. R. North, *Heathen Gods in Old English Literature*, (Cambridge: Cambridge University Press 1997), 52, 54. See also K.L. Jolly, *Popular Religion in Late Saxon England*, (Chapel Hill & London: University of North Carolina Press 1996), 133-8.

20. Herrick, *Imagining the Sacred Past*, 58-8, (quotation, 59), 61. Reff, *Plagues, Priests, Demons*, 67. B & P Sawyer, *Mediaeval Scandinavia*, 101-2. Russell, *op.cit.*, supra, 67-9. Strickland, *Saracens, Demons, and Jews*, 61-93, quotation from the *Life of Guthlac*, 67. Dendle, *Satan Unbound*, 43, 44, 49. Wright, *Art and Antichrist*, 15, 22, 67, 85. Strickland, *op.cit.*, 64, 74, 75, 76. Bede, *Expositio super Divi Jacobi epistolam* chap. 3 = *Patrologia Latina* 93.27. Mellinkoff, *Outcasts* Vol.2, IV.13. Cf. the mosaic of Hell by Coppo di Marcovaldo, dating from the 1260s and 1270s, in the Baptistery in Florence, which shows an immense humanoid with large curved bull's horns and immense snakes issuing from his temples, Lorenzi, *Devils in Art*, 31, 49. Russell, *Lucifer*, 130-3. Link, *The Devil*, 44-77. Satan's presence in a scene is sometimes conveyed by the symbol of a fly as in the painting of the Last Supper by the Master of the Housebook (c.1480-5), and Hans Baldung Grien's *Martyrdom of Saint Sebastian* (1507). See Mellinkoff, *op.cit.*, Vol.2, II.41 and II.14. Kennedy, *The Caedmon Poems*, 206-9, 213. On the date of the drawings, *Ibid.*, 191. Christina of Stommeln: Goodich, *Other Middle Ages*, 164-8.

21. Glaber, *Historiarum libri quinque*, 218-23, 217. Rudolf also recounted the experience of a dying man who was visited by a heretic noblewoman. She was accompanied by 'an innumerable army in deep black clothes and with absolutely horrible faces'. After the woman left, the leader of this 'army' started a conversation with the dying man, tempting him with the prospect of a cure and a long life. Recognising the spirit as Satan, the dying man made a profession of his faith in Jesus and traced the sign of the cross; whereupon the Devil and his attendant demons vanished 'like smoke', *Ibid.*, 178-81. Notice that once again both the Devil and the demons are human-like in appearance, even though their faces are very ugly. Guibert de Nogent, *Monodiae*, 87-8, 113-16, 84, 40-1, 52, 56-7, 110, 64-8, 52-3. Christina of Stommeln: Goodich, *Other Middle Ages*, 164-8. Beguines were members of lay sisterhoods, who devoted themselves to religious lives, but did not take vows and were free to leave and marry.

Chapter 4

22. Cox, *The Devil and the Sacred*, 5-6. Ogden, *The Staging of Drama*, 131, 137. Bevington, *Mediaeval Drama*, 805. Twycross & Carpenter, *Masks and Masking*, 201-16, (Wycliffe quotation, 289). R.E. Surtz, 'Masks in the Mediaeval Peninsular theatre' in M. Twycross (ed.), *Festive Drama*, Cambridge: D.S. Brewer 1996, 80-7. C.F. Strietman, 'The Low Countries' in E. Simon (ed.), *The Theatre of Mediaeval Europe*, Cambridge: Cambridge University Press 1991, 242. Cox, *op.cit.*, 90. Rudwin, *Der Teufel*, 108. C.W. Marshall, *The Stagecraft and Performance of Roman Comedy*, (Cambridge: Cambridge University Press 2006), 127-8. Lecoq cited *Ibid.*, 128.

23. Bevington, *op.cit.* supra, 85, 89, 90: quotation, 105. Twycross & Carpenter, *op.cit.* supra, 214. Jody Enders pertinently issues a warning against interpreting the possible reaction of Mediaeval audiences to the opportunities for slap-stick which demons' cavorting may have offered as the response of children, or of people with an undeveloped sense of the proprieties, *Death by Drama and Other Mediaeval Urban Legends*, (Chicago & London: University of Chicago Press) 2002, 105-17. Bevington, *op.cit.*, 479. Cox, *op.cit.* supra, 69-70. Bevington, *op.cit.*, 678, 479, 701, 261-2. See further Russell, *Lucifer*, 250-73.

24. Voragine, *Golden Legend* 2.205, 224, 193-5; 1.370. Shinners, *Mediaeval Popular Religion*, 324-5. M. Jones, *The Secret Middle Ages*, Stroud: Sutton Publishing 2004, 237-8. Shinners, *op.cit.*, 138, 217, 238-9. Dante, *Inferno*, Canto 34.28-57. Eliot, 'Dante', 251. For a three-headed Trinity, see Strickland, *Saracens, Demons, and Jews*, 244. There is a picture of a three-headed Antichrist in the Harley Manuscript 1527, fol.127r, (mid thirteenth century). See McGinn, *Antichrist*, 148. Colours: Pleij, *Colours Demonic and Divine*, 17, 77-8. Humours: Bartholomaeus Anglicus, *De proprietatibus rerum* Book 4, chaps. 7-11. Hildegard von Bingen, *Causae et Curae*, 72-6. Link, *The Devil*, 68. Note, however, that Alastair Smart rejected the attribution of these frescoes to Giotto and suggested they were by a group of painters of the late thirteenth or early fourteenth century, *The Assisi Problem and the Art of Giotto*, (New York: Hacker Art Books 1983), 233-60. Matteo Chiromono, *Chiose alla Commedia*, ed. A. Mazzucchi, Vol. 1, Rome: Salerno Editrice 2004, 512.

25. It is not clear who 'he' is or who 'they' are at this point.

26. 'He says' seems to be the wording of the clerk at this point, who is indicating what one of the ex-Cathars is telling him. One can see similar phrasing in the remaining items, too.

27. These appear to be the words of 'Andreas' who was one of the 'perfect' Cathars, that is, one of those granted salvation, as opposed to others who were still working towards it.

28. Russell, *Lucifer*, 159-90. McGinn, *Antichrist*, 100-3. Bogomils: Taylor, *Heresy in Mediaeval France*, 62-4, 116-22. Cathars: Lambert, *The Cathars*, 5-12, 23-44. Lansing, *Power and Purity*, 84-6. (I have retranslated the passages from the Latin text given in Lansing's Appendix A because the translation she gives is unsatisfactory). Oddities within the translation reflect the nature of the document. It was recorded by two secretaries, the first of whom cannot resist adding his own explanatory comments, ('that's to say'), while the second retains the immediacy of the interrogation, ('he believes', 'he says').

29. Lambert, *Mediaeval Heresy*, 105-46. Thouzellier, *Catharisme et Valdéisme en Languedoc*, 284-8. Russell, *Lucifer*, 193-206. Boureau, *Satan the Heretic*, 95-106. Strickland, *Saracens, Demons, and Jews*, 42-59, 77-8, 122-30. Martini, *Pugio fidei adversus Mauros et Judaeos*, Paris 1651, 363. Guibert, *Monodiae* Book 1, chap. 26. Trachtenberg, *The Devil and the Jews*, 57-75, 44-7. Strickland, *op.cit.*, 168-72, 173-88, 200-6. Tolan, 'Peter the Venerable on the diabolical heresy of the Saracens', 354-6.

30. Audisio, *The Waldensian Dissent*, 7-10, 45-59. Thouzellier, *Catharisme et Valdéisme en Languedoc*, 27-36. Behringer, 'How Waldensians became witches', 155-7, 182. Muchembled, *A History of the Devil*, 38-44. Eugenius IV: Hansen, *Quellen und Untersuchungen*, 17-18. The two Italian vernacular terms are *stregulae*, which is a diminutive of *stréga*, and *stregones*. Both were in use as early as the fourteenth century and both are derived from the Latin *striga*, 'an evil night spirit', 'a vampire', and then later 'witch'. Behringer, *op.cit*, 182-3.

Chapter 5

31. *Chronica de Mailros*, (Edinburgh: Ballantyne Club 1835), 80.

32. Reading *fauni* for *forni*, 'oven' or 'stove' which is the standard transcription, but does not seem to make particularly good sense.

33. Ginzburg, *Ecstasies*, 63-86. With Minucius Felix, compare Tertullian, *Apologeticus* 7.1; 8.7-8. Gregory IX's letter: *Monumenta Germaniae Historica*, Epistolae seculi xiii, Vol. 1, ed. C. Rodenberg, (Berlin 1883), 432-4 (no. 537). Danse macabre: Clark, *The Dance of Death*, 33 and

illustration opposite 36, (mid fourteenth century). *New York Times* 4 May, 1922. Caciola, 'Mystics, demoniacs, and the physiology of spirit possession', 279-80. Russell, *Witchcraft in the Middle Ages*, 130-1, 126-7, 161-2. Lambert, *The Cathars*, 76-7. Bodin, *Démonomanie*, 1711. Rémy, *Demonolatry* Book 1, chap. 11.

34. Aubri, *Chronica*, 931. Cohn, *Europe's Inner Demons*, 34-6, 56-7. John of Reading: quoted in S.K. Cohn, *The Black Death Transformed*, London: Hodder Headline 2003, 130. Cavendish, *The Magical Arts*, 296-7. Cf. Russell, *op.cit.* supra, 177-9. It is interesting, in view of the way this literary genre developed, that 1307 Templars were accused of worshipping or reverencing an idol, kissing the buttocks of their superiors in the Order, and engaging in illicit sex. Boureau, *Satan the Heretic*, 201-6. Russell, *op.cit.*, 75-7, 116, 135, 193, 206-7. L. Thorndike, *A History of Magic and Experimental Science* Vol. 4, (New York: Columbia University Press 1934), 229. *Errores Gazariorum*: Ostorero, Paravicini Bagliani, Utz Trump, *L'imaginaire du sabbat*, 272-4, 288, 290, 312-14.

35. Reading *supponant*. Ostorero etc. have *suppinant* which is surely a misprint, and the translation 'they turn [the vessel] over' does not fit any of the senses of *suppono*.

36. Tholosan: Ostorero etc., *op.cit.* supra, 357-8, 362-7, 423-5. Marx, *L'inquisition en Dauphiné*, 34.

37. Nider, *Formicarius* Book 5, chap. 3. Le Franc: Ostorero etc, *L'Imaginaire du Sabbat*, 441-4, 456-7. Perhaps the most extraordinary claim made about being transported to a Sabbat comes from Jubert of Bavaria who, at his trial in 1437, said that he and others were brought thither 'in the twinkling of an eye on top of a mule, or horse-shit', Hansen, *Quellen*, 542. *Recollectio*: Hansen, *op.cit.*, 157, 159-63. Muchembled, *A History of the Devil*, 43.

38. Mandrou, *Magistrats et sorciers*, 125-6, 133-7. Rémy, *Démonolatrie*, chap. 14. Aquitaine incident: Florimond de Raymond, *L'Antechrist*, quoted by De Lancre, *op.cit.*, 47. Del Rio, *Disquisitiones Magicae* Book 2, question 16. Cf. Rémy, *op.cit.*, Book 1, chap.17. On the wearing of masks, Rémy says the practice was invariable and done especially to protect the identities of the rich, *op.cit.*, Book 1, chap. 18. Quotation from Rémy, Book 1, chap. 20. On hell-mouths, see G.D. Schmidt, *The Iconography of the Mouth of Hell: Eighth-Century Britain to the Fifteenth Century*, Susquehanna University Press 1995. Lima, *Stages of Evil*, 14-43. Link, *The Devil*, 70-1, 76 (picture). Bodin, *La démonomanie des sorciers* Book 2, chap. 4. Rochelandet, *Sorciers, diables, et bûchers*, 104-5, 107-11. Boguet, *Discours des sorciers*, chaps. 1, 2, 22.

39. See further Davidson, 'Great black goats', 144, 147-8, and the illustrations on pp.150, 153.

40. De Lancre too emphasises the importance felt by the participants of dancing at the Sabbat. 'They say that they go to the Sabbat only to dance, as they always do in the Labourd, going to these places just as they would to a parish celebration', *Tableau de l'inconstance des mauvais anges et démons*, 223.

41. Guazzo, *Compendium*, chaps. 6, 8, 12. De Lancre, *op.cit.* supra, 463, 90-3, 99, 95-6, 398-9. Henningsen, *The Witches' Advocate*, 111, 70, 83. Rudwin, *Der Teufel*, 108.

Chapter 6

42. Rabelais, *Gargantua* Book 4, chap. 13 (translated J.M. Cohen). Jean Lermat emphasises the difference between Rabelais's belief in the Evil Spirit and his dismissal of the Devil of popular religion, *Le Moyen Age dans le Gargantua de Rabelais*, Paris: Les Belles Lettres 1973, 444-56. Murals: Bolvig, 'Mural paintings, oral society, visual linearity', 12-13, 20. Göttler, 'Fire, smoke and vapour', 24-36, 402, quotation p.43. Matheson, *The Imaginative World of the Reformation*, 27. Geisberg, *The German Single-Leaf Woodcut* 2.511. Strauss, *The German Single-Leaf Woodcut* 3.1271. Geisberg, *op.cit.* 1.140; 2.438-40. Alexander & Strauss, *The German Single-Leaf Woodcut* 1.384. Geisberg, *op.cit.*1.205. Cf. Lucan Cranach the Elder on a like subject, *Ibid.* 2.578. Strauss, *op.cit.* 1.259, 310. Oldridge, *The Devil in Early Modern England*, 28, 72-5, and plates 14 & 9. These illustrations to Bateman's pamphlet actually seem to have been cut from designs by Marcus Gheerhaerts the Elder. See E. Hodnett, *Marcus Gheerhaerts the Elder of Bruges, London, and Antwerp*, Utrecht: Haentjens Dekker & Gumbert 1971, 46-8. Strauss, *op.cit.* 3.1335;

2.488. Alexander & Strauss, *op.cit.* 2.450, 628. Strauss, *op.cit.* 2.754; 3.1337. Youngs & Harris, 'Demonising the night', 141-2.

43. Roos, *The Devil in 16ᵗʰ Century German Literature*, 52-60, 109. Midelfort, 'The Devil and the German people', 242. Muchembled, *History of the Devil*, 111-14, 124-9, 131, 137, 139. Cox, *The Devil and the Sacred in English Drama*, 125, 210-11, 84-5, 194, 201-8; 'Stage devilry in two plays', 940-1. Matheson, *The Imaginative World of the Reformation*, 15, 58-9, 83, 91, 92, quotation p.86.

44. *The Realities of Witchcraft and Popular Magic*, 92.

45. Sinclair, *Satan's Invisible World Discovered*, 47, 160-1, 163, 10-16. See also Miller, 'Men in black', 149-54.

46. National Archives of Scotland: Records of the Presbytery of Stirling, *CH2/722/6*.

47. On hallucination and stress, see Bever, *op,cit,* supra, 30-3.

48. Bever, *op.cit.* supra, 82-3. Krause, *The German Single-Leaf Woodcut* 2.554.

49. On stress as a factor in witchcraft, see Bever, *op.cit.* supra, 15-28. See also Maxwell-Stuart, *An Abundance of Witches*, 31-3, 80-2.

50. M.F. Graham, *The Uses of Reform: Godly Discipline and Popular Behaviour in Scotland and Beyond, 1560-1610*, Leiden: Brill 1996, 145, 157, 112, 218.

51. De Lancre, *op.cit.* supra, 234-5.

52. De Lancre, *op.cit.* supra, 129-30.

53. Wier, *De praestigiis daemonum*, Book 3, chap.7. R. Scot, *The Discoverie of Witchcraft*, Book 1, chap.3. Salazar in Henningsen, *The Salazar Documents*, 314-22. F. Spee, *Cautio Criminalis*, question 51.

54. M. Gibson, *Reading Witchcraft: Stories of Early English Witches*, London: Routledge 1999, 190. Bechtel, *La sorcière et l'occident*, 493. Del Rio, *Disquisitiones Magicae* Book 2, question 26, section 5.

55. Krause, 'Confessional fictions and demonology in Renaissance France', 331. Ekirch, *At Day's Close*, 300-23. Cf. Camporesi, *Bread of Dreams*, 92-102. Charms: see C. Hole, *A Mirror of Witchcraft*, (London: Chatto & Windus 1957), 239-40, 241-2.

56. Groebner, *Who Are You?* 81-2.

57. Corstorphine Kirk session records: Scottish National Archives, *CH2/234/1*; Liberton Kirk session records, *CH2/383/1-2*; Synod of Moray records, *CH2/271/2*. On the Devil's appearance as a dog, see Oldridge, *The Devil in Early Modern England*, 59-60. Diabolic re-baptism was not confined to Scotland, of course. In Bamberg, a new witch was re-baptised in company, usually at a brook, when one of those present cast water over her and muttered unintelligible words. She was 'baptised' in the Devil's name and received another name herself. See Lea, *Materials Towards a History of Witchcraft* 3.1168.

58. Bamberg: Lea, *op.cit.* supra, 3.1167. Le Loyer, cited by Bechtel, *La sorcière et l'occident*, 468. Jordannes of Bergamo, *Quaestio de strigis* in Hansen, *Quellen*, 198-9. Andrés de Laguna: see Rothman, De Laguna's commentaries', 562-7. Simms, 'Andrés Laguna', 4-9.

59. Bever, *op.cit.* supra, 139-44.

60. Behringer, *Shaman of Oberstdorf*, 155, 17-21, 22-4, 70-1, 88. Luther, *Table-Talk*, 78, 83. Narwood quotation in Johnstone, *The Devil and Demonism in Early Modern England*, 215. Bever, *op.cit.* supra, 84-5.

Chapter 7

61. Alexander & Strauss, *The German Single-Leaf Woodcut* 2.668.

62. Harrer, *Seven Years in Tibet*, English trans. London: Reprint Society 1955, reprint of 1953 edition, 206-8. Fine, 'Benevolent spirit possession', 103-17. Goldish, 'Vision and possession', 219-21. Tuczay, 'Trance prophets and diviners in the Middle Ages', 216-19, 223-4. Pócs, 'Possession phenomena, possession-systems', 100-4, 109-21. Charm: W. MacKenzie, *Gaelic Incantations, Charms and Blessings*, (Inverness: North Counties Newspaper and Printing and Publishing Co. Ltd 1895), 53.

63. Boguet, *Discours des Sorciers*, chap.1. Camporesi, *Bread of Dreams*, 121, 123. Marthe Brossier: Mandrou, *Magistrats et sorciers*, 163-80. Sluhovsky, *Believe Not Every Spirit*, 61-93: quotation, 87-8. *Rituale Romanum*, 414-15, 423-4, 429. See also G. Romeo, *Inquisitori, esorcisti, e streghe nell'Italia della Contrariforma*, (Firenze: Sansoni Editore 1990), 145-68.

64. Caciola, 'Breath, heart, guts', 27-35. She discusses this at greater length in *Discerning Spirits*, chapter 3. Caesarius, quoted in Caciola, *Discerning Spirits*, 200. See also Oldridge, *The Devil in Early Modern England*, 115, and Almond, *Demonic Possession*, 379-80. Coventry, *Demonic Possession in Trial*, 49. Ekirch, *At Day's Close*, 139-40. J. Millar (ed.), *A History of the Witches of Renfrewshire*, new ed., (Paisley: Alex Gardner 1877), 75-6.

65. Harline, *The Burdens of Sister Margaret*, 35-6. Sluhovsky, 'The Devil in the convent', 1405-7. Women's bodies: quotations from D. Purkiss, *The Witch in History*, London & (New York: Routledge 1996), 120-1. Sluhovsky, *op.cit.*, 1382-6. Mandrou, *Magistrats et sorciers*, 219-26. Ferber, *Demonic Possession and Exorcism*, 94-108, 111-12. Sluhovsky quotation, *op.cit.*, 1399. Mandrou, *op.cit.*, 173-9. Ferber, *op.cit.*, 47-54. Almond, *Demonic Possession*, 240-3, 250. J. Sharpe, *The Bewitching of Anne Gunter*, London: Profile Books 1999, 45, 103-4. French woman: Harline, *op.cit.*, 56.

66. Almond, *op.cit.* supra, 218-20. Ferber, *op.cit.* supra, 30-6. Walker, 'Demonic possession', 239-42. Sluhovsky, *Believe Not Every Spirit*, 19-23. Almond, *op.cit.*, 199. Deacon and Walker quoted in Sands, 'The doctrine of transubstantiation', 459. Oldridge, *The Devil in Early Modern England*, 122-33.

67. *Attachiatis*. This is an English word given a Latin verbal ending. The speaker is not called 'Ignoramus' for nothing.

68. Latin does not necessarily use its possessive adjectives, and here the text says merely 'name is ... name is', thereby allowing the 'misunderstanding' to take place. This cannot be reproduced in English.

69. Munday: Johnstone, *The Devil and Demonism in Early Modern England*, 39-40, 206, 39 footnote 59, 293. Kallendorf, *Exorcism and its Texts*, 19-23. Oldridge, *The Devil in Early Modern England*, 182. Kallendorf, *op.cit.*, 52, 46-7, 33-4, 53-4. Van Dijkhuizen, *Devil Theatre* 96-9, 116-18. Kallendorf, *op.cit.*, 26-9. Quotation: Ruggle, *Ignoramus comoedia*, ed. J.S. (Hawkins, London 1787).

70. Clark, *Thinking With Demons*, 396. Kallendorf, *op.cit.* supra, 206.

Chapter 8

71. Baker, *The Devil of Great Island*, 190-1. It is a picture interestingly reminiscent of that allegedly held by coloured people in the southern states of the USA at the beginning of the twentieth century. 'Most of the time ... when going about on the earth', wrote Newbell Puckett, 'the Negro devil has the appearance of a gentleman, wearing a high silk hat, and a frock coat, and having an "ambrosial curl" in the centre of his forehead to hide the single horn which is located there', *Folk Beliefs of the Southern Negro*, (Chapel Hill: University of North Carolina Press 1926), 550. Midelfort, 'Catholic and Lutheran reactions to demon possession', 633. Mitter, *Much Maligned Monsters*, 3, 10-27, 54-5, 57; quotation, 17.

72. Cervantes, *The Idea of the Devil*, 8; *The Devil in the New World*, 14, 17, 48. Reff, *Plagues, Priests, Demons*, 136-7; quotation, 229-30; 155, 178-9. Griffiths, *Sacred Dialogues*, 245-7; quotation, 249. De Mello e Souza, *The Devil and the Land of the Holy Cross*, 32-5; quotation, 80; 156-7, 162-3. Pachoud, *Le monde amérindien*, 51-65.

73. Brendbekken, 'Beyond Vodou and anthroposophy', 43, 50. Meyer, *Translating the Devil*, 51, 83-5, 99-101, 216. On the link between Pentecostalism and Satan-awareness, see Marshall, 'Power in the name of Jesus', 213-46.

74. Percy, 'A True Relation, etc.' in E.W. Haile (ed.), *Jamestown Narratives: Eyewitness Accounts of the Virginia Colony, the First Decade 1607-1617*, Champlain, (VA: RoundHouse 1998), 515. Hall, *Witch-Hunting*, 149-50, 336. Cf. *Ibid.*, 137, 141 where we find that in Cambridge Massachusetts

1659, John Gibson's daughter, Rebecca, a married woman, fell into fits and claimed she saw Satan at her bedside, later saying she was frightened by his appearing to her in different shapes. Demos, *Entertaining Satan*, 58, 166-7, 173-4. Norton, *In the Devil's Snare*, 65, 80, 81, 148, 234, 258, 260. On 'black' American Indians, see Norton, *op.cit.*, 58-9, 252. Demos, *op.cit.*, 311. Cf. the observation of Cotton Mather, 'That the Devil is come down unto us with great wrath, we find, we feel, we now deplore. In many ways, for many years, hath the Devil been essaying to extirpate the kingdom of our Lord Jesus here ... The things confessed by witches, and the things endured by others, laid together, amount unto this account of our affliction. The Devil, exhibiting himself ordinarily as a small black man, has decoyed a fearful knot of proud, froward, ignorant, envious and malicious creatures to lift themselves in his horrid service by entering their names in a book by him tendered unto them. These witches, whereof above a score have now confessed and shown their deeds, and some are now tormented by the devils for confessing, have met in Hellish rendezvous ... In these Hellish meetings, these monsters have associated themselves to do no less a thing here than to destroy the kingdom of our Lord Jesus Christ in these parts of the world ... In such extravagant ways have these wretches propounded the dragooning of as many as they can, in their own combination, and the destroying of others, with lingering, spreading, deadly diseases, till our country should at last become too hot for us. Among the ghastly instances of the success which those bloody witches have had, we have seen even some of their own children so dedicated unto the Devil that in their infancy, it is found, the imps have sucked them and rendered them venomous to a prodigy. We have also seen the Devil's first batteries upon the town, where the first church of our Lord in this colony was gathered, producing those distractions which have almost ruined the town. We have seen likewise the plague reaching afterwards into other towns far and near, where the houses of good men have the Devil's filling of them with terrible vexations', *The Wonders of the Invisible World*, (London: J.R. Smith 1862), 80-3.

75. The Chinese, for example, were considered to be the least superstitious of peoples, whereas the Jews were not only superstitious, but ignorant as well. See V. Volpilhac-Auger, 'Paysage de la superstition' in B. Dompnier (ed.), *La superstition à l'âge des lumières*, (Paris: Honoré Champion 1998), 100.

76. Muchembled, *A History of the Devil*, 153-7, 164-6. Porter, 'Witchcraft and magic', 197-211. Schmidt, 'From demon possession to magic show', 281-4. Connor, *Dumbstruck*, 209-25. Muchembled, *op.cit.*, 167, 171-2. Lewis, *The Monk*, Vol.3, chap.5; quotation, 433.

77. Dömötör, *Hungarian Folk Beliefs*, 66. Davies, 'Talk of the Devil', 2, 11-13, (ballad quotation, 12), 17-19. Freytag, 'Witchcraft, witch doctors, and the fight against "superstition"', 39-40, 35. Barry, 'Public infidelity and private belief?' 118-19, 134-5. Davies, 'Witchcraft accusations on France', 109. Midelfort, *Exorcism and Enlightenment*, 11-31, 59-65; illustration, 21. Olli, 'The Devil's pact', 103-5. Torquemada, *La Inquisicion y el Diablo*, 97-100, 194-211, 113-17. Devlin, *The Superstitious Mind*, 169-70.

78. Porter, 'Witchcraft and magic', 219, 266-72. Charcot & Richer, *Les démoniaques dans l'art*, v-xii, 91-100; quotation, 55. Kimball, 'From Anna O to Bertha Pappenheim', 20-2. Muchembled, *A History of the Devil*, 208-11. Baudelaire, *Les Fleurs du Mal* in *Oeuvres Complètes*, revised by Y.G. le Dantec & C. Pichois, (Paris: Éditions Gallimard 1961), 105, 116, 118; 'The Generous Gambler' in *Le Spleen de Paris*, *op.cit.*, 274-7. J.A. Hiddleston, *Baudelaire and Le Spleen de Paris*, (Oxford: Clarendon Press 1987), 56.

79. Beard, *The Autobiography of Satan*, v, 1, 234, 292, 417.

80. J. Simpson, 'Sussex local legends', *Folklore* 84 (1973), 209. T. Brown, 'A further note on the Stag Hunt in Devon', *Folkore* 90 (1979), 20-1. D.A. Barrowclough & J. Hallam, 'The Devil's footprints and other folklore: local legend and archaeological evidence in Lancashire', *Folklore* 119 (2008), 93. Respect (ironic or otherwise) for the Devil was to be found in the west country of England as late as 1967 when R.L. Tongue observed that 'in Somerset, we speak of His Satanic Majesty respectfully as "The Gentleman in Black". An old farmer I know, after carefully touching his forelock, says, "The Gentleman downstairs",' 'Folk song and folklore', *Folklore* 78 (1967), 301. B.S. Benedikz, 'Basic themes in Icelandic folklore', *Folklore* 84 (1973), 17. M. Puhvel, 'The mystery of the cross-roads', *Folklore* 87 (1976), 169. Valk, *The Black Gentleman*,

25, 41-4, 63-6, 111-16; quotation, 117. This anecdote was gathered in 1930. For the full range of the Devil's manifestations in Estonian and Lithuanian folk belief, see *Ibid.*, 197-8, 201.

81. Paul VI's suppression of the order of exorcist is contained in his Apostolic Letter, *Ministeria quaedam*. Muchembled, *A History of the Devil*, 230-4. Fr. Amorth: *www.freerepublic.com/focus/f-religion/1260364/posts*. Alexander, *To Anger the Devil*,25, 26. Cuneo, *American Exorcism*, 326; quotation, 298. Ellis, *Raising the Devil*, 15-30, 79-85; quotation, 81; 87-9, 115-19, 125-34. Griffiths, 'Le mythe de satanisme au xixe siècle', 213-33. Sunday Pictorial: quoted in Medway, *Lure of the Sinister*, 143. Doreen Irvine, *Ibid.*, 159-60, 217, 222, 226, 234-45; quotation, 243. See further La Fontaine, *Speak of the Devil*, 61-7, 180-92. Frankfurter, *Evil Incarnate*, 57-72.

82. Nelson, *The Secret Life of Puppets*, 18-19. Goodman, *How About Demons?* 26-7. See also Muchembled, *A History of the Devil*, 242-62 where he discusses the preternatural and demonic in films. LaVey, *Satanic Bible*, 69. Frankfurter, *Evil Incarnate*, 200-3. Ellis, *Raising the Devil*, 169-73, 179-80; quotation, 180. Ayn Rand (1905-82) was a Russian-born American novelist and philosopher whose central philosophical proposition was that the pursuit of one's own rational self-interest and happiness is the highest moral purpose in life. It is worth comparing a manifesto of Satanism proclaimed by an adherent of the religion-philosophy at the end of the 1980s. 'Satanists do not believe that some mysterious and awesome deity (whether he has horns and tail or no) is going to hand us that knowledge in return for our allegiance or our "soul". Knowledge is achieved by learning, working, experimenting, experiencing and thinking. That is why the orthodox religions fulminate against Satanism, because they are aware of the insecure foundations of their own dogma. It is not what we say or do. The simple fact that we exist threatens them above all else', Anon, *The Occult Census*, 39-40.

83. Brendbekken, 'Beyond Vodou and anthroposophy', 43, 50. Meyer, *Translating the Devil*, 51, 83-5, 99-101, 216. On the link between Pentecostalism and Satan awareness, see Marshall, 'Power in the name of Jesus', 213-46. Weber, *Apocalypses*, 193-222; quotation, 206. Muchembled, *A History of the Devil*, 275. Lucia de Jesus, *Fátima in Lucia's Own Words*, (Cambridge: Ravensgate Press 1995), 105. Fernandino, 'Screwtape revisited', 107-8.

Illustrations

Select Bibliography

Alexander D. & Strauss W.L., *The German Single-Leaf Woodcut, 1600-1700*, 2 vols. New York: Abaris
 Books 1977
Alexander M., *To Anger the Devil*, Suffolk: Neville Spearman 1978
Almond P.C., *Demonic Possession and Exorcism in Early Modern England*, Cambridge: Cambridge
 University Press 2004
Anon, *The Occult Census 1989*, Leeds: The Sorcerer's Apprentice Press 1989
Athanasius of Alexandria, *The Life of Antony*, trans. T. Vivian & N. Athanassakis, Kalamazoo,
 Michigan: Cistercian Publications 2003
Aubri de Trois Fontaines, *Chronica* in *Monumenta Germaniae Historica*, Scriptores 23.931-2
Audisio G., *The Waldensian Dissent: Persecution and Survival, c.1170-c.1570*, English trans.,
 Cambridge: Cambridge University Press 1999
Awn P.J., *Satan's Tragedy and Redemption: Iblis in Sufi Psychology*, Leiden: Brill 1983
Baker E.W., *The Devil of Great Island: Witchcraft and Conflict in Early New England*, New York:
 Palgrave Macmillan 2007
Barber M., *The Cathars: Dualist Heretics in Languedoc in the High Middle Ages*, New York: Pearson
 Education 2000
Barry J., 'Public infidelity and private belief? The discourse of spirits in enlightenment Bristol'
 in O. Davies & W. de Blécourt (eds), *Beyond the Witch Trials: Witchcraft and Magic in
 Enlightenment Europe*, Manchester & New York: Manchester University Press 2004, 117-43
Battista S., 'Blámenn, *djöflar*, and other representations of evil in Old Norse translation literature',
 www.dur.ac.uk/medieval.www/sagaconf/battista.htm
Baynes N.H., 'St Antony and the demons', *Journal of Egyptian Archaeology* 40 (1954), 195-230
Beard J.R., *The Autobiography of Satan*, Edinburgh & London: Williams and Norgate 1872
Bechtel G., *La sorcière et l'occident: la destruction de la sorcellerie en Europe des origines aux grands
 bûchers*, Paris: Librairie Plon 1997
Behringer W., *Shaman of Oberstdorf: Chonrad Stoecklin and the Phantoms of the Night*, English
 trans., Charlottesville:University Press of Virginia 1998, 'How Waldensians became witches:
 heretics and their journey to the other world' in Klaniczay & Pócs (eds), *Communicating with
 the Spirits* q.v. 1.155-92
Bekker H., 'The Lucifer motif in the German drama of the sixteenth century', *Monatshefte* 51
 (1959), 234-47
Bever E., *The Realities of Witchcraft and Popular Magic in Early Modern Europe: Culture, Cognition,
 and Everyday Life*, Basingstoke: Palgrave, Macmillan 2008
Bevington D. (ed.), *Mediaeval Drama*, Boston: Houghton Mifflin Co. 1975
Black J. & Green A., *Gods, Demons, and Symbols of Ancient Mesopotamia: An Illustrated Dictionary*,
 London: British Museum Press 1992

Bolvig A., 'Mural paintings, oral society, visual linearity: the act of looking at a picture' in L. Urbano Afonso & V. Serrão (eds), *Out of the Stream: Studies in Mediaeval and Renaissance Mural Painting*, Newcastle: Cambridge Scholars Publishing 2007, 10-21

Bottéro J., *Religion in Ancient Mesopotamia*, English trans., Chicago & London: University of Chicago Press 2001

Boureau A., *Satan the Heretic: The Birth of Demonology in the Mediaeval West*, English trans., Chicago & London: University of Chicago Press 2006

Bourke C., 'The iconography of the Devil: St Vigean's, Eassie, and the Book of Kells', *Innes Review* 58 (2007), 95-100

Boyce M., *A History of Zoroastrianism*, Vol. 1, Leiden: Brill 1975

Brandon S.G.F., 'The Devil in faith and history', *History Today* 13 (1963), 468-78

Brann E.T.H., *The World of the Imagination: Sum and Substance*, Lanham: Rowman & Littlefield 1991

Brendbekken M., 'Beyond Vodou and anthroposophy in the Dominican –Haitian borderlands' in B. Kapferer (ed.), *Beyond Rationalism: Rethinking Magic, Witchcraft and Sorcery*, New York & Oxford: Berghahn Books 2002, 31-74

Brennan B.R., 'Dating Athanasius's Vita Antonii', *Vigiliae Chrisianae* 30 (1976), 52-4

Breytenbach C. & Day P.L., 'Satan', in K. Van der Toorn, R. Becking, P. van der Horst (eds), *Dictionary of Deities and Demons in the Bible*, Leiden: Brill 1999, cols. 726-32

Brock S. & Ashbrook H.S., *Holy Women of the Syrian Orient*, Berkeley: University of California Press 1987

Caciola N., 'Mystics, demoniacs, and the physiology of spirit possession in Mediaeval Europe', *Comparative Studies in Society and History* 42 (April 2000), 268-306

——, *Discerning Spirits: Divine and Demonic Possession in the Middle Ages*, Ithaca & London: Cornell University Press 2003

——, 'Breath, heart, guts: the body and spirits in the Middle Ages' in G. Klaniczay & E. Pócs (eds), *Demons, Spirits, Witches* Vol. 1: *Communicating with the Spirits*, Budapest & New York: Central European University Press 2005, 21-39

Camporesi P., *Bread of Dreams*, English trans. Cambridge: Polity Press 1989

Cardelle de Hartmann C., *Lateinische Dialoge 1200-1400: Literaturhistorische Studie und Repertorium*, Leiden: Brill 2007

Carus P., *The History of the Devil and the Idea of Evil*, New York: Grammercy Books 1996

Cavendish R., *The Magical Arts*, London: Arkana 1984

Cervantes F., *The Idea of the Devil and the Problem of the Indian: The Case of Mexico in the Sixteenth Century*, University of London, Institute of Latin American Research Papers 24, London 1991

——, *The Devil in the New World: The Impact of Diabolism in New Spain*, New Haven & London: Yale University Press 1994

Chabbi J., 'Jinn' in *Encyclopaedia of the Qur'ān* Vol. 3, Leiden: Brill 2003, 43-9

Charlesworth J.H. (ed.), *The Old Testament Pseudepigrapha* 2 vols. London: Darton, Longman & Todd 1983-5

Charcot J.-M. & Richer P., *Les démoniaques dans l'art*, originally published Paris 1887, Amsterdam: M.M. Israel 1972

Clark J.M., *The Dance of Death in the Middle Ages and Renaissance*, Glasgow: Jackson 1950

Cohn N., *Europe's Inner Demons: An Inquiry Inspired by the Great Witch-Hunt*, London: Book Club Associates 1975

Colliot R., 'Rencontres du moine Raoul Glaber avec le diable d'après ses histoires', in *Le Diable au Moyen Âge: doctrine, problèmes moraux, representations*, Aix-en-Provence: Publications du CUER MA 1979, 117-33

Connor S., *Dumbstruck: A Cultural History of Ventriloquism*, Oxford: Oxford University Press 2000

Costen M.D., *The Cathars and the Albigensian Crusade*, Manchester: Manchester University Press 1997

Coventry W.W., *Demonic Possession on Trial: Case Studies in Early Modern England and Colonil America, 1593-1692*, iUniverse.com 2003

Cox J.D., 'Stage devilry in two King's Men plays of 1606', *Modern Language Review* 93 (1998), 934-47

––––––, *The Devil and the Sacred in English Drama, 1350-1642*, Cambridge: Cambridge University Press 2000

Cuneo M.W., *American Exorcism: Expelling Demons in the Land of Plenty*, London: Bantam Books 2002

Curta F., 'Colour perception, dyestuffs, and colour terms in twelfth-century French literature', *Medium Aevum* 73 (2004), 43-65

Czarnecki P., 'Luciferianism in the thirteenth century: a forgotten offshoot of Catharism', *Studia Historyczne* 47 (2004), 3-19

Dante Alighieri, *Hell*, trans. S. Ellis, London: Chatto & Windus 1994

Daston L., 'Marvellous facts and miraculous evidence in early modern Europe', *Critical Inquiry* 18 (Autumn 1991), 93-124

Dastur M.N., *The Moral and Ethical Teachings of Zarathushtra*, Bombay: University of Bombay 1928

Davidson J.P., 'Black goats and evil little women: the image of the witch in sixteenth-century German art', *Journal of the Rocky Mountain Mediaeval and Renaissance Society* 6 (1985), 141-57

Davies O., 'Witchcraft accusations in France, 1850-1990' in W. de Blécourt & O. Davies (eds), *Witchcraft Continued: Popular Magic in Modern Europe*, Manchester & New York: Manchester University Press 2004, 107-32

––––––, 'Talk of the Devil: crime and Satanic inspiration in eighteenth-century England', *www.karisgarden.com/cunningfolk/devil.pdf*

Day P.L., *An Adversary in Heaven: Satan in the Hebrew Bible*, Atlanta: Scholars Press 1988

De Jesus-Marie B. (ed.), *Satan*, New York: Sheed & Ward 1952

De Mello e Souza L., *The Devil and the Land of the Holy Cross: Witchcraft, Slavery, and Popular Religion in Colonial Brazil*, English trans. Austin: University of Texas Press 2003

Defoe D., *The Political History of the Devil*, ed. I.N. Rothman & R.M. Bowerman, New York: AMS Press 2003

Demos J.P., *Entertaining Satan: Witchcraft and the Culture of Early New England*, Oxford: Oxford University Press 1982

Dendle P., *Satan Unbound: The Devil in Old English Narrative Literature*, Toronto: University of Toronto Press 2001

Devlin J., *The Superstitious Mind: French Peasants and the Supernatural in the Nineteenth Century*, New Haven & London: Yale University Press 1987

Dömötör T., *Hungarian Folk-Beliefs*, Bloomington: Indiana University Press 1981

Doughty C.M., *Travels in Arabia Deserta* 2 vols, London: Warner & Cape 1921

Dubois T.A., *Nordic Religions in the Viking Age*, Philadelphia: University of Pennsylvania Press 1999

Ekirch A.R., *At Day's Close: Night in Times Past*, London: Weidenfeld & Nicolson 2005

Ellis B., *Raising the Devil: Satanism, New Religions, and the Media*, Lexington: University Press of Kentucky 2000

––––––, *Lucifer Ascending: The Occult in Folklore and Popular Culture*, Kentucky: University of Kentucky Press 2004

Eliot T.S., 'Dante' in *Selected Essays*, 3rd ed. London: Faber & Faber Ltd 1951, 237-77

Fernandino K., 'Screwtape revisited: demonology western, African, and Biblical' in A.N.S. Lane (ed.), *The Unseen World: Christian Reflections on Angels, Demons, and the Heavenly Realm*, Carlisle: Paternoster Press 1996, 103-32.

Ferreiro A. (ed.), *The Devil, Heresy, and Witchcraft in the Middle Ages: Essays in Honour of Jeffrey B. Russell*, Leiden: Brill 1998

Fine L., 'Benevolent spirit possession in sixteenth-century Safed' in Goldish M (ed.), *Spirit Possession in Judaism* q.v. 101-23

Fletcher R., *The Conversion of Europe from Paganism to Christianity, 371-1386 AD*, London: Harper Collins 1997

Flint V., 'The demonisation of magic and sorcery in late antiquity' in B. Ankarloo & S. Clark (eds), *The Athlone History of Witchcraft and Magic in Europe*: Vol. 2, *Ancient Greece and Rome*, London: Athlone Press 1999, 279-348

Forsyth N., *The Old Enemy: Satan and the Combat Myth*, Princeton: Princeton University Press 1987

——, 'Satan: making a Heaven of Hell, a Hell of Heaven' in A. Ferreiro (ed.), *The Devil, Heresy, and Witchcraft* q.v. 241-58

Frankfurter D., 'Syncretism and the holy man in late antique Egypt', *Journal of Early Christian Studies* 11 (2003), 339-85

——, *Evil Incarnate: Rumours of Demonic Conspiracy and Satanic Abuse in History*, Princeton & Oxford: Princeton University Press 2006

Freytag N., 'Witchcraft, witch doctors, and the fight against "superstition" in nineteenth-century Germany' in W. de Blécourt & O. Davies (eds), *Witchcraft Continued: Popular Magic in Modern Europe*, Manchester & New York: Manchester University Press 2004, 29-45

Frost P., 'Attitudes towards blacks in the early Christian era', *The Second Century* 8 (1991), 1-11

Geisberg M., *The German Single-Leaf Woodcut, 1500-1550*, revised ed. 4 vols. New York: Hacher Art Books 1974

Ginzburg C., *Ecstasies: Deciphering the Witches' Sabbath*, English trans., London: Hutchinson Radius 1990

Glaber Rudolf, *Historiarum libri quinque*, trans. J. France, Oxford: Clarendon Press 1989

Goldish M (ed.), *Spirit Possession in Judaism: Cases and Contexts from the Middle Ages to the Present*, Detroit: Wayne State University Press 2003

——, 'Vision and possession: Nathan of Gaza's earliest prophecies in historical context' in Goldish, *Spirit Possession in Judaism*, q.v. 217-36

Goodich M. (ed.), *Other Middle Ages: Witnesses at the Margins of Mediaeval Society*, Philadelphia: University of Pennsylvania Press 1998

Goodman F.D., *How About Demons? Possession and Exorcism in the Modern World*, Bloomington & Indianapolis: Indiana University Press 1988

Göttler C., 'Fire, smoke, and vapour. Jan Breughel's poetic Hells: "ghespook" in early modern art' in C. Göttler & W. Neuber (eds), *Spirits Unseen: The Representation of Subtle Bodies in Early Modern European Culture*, Leiden: Brill 2008, 19-46

Griffiths N., *Sacred Dialogues: Christianity and Native Religions in the Colonial Americas, 1492-1700*, England: Lulu Enterprises 2006

Griffiths R., 'Le mythe de Satanisme au xixe siècle' in M. Milner (ed.), *Entretiens sur l'homme et le diable*, Paris: Mouton & Co. 1965, 213-33

Griffiths J. Gwyn, *The Conflict of Horus and Seth*, (Liverpool: Liverpool University Press 1960)

Groebner V., *Who Are You? Identification, Deception, and Surveillance in Early Modern Europe*, English trans., New York: Zone Books 2007

Guazzo, Francesco Maria, *Compendium Maleficarum*, English trans. (originally published London 1929), New York: Dover Publications 1988

Guibert de Nogent, *Monodiae = A Monk's Confession: The Memoirs of Guibert de Nogent*, trans. P.J. Archambault, Pennsylvania: Pennsylvania State University Press 1996

Hall D.D. (ed.), *Witch-Hunting in Seventeenth-Century New England*, 2nd ed. Boston: Northeastern University Press 1999

Hall R.G., 'The Ascension of Isaiah: community situation, date, and place in early Christianity', *Journal of Biblical Literature* 109 (1990), 289-306

Harline C., *The Burdens of Sister Margaret*, revised and abridged ed., New Haven & London: Yale University Press 2000

Hawting G.R., *The Idea of Idolatry and the Emergence of Islam: From Polemic to History*, Cambridge: Cambridge University Press 1999

Henniger J., 'Pre-Islamic Bedouin religion' in M.L. Swartz (ed.), *Studies on Islam*, Oxford: Oxford University Press 1981, 3-22

Henningsen G., *The Witches' Advocate: Basque Witchcraft and the Spanish Inquisition (1609-1614)*, Reno, Nevada: University of Nevada Press 1980

——, (ed.), *The Salazar Documents: Inquisitor Alonso de Salazar Frías and Others on the Basque Witch Persecution*, Leiden: Brill 2004

Hildegard von Bingen, *Causae et curae*, ed. P. Kaiser, Leipzig: Teubner 1903

Jacobsen T., *The Treasures of Darkness: a History of Mesopotamian Religion*, New Haven & London: Yale University Press 1976

James M.R., *The Apocryphal New Testament*, Oxford: Clarendon Press reprint 1983

Johnstone N., *The Devil and Demonism in Early Modern England*, Cambridge: Cambridge University Press 2006

Jolly K.L., 'Elves in the Psalms: the experience of evil from a cosmic perspective' in A. Ferreiro (ed.), *The Devil, Heresy, and Witchcraft in the Middle Ages*, Leiden: Brill 1998, 19-44

Jones P. & Pennick N., *A History of Pagan Europe*, London & New York: Routledge 1995

Kallendorf H., *Exorcism and its Texts: Subjectivity in Early Modern Literature of England and Spain*, Toronto: University of Toronto Press 2003

Kelley H.A., *The Devil, Demonology and Witchcraft*, New York: Doubleday 1968

——, *Satan, A Biography*, Cambridge: Cambridge University Press 2006

Kennedy C.W. (trans.), *The Caedmon Poems*, London: George Routledge & Sons Limited 1916

Kerrick S.K., *Imagining the Sacred Past: Hagiography and Power in Early Normandy*, Cambridge, Mass: Harvard University Press 2007

Kimball M.M., 'From "Anna O" to Bertha Pappenheim: transforming private pain into public action', *History of Psychology* 3 (February 2000), 20-43

Klaniczay G., 'The process of trance, heavenly and diabolic apparition in Johannes Nider's Formicarius' = *Collegium Budapest Discussion Papers*, Series 65 (June 2003)

Klaniczay G. & Pócs E. (eds), *Demons, Spirits, Witches* Vol.2: *Christian Demonology and Popular Mythology*, Budapest: Central European University Press 2006

Klüger R.S., *Satan in the Old Testament*, Evanston, Illinois: Northwestern University Press 1967

Knust J., 'Enslaved to demons: sex, violence, and the Apologies of Justin Martyr' in T. Penner & C. Vander Stichele (eds), *Mapping Gender in Ancient Religious Discourses*, Leiden: Brill 2007, 431-55

Koopmans J., *Le théâtre des exclus au Moyen Âge: hérétiques, sorcières, et marginaux*, Paris: Editions Imago 1997

Koran, trans. A.J. Arberry, Oxford: Oxford University Press 1986

Krause V., 'Confessional fictions and demonology in Renaissance France', *Journal of Mediaeval and Early Modern Studies* 35 (Spring 2005), 327-48

Ladurie Le Roy E., *Montaillou*, English trans., London: Penguin Books 1978

La Fontaine J.S., *Speak of the Devil: Tales of Satanic Abuse in Contemporary England*, Cambridge: Cambridge University Press 1998

Lambert M., *Mediaeval Heresy: Popular Movements from the Gregorian Reform to the Reformation*, 2nd ed. Oxford: Blackwell 1992

——, *The Cathars*, Oxford: Blackwell 1998

Lash C.J.A., 'Where do devils live? A problem in the textual criticism of Ephesians 6.12', *Vigiliae Christianae* 30 (1976), 161-74

LaVey A., *Satanic Bible*, Avon Books 1969

Lea H.C., *Materials Towards A History of Witchcraft*, ed. A.C. Howland, 3 vols. Philadelphia: University of Pennsylvania Press 1939

Lehtipu O., *The Afterlife Imagery in Luke's Story of the Rich Man and Lazarus*, Leiden & Boston: Brill 2007

Leloir L., 'Le diable chez les pères du desert et dans les écrits du Moyen-Âge', in *Typus, Symbol, Allegorie bei den Östlichen Vätern und ihren Parallelen im Mittelalter*, Regensburg: Friedrich Pustet 1982, 218-37

Lewis M., *The Monk*, first published 1796, London: Oxford University Press 1973

Lieu S.N.C., *Manichaeism in Mesopotamia and the Roman East*, Leiden: Brill 1994

Lima R., *Stages of Evil: Occultism in Western Theatre and Drama*, Lexington, Kentucky: University of Kentucky Press 2005

Link L., *The Devil: A Mask without a Face*, London: Reaktion 1995

Lorenzi L., *Devils in Art: Florence, from the Middle Ages to the Renaissance*, English trans. Florence: Centro Di 1997

Luther M., *Table Talk*, ed. T.G. Tappert = *Luther's Works* Vol.54, ed. H.T. Lehmann, Philadelphia: Fortress Press 1967

MacDonald D.B., Boratav P.N., Nizami K.A., 'Djinn' in *Encyclopaedia of Islam* Vol. 2, Leiden & London: Brill & Luzac 1965, 546-9

Mandrou R., *Magistrats et sorciers en France au xviie siècle*, Paris: Librairie Plon 1968

Mango C., 'Diabolus Byzantinus', *Dumbarton Oaks Papers* 46 (1992), 215-23

Marshall R., 'Power in the name of Jesus: social transformation and Pentecostalism in Western Nigeria revisited' in T.O. Rnager & O. Vaughan (eds), *Legitimacy and the State in Twentieth Century Africa*, London: Macmillan 1993, 213-46

Marx J., *L'Inquisition en Dauphiné: Étude sur le développement et la répression de l'hérésie et de la sorcellerie du xive siècle au début du regne de François Ier*, Paris: E. Champion 1914

Matheson P., *The Imaginative World of the Reformation*, Edinburgh: T&T Clark 2000

Maxwell-Stuart P.G., *An Abundance of Witches: The Great Scottish Witch-Hunt*, Stroud: Tempus Publishing 2005

McGinn B., *Antichrist*, New York: HarperSanFrancisco 1994

McHugh M., 'Satan and Saint Ambrose', *Classical Folia* 26 (1972), 94–106

Medway G.J., *Lure of the Sinister: The Unnatural History of Satanism*, New York & London: New York University Press 2001

Mellinkoff R., *Outcasts: Signs of Otherness in Northern European Art of the Late Middle Ages*, 2 vols., Berkeley, Los Angeles: University of California Press 1993

Meyer B., *Translating the Devil: Religion and Modernity Among the Ewe in Ghana*, Edinburgh: Edinburgh University Press 1999

Midelfort H.C.E., 'Catholic and Lutheran reactions to demonic possession in the late seventeenth century', *Daphnis* 15 (1986), 623-48

——, 'The Devil and the German people' in D. Oldridge (ed.), *The Witchcraft Reader*, London & New York: Routledge 2002, 240-53

——, *Exorcism and Enlightenment: Johann Joseph Gassner and the Demons of Eighteenth-Century Germany*, New Haven & London: Yale University Press 2005

Miller J., 'Men in black: appearances of the Devil in early modern Scottish witchcraft discourse' in J. Goodare, L. Martin, J. Miller (eds), *Witchcraft and Belief in Early Modern Scotland*, Basingstoke: Palgrave Macmillan 2008, 144-65

Milner M. (ed.), *Entretiens sur l'homme et le diable*, Paris: Mouton & Co 1965

Mitter P., *Much Maligned Monsters: A History of European Reaction to Indian Art*, Chicago & London: Chicago University Press 1992

Mitter P., *Much Maligned Monsters: A History of European Reactions to Indian Art*, Chicago & London: University of Chicago Press 1992

Muchembled R., *A History of the Devil: From the Middle Ages to the Present*, English trans., Cambridge: Polity Press 2003

Mullen E.T., *The Divine Council in Canaanite and Early Hebrew Literature*, Chico, California: Scolars Press 1980

Nagel M.B., *Deliver Us From Evil: What the Bible Says about Satan*, Cleveland: United Church Press 1999

Nelson V., *The Secret Life of Puppets*, Cambridge, Mass: Harvard University Press 2001

Norton M.B., *In the Devil's Snare: The Salem Witchcraft Case of 1692*, New York: Alfred A. Knopf 2002

Nugent A., 'Black demons in the desert', *American Benedictine Review* 49 (June 1998), 209-21

Ogden D.H., *The Staging of Drama in the Mediaeval Church*, Newark: University of Delaware Press 2002

O'Grady J., *The Prince of Darkness: The Devil in History, Religion, and the Human Psyche*, Shaftesbury: Element Books 1989

Oldridge D., *The Devil in Early Modern England*, Stroud: Sutton Publishing 2000

Olli S.-M., 'The Devil's pact: a male strategy' in O. Davies & W. de Blécourt (eds), *Beyond the Witch Trials: Witchcraft and Magic in Enlightenment Europe*, Manchester & New York: Manchester University Press 2004, 100-16

Ostorero M., Paravicini Bagliani A., Utz Trump K (eds), *L'imaginaire du sabbat*, Lausanne: Université de Lausanne 1999

Pagels E.H., *The Origin of Satan*, London: Allen Lane 1995
——, 'The social history of Satan, Part Three: John of Patmos and Ignatius of Antioch: Contrasting visions of God's people', *Harvard Theological Review* 99 (2006), 487-505
Papini G., *The Devil*, London: Eyre & Spottiswood 1955
Paschaud A., *Le monde amérindien au miroir des Lettres édifiantes et curieuses*, Oxford: Voltaire Foundation 2008
Pleij H., *Colours Demonic and Divine: Shades of Meaning in the Middle Ages and After*, English trans., New York: Columbia University Press 2004
Pócs E., 'Possession phenomena: possession-systems. Some east-central European examples' in G. Klaniczay & E. Pócs (eds), *Demons, Spirits, Witches* Vol. 1: *Communicating with the Spirits*, Budapest & New York: Central European University Press 2005, 84-51
Porter R., 'Witchcraft and magic in enlightenment, romantic, and liberal thought' in B. Ankarloo & S. Clark (eds), *The Athlone History of Witchcraft and Magic* Vol. 5, *The Enlightenment and Nineteenth Centuries*, London: Athlone Press 1999, 193-282
Reed A.Y., *Fallen Angels and the History of Judaism and Christianity: The Reception of Enochic Literature*, Cambridge: Cambridge University Press 2005
Reff D.T., *Plagues, Priests, Demons: Sacred Narratives and the Rise of Christianity in the Old World and the New*, Cambridge: Cambridge University Press 2005
Rémy N., *Demonolatry*, English trans., originally London 1930, New York: Dover Publications 2008
Rippin A., 'Devil' in *Encyclopaedia of the Qur'ān*, Vol. 1, Leiden: Brill 2001, 524-7
Rituale Romanum Pauli V Pontificis Maximi iussu editum, Mechlin: H. Dessain 1856
Roberts A. & Donaldson J. (eds), *The Ante-Nicene Fathers: Translations of the Writings of the Fathers down to AD 325*, 10 vols.: Vol. 8, Michigan: W.B. Eerdmans Pubishing Company, reprint 1995
Roberts J.J.M., *The Earliest Semitic Pantheon*, Baltimore & London: The John Hopkins University Press 1972
Rochelandet B., *Sorcières, diables et bûchers en Franche-Comté au xvie et xviie siècles*, Besançon: Éditions Cêtre 1997
Roos K.L., *The Devil in 16ᵉ Century German Literature: The Teufelbücher*, Bern: Herbert Lang 1972
Rothman T., 'De Laguna's commentaries on hallucinogenic drugs and witchcraft in Dioscorides's Materia Medica', *Bulletin of the History of Medicine* 46 (1972), 562-7
Rudwin M., *Der Teufel in den deutschen geistlichen Spielen des Mittelalters und der Reformationszeit*, Göttingen: Vandenhoed & Ruprecht 1915
Russell R.B., *Witchcraft in the Middle Ages*, Ithaca & London: Cornell University Press 1972
——, *The Devil: Perceptions of Evil from Antiquity to Primitive Christianity*, Ithaca, New York: Cornell University Press 1977
——, *Satan: The Early Christian Tradition*, Ithaca, New York: Cornell University Press 1981
——, *Lucifer: The Devil in the Middle Ages*, Ithaca, New York: Cornell University Press 1984
——, *Mephistopheles: The Devil in the Modern World*, Ithaca, New York: Cornell University Press 1986
Sands K.R., 'The doctrine of transubstantiation and the English Protestant dispossession of demons', *History* 85 (2000), 446-62
San Juan R.M., 'Dizzying visions. St Teresa of Jesus and the embodied visual image' in C. Göttler & W. Neuber (eds), *Spirits Unseen: The Representation of Subtle Bodies in Early Modern European Culture*, Leiden: Brill 2008, 245-67
Satran D., 'Deceiving the deceiver: variations on an early Christian theme', in E.G. Chazon, D. Satran, R.A. Clements (eds), *Things Revealed: Studies in Early Jewish and Christian Literature in Honour of Michael E. Stone*, Leiden & Boston: Brill 2004, 57-64
Schofield Clark L., *From Angels to Aliens: Teenagers, the Media, and the Supernatural*, Oxford: Oxford University Press 2003
Sawyer B. & P., *Mediaeval Scandinavia: From Conversion to Reformation, circa 800-1500*, Minneapolis: University of Minnesota Press 1993
Schmidt L.E., 'From demon possession to magic show: ventriloquism, religion, and the enlightenment', *Church History* 67 (1998), 274-304

Schock P., *Romantic Satanism: Myth and the Historical Moment in Blake, Shelley and Byron*, Basingstoke: Palgrave Macmillan 2003

Shinners J. (ed.), *Mediaeval Popular Religion, 1000-1500*, Peterborough, Ontario: Broadview Press 1997

Sidky H., *Witchcraft, Lycanthropy, Drugs, and Disease*, New York: Peter Lang 1997

Sinclair G., *Satan's Invisible World Discovered*, Edinburgh: Thomas George Stevenson 1871, reprint of 1685

Simms N., 'Andrés Laguna, Marrano physician, and the discovery of madness', *www.geocities. com/psychohistory 2001/ SimmsAndresLaguna.html*

Sluhovsky M., 'The Devil in the convent', *American Historical Review* 107 (December 2002), 1378-1411

——, *Believe Not Every Spirit: Possession, Mysticism, and Discernment in Early Modern Catholicism*, Chicago & London: University of Chicago Press 2007

Steinschneider M. (ed.), *Alphabeticum Syracidis utrumque, cum expositione antiqua narrationes et fabulas continente*, Berlin: Friedländer 1858

Stern D. & Mirsky M.J. (eds), *Rabbinic Fantasies: Imaginative Narratives from Classical Hebrew Literature*, New Haven & London: Yale University Press 1998

Stewart P.J. & Strathern A., *Witchcraft, Sorcery, Rumours, and Gossip, Cambridge*: Cambridge University Press 2004

Strauss W.L., *The German Single-Leaf Woodcut, 1550-1600*, 3 vols., New York: Abaris Books 1975

Strickland D.H., *Saracens, Demons, and Jews: Making Monsters in Mediaeval Art*, Princeton: Princeton University Press 2003

Szacsvay E., 'Protestant Devil figures in Hungary', in Klaniczay G. & Pócs E. (eds), *Demons, Spirits, Witches* Vol.2, q.v., 89-108

Tatai E., 'An iconographical approach to representations of the Devil in Mediaeval Hungary', in Klaniczay G. & Pócs E. (eds), *Demons, Spirits, Witches* Vol.2, q.v., 54-71

Taylor C., *Heresy in Mediaeval France: Dualism in Aquitaine and the Agenais, 1000-1249*, Woodbrideg: Boydell Press 2005

Thouzellier C., *Catharisme et Valdéisme en Languedoc à la fin du xiie et au début du xiiie siècle*, Louvian-Paris: Nauwelaerts, Béatrice-Nauwelaerts 1969

Thurston R.W., 'The spawning of Satan', *BBC History* (May 2002), 20-3

Tolan J., 'Peter the Venerable on the "diabolical heresy of the Saracens"' in A. Ferreiro (ed.), *The Devil, Heresy, and Witchcraft* q.v., 345-67

Torquemada M.J., *La Inquisicion y el Diablo: Supersticiones en el siglo XVIII*, Seville: Universidad de Sevilla 2000

Trachtenberg J., *The Devil and the Jews: The Mediaeval Conception of the Jew and its Relation to Modern Anti-Semitism*, 2nd pbk ed., Philadelphia & Jerusalem: The Jewish Publication Society 1983

Trombley F.R., *Hellenic Religion and Christianisation, c.370-529*, Vol.2, Leiden: Brill 1994

Tschaikner M., *Der Teufel und die Hexen müssen aus dem Land*, Liechtenstein 1998

Tuczay C., 'Trance prophets and diviners in the Middle Ages' in G. Klaniczay & E. Pócs (eds), *Demons, Spirits, Witches* Vol.1, *Communicating with the Spirits*, Budapest & New York: Central European University Press 2005, 215-33

Turner A.K., *The History of Hell*, New York: Harcourt Brace & Co 1993

Twycross M. & Carpenter S., *Masks and Masking in Mediaeval and Early Tudor England*, Aldershot: Ashgate 2002

Valk Ü., *The Black Gentleman: Manifestations of the Devil in Estonian Folklore*, Helsinki: Academia Scientiarum Fennica 2001

VanderKam J.C., '1 Enoch, Enochic motifs, and Enoch in early Christian literature' in J.C. VanderKam & W. Adler (eds), *The Jewish Apocalyptic Heritage in Early Christianity*, Minneapolis: Fortress Press 1996, 33-101

Van der Vliet J., 'Satan's fall in Coptic magic', in M.W. Meyer & P. Mirecki (eds), *Ancient Magic and Ritual Power*, (Leiden: Brill 1995), 410-18

Van Dijkhuizen J.F., *Devil Theatre: Demonic Possession and Exorcism in English Renaissance Drama, 1558-1642*, Woodbridge: D.S. Brewer 2007

Velde H. te, *Seth, God of Confusion*, (Leiden: Brill 1967)

Voragine Jacobus de, *The Golden Legend* 2 vols., trans. W. Granger Ryan, Princeton: Princeton University Press 1993

Walker D.P., *The Decline of Hell: Seventeenth-Century Discussions of Eternal Torment*, Chicago: University of Chicago Press 1964

——, 'Demonic possession used as propaganda in the later 16th century' in *Scienze, Credenze Occulti Livelli di Cultura*, Firenze: Olschki 1982, 237-48

Walsham A., *Providence in Early Modern England*, Oxford: Oxford University Press 2001

Warner M., *From the Beast to the Blonde: On Fairy Tales and their Tellers*, London: Vintage 1995

——, *No Go the Bogeyman: Scaring, Lulling, and Making Mock*, London: Vintage 2000

Watson G., 'The concept of "phantasia" from the late Hellenistic period to early Neoplatonism', *Aufstieg und Niedergang der Römischen Welt* II.36.7, 4765-810

Watterson B., *Coptic Egypt*, Edinburgh: Scottish Academic Press 1988

Weber E., *Apocalypses: Prophecies, Cults, and Millennial Beliefs Throughout the Ages*, London: Hutchinson 1999

Wensinck A.J., 'Iblis' in *Encyclopaedia of Islam* Vol. 3, Leiden & London: Brill & Luzac 1971, 668-9

Wolf-Knuts U., 'The Devil and birthgiving', in Klaniczay G. & Pócs E. (eds), *Demons, Spirits, Witches* Vol.2 q.v., 109-18

Wolfson H.A., 'The internal senses in Latin, Arabic, and Hebrew philosophic texts', *Harvard Theological Review* 28 (1935), 69-133

Woods W., *The History of the Devil*, New York: G.P. Putnam's Sons 1973

Woolf R., 'The Devil in Old English poetry', *Review of English Studies* ns 4.13 (1953), 1-1

Wray T.J. & Mobley G., *The Birth of Satan: Tracing the Devil's Biblical Roots*, New York: Palgrave Macmillan 2005

Wright J.E., *The Early History of Heaven*, New York & Oxford: Oxford University Press 2000

Wright R.M., *Art and Antichrist in Mediaeval Europe*, Manchester: Manchester University Press 1995

Youngs D. & Harris S., 'Demonising the night in Mediaeval Europe: a temporal monstrosity?' in B. Bildhauer & R. Mills (eds), *The Monstrous Middle Ages*, Cardiff: University of Wales Press 2003, 134-54

Index